LABOUR MARKET POLICY

Nick Adnett

Longman
London and New York

Longman Group UK Limited,
Longman House, Burnt Mill, Harlow,
Essex CM20 2JE, England
and Associated Companies throughout the world.

*Published in the United States of America
by Longman Inc., New York*

First published 1989

British Library Cataloguing in Publication Data
Adnett, Nick
    Labour market policy.
    1. Great Britain. Labour market
    I. Title
    331.12'0941

ISBN 0-582-00962-6

Library of Congress Cataloging in Publication Data

Set in Linotron 202 10/12pt Palatino

Produced by Longman Group (FE) Limited
Printed in Hong Kong

CONTENTS

Preface   vi
Acknowledgements   vii

1 Introduction   1

   1.1 The development of labour market policy   2
   1.2 The evolution of the Manpower Services
       Commission 1973–88   4
   1.3 Plan of the book   8

2 Labour market economics   10

   2.1 The basic neoclassical model   10
   2.2 Extensions to the basic neoclassical model   16
   2.3 Alternative approaches to the analysis of the
       labour market   21
   2.4 Competitive v. structural models of the labour market   25
   2.5 Policy implications   27
       Further reading   29

3 The labour market   31

   3.1 The structure of the UK labour market   32
   3.2 Theory and practice in the labour market   47
   3.3 Conclusions   57
       Further reading   58

4 Education and training   60

4.1 Current patterns of education and training 62
4.2 The competitive approach to education and training: human capital theory 66
4.3 Structuralist approaches to education and training: screening hypothesis 77
4.4 Policy issues 80
4.5 Conclusions 97
Further reading 100

5 Search and mobility in the labour market 101

5.1 Job search: theory and evidence 102
5.2 Search policy issues 117
5.3 Geographical mobility: theory and evidence 121
5.4 Mobility policy issues 126
Further reading 129

6 Discrimination 130

6.1 Evidence 131
6.2 Defining labour market discrimination 134
6.3 Pre-entry discrimination 139
6.4 Post-entry discrimination 140
6.5 Empirical studies 146
6.6 Policy implications of theory 154
6.7 The impact of current policies 160
6.8 Conclusions 166
Further reading 167

7 Unemployment 169

7.1 Unemployment: methodology and evidence 170
7.2 An introduction to the development of modern theories of unemployment 177
7.3 Deviations from the natural rate of unemployment: theories of wage rigidity 184
7.4 Determinants of the natural rate of unemployment 189
7.5 Towards an assessment: accounting for the rise in British unemployment 194
7.6 Policy implications 203
7.7 Current British Government policies 204
7.8 Alternative policies to reduce unemployment 215

7.9 Conclusions   221
    Further reading   221

8 Wage-fixing, social insurance and taxation   223

    8.1 Pay determination   224
    8.2 Reducing union power   225
    8.3 Conventional incomes policies   229
    8.4 Tax-based incomes policies   232
    8.5 Share economy   234
    8.6 Social insurance and taxation   240
        Further reading   250

9 Conclusions   251

References   255
Index   275

PREFACE

The last two decades have been exciting times for students of labour economics. During this period labour market behaviour has been at the heart of the major theoretical debates and labour market policies have to a large extent displaced demand management policies at the centre of the British Government's strategies. These developments have generated much research and this book considers what we have learnt about these two areas in recent years. The inclusion of an introductory theory chapter and minimal usage of mathematical analysis make the arguments and assessments accessible to all readers who have completed an introductory course in economic theory. The book was designed originally for advanced undergraduate students in economics and business studies, though its comprehensive review of recent applied work may attract graduate students in economics and management.

Although the book concentrates on labour market policy it is the intention that it should be used as a textbook for courses in labour economics, with each chapter providing a rigorous review of both theoretical developments and associated empirical studies. A further difference is that the recent contributions made to understanding labour market behaviour by insider–outsider and efficiency wage models are recognised by devoting almost equal time to the explanation and assessment of non-neoclassical models. An extensive bibliography is provided and though the key theoretical and empirical works are integrated into the text, each chapter concludes with a guide to further reading. Throughout the book evidence is presented which summarises recent labour market trends in the UK and other developed capitalist economies. A full introduction to the book is contained in Chapter 1.

The book was started while I was a visiting professor in the Department of Economics, California State University, Sacramento:

I owe a debt of gratitude to library and departmental colleagues at that institution. I am also grateful for the support I have received in my home college. Few of the ideas in this book are original and I have tried to indicate the origins of particular arguments in the text; for any omissions I apologise. I would specifically like to thank the following economists who have provided critical comments on earlier versions of this manuscript: Sam Cameron; Steve Hurd; William Forbes; Peter Reynolds and Jim van Heuit. Amstrad PCWs worked efficiently at both voltages, but I required Kath Gannon to provide the expertise for the tables and Liz Adnett for the diagrams, many thanks to both.

Nick Adnett
January 1988

ACKNOWLEDGEMENTS

We are grateful to the following for permission to reproduce copyright material:

Gower Publishing Co Ltd for table 7.3 from table 8.5 in 'Labour Demand' by R Lindley p 167 *Unemployment and Labour Market Policies* ed P Hart (1986); the Controller of Her Majesty's Stationery Office for table 6.3 from table 5 p 570 *Employment Gazette* Nov 1987 and table 4.2 from table 3.11 *Social Trends* 17, 1987; the Organisation For Economic Co-operation and Development for table 7.1 adapted from *OECD Quarterly Labour Force Statistics* No 4, 1987 (pub OECD, Paris); Oxford University Press for table 7.2 adapted from table 8 p 68 *How To Beat Unemployment* by R Layard (c) R Layard 1986 (pub Oxford Univ Press); The University of Chicago Press for table 6.1 from table 3 of the article 'Inter Country Companion' by J Mincer p 56 *Journal of Labor Economics* 3 Supp, 1986.

ACKNOWLEDGEMENTS

For Liz, Richard and Katherine – Sorry!

Chapter 1

INTRODUCTION

The subject of this text is the analysis of governments' attempts
to improve the operation of the labour market. The concern
is with means of improving levels of output and productivity
rather than equity, hence the concentration on policies related
to education, training, search, discrimination and unemployment.
The form and extent of labour market policy will be influenced by
the economic environment, the prevailing economic and political
philosophy and, given our imperfect and changing understanding,
inevitably pragmatism. Any investigation of policy should start
from a consideration of objectives and conclude on the success
of policy initiatives in meeting those objectives. The reluctance
of governments to specify detailed objectives and the difficulty in
evaluating often small-scale, uncontrolled and short-term policies
prevent such an approach. Instead in this work policy is reviewed
and assessed with reference to contemporary analyses of labour
market behaviour. Since our primary interest is with labour market
efficiency this text concentrates on labour economics; though the
traditional structure of a text in that area is avoided, this book
is intended to provide an introduction to contemporary theory.
Recent theoretical developments have emphasised the importance
of behavioural, sociological and institutional factors in labour market
behaviour and this emphasis is reflected in the following pages.
While the discussion concentrates upon labour market policy in
the UK reference is made to relevant policies and analyses in
other developed capitalist economies. Indeed given the level of
sophistication, data availability and the sheer quantity of American
research, US studies often dominate the literature in particular
topics. However, dissimilarities between the British labour market
and those of other Western economies suggest that results obtained
in foreign studies need not be duplicated in the UK.

In this chapter we initially consider the evolution of labour market policies, concentrating on the last fifty years. The rise and fall of interventionist policies are recorded and contrasted with the present voluntarist or passive approach, and the growth of the Manpower Services Commission/Training Commission is given special prominence. The present nature and administration of British policy are summarised and the chapter concludes with an outline and explanation of the structure of the remainder of the book.

1.1 The development of labour market policy

The unique demands of a war economy tend to generate widespread government intervention in the economy, and in the UK the two World Wars established the labour market as a major area for government concern. Before this time intervention had been largely concerned with issues perceived as social, such as the Education and Factory Acts, Poor Laws and National Insurance, or with establishing the institutional framework for collective bargaining. As the twentieth century progressed labour market efficiency featured more centrally, indicated by the establishment of a national system of employment exchanges and government provision of industrial training. During the Second World War the British Government took direct control of the labour market, controls which it was reluctant to relax in the immediate post-war period, given the persistence of critical labour shortages. Both Conservative and Labour Governments in the late 1940s and 1950s utilised hiring restrictions to direct workers towards employment in the energy and export sectors.

The achievement of acceptable levels of employment in post-war Western economies caused labour market policy to shift towards qualitative aspects of employment. In the UK the economy failed to grow steadily at the rates achieved by other Western economies in the decades after the war. The newly adopted demand–management policies merely generated 'stop–go' cycles, reflecting the constraint of the chronic weakness of the balance of payments at prevailing exchange rates. The search for new policy instruments to circumvent this 'vicious circle' of slow growth coincided with the universal acceptance of the Phillips curve relationship between 'tightness' in the labour market and wage inflation. To prolong the 'Go' phase of the cycle 'bottlenecks', causing inflation and increased imports, needed to be eliminated. In short, the Phillips curve needed to be shifted to the left. Following this diagnosis the 1960s saw widespread policy initiatives in the labour market. In particular, confidence in both the ability of government to forecast manpower requirements accurately and to redirect jobs and workers, induced concentration on the reduction of mismatch. Taxes and subsidies such as the selective employment tax and Regional Employment Premium were introduced to alter the structure and location of employment. Skill shortages were attacked by a massive increase in government-financed off-the-job training, while the 1964 Industrial Training Act introduced a levy–grant system to encourage private sector on-the-job training. Finally, the 1973 Employment and Training Act established the Manpower Services Commission (MSC) to devise and supervise a comprehensive manpower policy. Economists could then fine-tune on the basis of marginal cost–benefit analysis of existing schemes.

Two other elements were important in influencing the evolution of British labour market policy in the 1960s and 1970s. Firstly, across all Western economies there was a movement towards government producing greater protection and security for workers and improving the relative position of minorities in the labour market. In the USA, President Johnson launched the 'Great Society' with the 1963 Equal Pay Act and the 1964 Civil Rights Act, which sought to reduce racial and sex discrimination. These measures were imitated by the 1970 Equal Pay Act and the 1968 Race Relations Act in the UK, where in addition the 1965 Redundancy Payments Act recognised that workers could establish some property rights to their jobs. Secondly, the relatively high inflation rate caused the system of British industrial relations and wage-fixing to come under scrutiny, the 1968 Donovan Royal Commission being an important example. The fear that the British system of collective bargaining had an inflationary bias induced successive governments to accept direct responsibility for the supervision of the level of wage settlements.

All of these influences contributed to the rapid growth of labour market policies in the UK in the 1960s and 1970s. Implicit in this growth was a belief that the costs of subverting market forces were low compared to the benefits gained. Market imperfections in the form of imperfect information, high transaction costs, imperfect capital and product markets, produced rigidities which together with widespread externalities were assumed to prevent efficient operation of the labour market. Hence intervention might produce both efficiency and equity gains, hence the gradual displacement of *laissez-faire* by corporatism. Nowhere was the corporatist labour market more fully developed than in Sweden, where bargaining became economy-wide in 1956 and the National Labour Board (or AMS) supervised a staggering array of labour market selective policies (Ginsburg 1983). Scandinavia apart, the last two decades have seen a retreat from such beliefs, reflecting the eclipse of Keynesian economics, the reassertion of a belief in the efficiency of competitive markets and perversely, the reappearance of mass unemployment. The British Government has radically redirected Department of Employment and MSC intervention in the labour market since 1979. Wages Councils, Industrial Training Boards and employment security legislation have been abolished or weakened and interventionist policy has been largely limited to the use of 1930s-style *ad hoc* public works or an alphabet of targeted subsidies to reduce measured unemployment. The one area which has seen new intervention has been the school-to-work transition aimed at rectifying the perceived failure of the education system to provide suitably qualified and motivated workers. To illustrate these developments and to summarise present policy the development of the MSC is now considered.

1.2 The evolution of the Manpower Services Commission: 1973–88

In 1970 Crossley defined manpower policy as being concerned with public investments in human assets, using 'selective taxes and subsidies to alter the structure of incentives so as to bring optimising individual behaviour closer to that which is also optimal from the social point of view' (p. 129). This definition reflected contemporary economists' optimistic view of the effects of such policies on increasing the stock of human capital and reducing frictional unemployment. These arguments lay behind the growth of interventionist labour market policy chronicled above, and the establishment of the MSC on 1 January 1974 to run the public employment and training services. Loosely based on the Swedish AMS with the governing body representing government, employers and trade unions, it was given the long-term aim of developing a comprehensive manpower policy with a dual function:

1. To enable the country's manpower resources to be developed and contribute fully to economic well-being; and
2. To ensure that there are available to each worker the opportunities

and services he or she needs in order to lead a satisfying working life.

MSC (1977: 1)

Table 1.1   MSC expenditure by major programmes

	Percentage of total expenditure		
	1976/77	1982/83	1986/87
Placing services Jobcentre and other Employment services	20	11	5
Training services Adult training (TOPS, etc.)	43	18	9
School-to-work transition (YOPS, YTS, TVEI, NAFE)	—	45	38
Employment measures JCP/Community Programme	9	13	35
Total expenditure, current prices (£m.)*	430	1343	3032
Total expenditure, 1980 prices (£m)†	714	1129	2132

Source: MSC Annual Report 1976/77, 1982/83 and 1986/87
* Includes MSC expenditure on behalf of the Department of Employment.
† Using total final expenditure price index of the earlier year.

Perusal of successive Annual Reports of the MSC provides an introduction to its changing priorities. Three major internal reorganisations have occurred since 1974, and keywords appear and disappear from the reports with great frequency. As Table 1.1 shows, in 1976/77 the MSC spent a total of about £430m., in 1986/87 gross expenditure had risen to £3155m., a threefold increase in real terms. The growth of MSC expenditure is startling especially when compared with restrictions elsewhere in the public sector, but the changing composition of that expenditure is equally significant; Tables 1.1 and 1.2 provide an overview of these changes. In the early years, two-thirds of MSC expenditure was on adult training and the employment service, with a further fifth supporting private sector training largely through Industrial Training Boards. In recent years two-thirds has been spent on the school-to-work transition and job creation for the long-term unemployed, with more being spent on the Enterprise Allowance Scheme (EAS) than on Jobcentres and other employment services. There has been a relative and absolute decline of expenditure on Jobcentres, and programmes to influence geographical mobility of workers have virtually disappeared. Gradually the emphasis has changed from a concern for the needs of the individual to a belief that these coincide with the needs of employers, and that it is the latter needs which must be allowed to drive the labour market. Increasingly simple financial targets have replaced more general economic and social objectives; one illustration is that the Skills Training Agency was required to break even annually from 1986/87. The key measure of efficiency throughout the MSC has become average unit cost of services provided.

Table 1.2   Comparisons of MSC outputs in 1976/77 and 1986/87

	1976/77	1986/87
Employment service		
Vacancies notified	2 131 000	2 610 000
Placings	1 484 000	1 910 000
Training services		
TOPS/adult training	89 000	68 000*
(occupational, full-time		
at least 6 months)		
Training for young		
people	15 000	360 000*
Special measures		
JCP/Community Programme	55 500	307 500

Source: MSC Annual Report 1976/77 and 1986/87
* Entrants.

Within continuing schemes increasing emphasis has been placed on training on the job, and direct training provision has become targeted on the unemployed. The MSC has become increasingly involved in secondary, further and higher education. Increased reliance has been placed upon private sector employers deciding upon the form and content of all education and training provided or financed by the government or MSC. The reduced emphasis upon the specific needs of individual workers has been shown by the closure of Occupational Guidance Units and introduction of self-service Jobcentres. This changed role of the MSC was reflected in the responsibility for operating the employment service being returned to the Department of Employment in October 1987, with the MSC's more limited functions being reflected in a name change to the Training Commission. Some of these changes were largely cosmetic, reflecting the continued pragmatism of policy in this area. In 1986 the MSC still supported over 100 statutory and non-statutory industry training bodies, and operated schemes to encourage the quality and quantity of private sector training provision in shortage occupations. Taxes and subsidies were still used to stimulate employment and training opportunities for disadvantaged groups in the labour market, though sticks as well as carrots now feature.

The division of major programme responsibilities between the Department of Employment and Training Commission at the beginning of 1988 is outlined below, at which time around a million individuals were benefiting from training or employment schemes. Expenditure figures refer to net provisional expenditures in 1986/87 (MSC 1987).

Department of Employment

Jobcentres: about 1000 offices, expenditure £140m. Provide a no-charge placing service and recruit entrants to the employment, training and enterprise programmes of the two bodies

Restart Programme: 1.3 million interviews in 1986/87, expenditure £50m. Consultations with all long-term unemployed aimed at increasing their job search or entering rehabilitation or training programme

Jobclubs: about 1300 in March 1988. Job-searching assistance provided to groups of unemployed workers

Services to the disabled: 27 Employment Rehabilitation Centres, cost £102m. Assisting the re-employment of disabled workers and provision of sheltered employment such as in Remploy

Enterprise Allowance Scheme (EAS): 110 000 annual entrants in 1987/8, expenditure £150m. Provides financial and training assistance to unemployed workers who wish to become self-employed

Training Commission

Job Training Scheme Community Programme (JTS/CP): target 600 000 annual entrants, expenditure £1350m. Adult training for long-term unemployed, to be combined and relaunched in September 1988

Youth Training Scheme (YTS): 360 000 entrants in 1986/87, expenditure £940m. Provides up to two years' work experience/training for unemployed 16- and 17-year-old school-leavers

Non-Advanced Further Education (NAFE): expenditure £110m., transferred from Rate Support Grant. Ensures that work-related NAFE

relates more closely and cost-effectively to local employers' perceptions of needs
Technical and Vocational Education Initiative (TVEI): 61 000 students in 1986/87, expenditure £72m. Provides financial incentives to increase the provision of technical and vocational education to fourteen- to eighteen-year-olds

Smaller schemes, programmes administered by other departments and bodies and the legal framework within which the labour market operates are discussed in the relevant later chapters. In those chapters comparisons are also made with labour market policies in other countries. The above review has shown how labour market policy has shifted away from a concern with improving the quality of employment. In recent years, adult training and job search assistance have been displaced as priority areas by youth training and job creation for the unemployed. It remains to be discovered in the following pages the extent to which these changes reflect either better or different understanding of labour market behaviour, or alternatively different labour market conditions and different government objectives.

1.3 Plan of the book

With our primary concern to understand the origins and assess the success of labour market policy, the starting-point chosen is to establish the nature of the British labour market and the current state of economic analysis of labour market behaviour. In Chapter 2 the dominant neoclassical approach in labour economics is introduced, the gradual movement away from the auction market model is plotted and the variety of behaviour consistent with contemporary neoclassical theory examined. In this chapter the structuralist interpretation of internal labour markets is also considered, and the diversity of models within this approach is explored from their modern revival in the dual labour market model to insider–outsider and efficiency wage theories. Both the neoclassical and structuralist approaches feature in the remaining chapters since it is argued that each model gives important and unique insights into the behaviour of individual labour markets. A guide to more comprehensive treatments of labour economics appends this chapter. Chapter 3 provides a broad summary of the structure of the British labour market, and recent trends in employment and wages are examined. Particular consideration is given to the nature of labour market adjustment to external shocks and the relatively small response of wages to contractions, and consequential large response of employment, is noted. The final part of this chapter attempts to assess the relative importance of neoclassical and structuralist models to an understanding of the British labour market. It concludes that the variety and flexibility of these markets precludes a universal model of labour market behaviour. Guides to further reading and major sources of labour market information are provided at the end of this chapter.

The following chapters address specific policy areas and adopt a common approach. Firstly, a statistical introduction to the nature of the topic is provided, relating British experience to that of other developed economies. This is followed by a review of relevant theoretical contributions from both analytical traditions linked with a survey of major empirical studies utilising these models. Current policy is then outlined and evaluated in the light of the previous discussion. Each chapter ends with suggestions for further reading. The topics covered by the individual chapters are as follows. Chapter 4 examines current education and training policy, an area which has been the subject of continual and vehement debate for the last century in the UK. In contrast Chapter 5 considers search and mobility, areas neglected in recent policy discussions, though not in theoretical literature. Discrimination is the subject of Chapter 6, here the dominance of American studies is most noticeable, partly reflecting the more varied and extensive policy response in the USA. Many of the issues raised in the previous chapters reappear in Chapter 7 which examines recent unemployment and the varied policy responses. The penultimate chapter investigates a wide range of policy issues peripheral to the previous topics: trade unions; tax and benefits, and systems of wage-fixing. In Chapter 9, we conclude with a review of the principles which should determine the design and implementation of labour market policy.

Chapter 2

LABOUR MARKET ECONOMICS

Since Adam Smith the dominant approach to the analysis of labour market behaviour has been to examine the interaction of labour supply and demand. In this chapter we examine how this approach has developed over recent times. Labour market behaviour is central to both micro and macro models and, as we shall see, at the heart of most contemporary debates about appropriate economic policies lie disagreements about how labour markets react to changes in the economic environment.

The neoclassical analysis of the labour market developed by Jevons and Marshall at the end of the last century forms the basis of modern approaches. Their approach was to treat the labour market as comparable to any goods market and apply the emerging tools of marginal analysis to participants' behaviour. The evolution of modern neoclassical analysis from this base is the initial task of this chapter; for those requiring a detailed introduction a guide to further reading concludes the chapter.

2.1 The basic neoclassical model

Consider a world of individual decision-takers where potential workers are motivated by a desire to maximise utility and firms by a desire to maximise profits. Initially also assume that the labour market approximates to an auction market, where decision-makers are price-takers and cannot by their own actions influence the outcome of the interaction of market forces. A uniform wage prevails in the market. We are accordingly in a world of perfectly competitive labour and goods markets. The labour market is characterised by large numbers of small independent firms wishing to hire labour and unorganised workers seeking to find employment. Workers and jobs are homogeneous, so that firms view all applicants as having the same productivity characteristics and workers view all job offers as identical in non-wage characteristics. All job offers and acceptances are for a single, infinitely divisible time period and there are no barriers to mobility in the market. Finally firms and workers have perfect information about existing conditions in the labour market. Firms wish to hire labour because they wish to generate profits from additional production. Workers are incapable of producing for themselves all of the goods which they wish to consume, and in a capitalist and monetary economy seek employment to earn wages which enable them to increase their total utility. Let us now consider how the labour market would operate in such an economy during the short run: a period of time when firms operate with given technology and fixed quantities of plant and machinery.

2.1.1 The demand for labour

Consider initially the demand for labour of an individual firm in the short run. There can be no substitution between factors of production and thus there is a direct relationship between the desired production and employment levels. This relationship is specified by the production function. Given that the firm has a fixed quantity of machinery and plant in the short run, as the firm hires additional inputs of labour output will tend to rise, but not proportionally. As more and more labour is employed, workers become capital starved, having to share their machines with more fellow workers. Once machines are being operated by the designed number of operatives at the optimal capacity, further hiring of labour is likely to lead to the extra workers having a smaller impact on production levels than previous recruits. If we define the marginal physical product of labour as the additional units of output produced by the employment of an extra unit of labour, then the argument implies that the marginal physical product of labour must eventually fall as labour input rises. This relationship is called the law of diminishing returns and it determines the general shape of the firm's production function. The firm's output will generally rise with employment increases, but at a decreasing rate.

Given this relationship between employment and output what determines how much labour the firm will wish to try to hire? The firm is motivated by the desire to increase profits and its desired employment level must correspond to that level which maximises profits from the sale of production. Consider a firm which is already producing profitably: it has to decide whether its current production and employment levels are optimal, that is whether it is consistent with profit maximisation. It can solve this problem by considering whether it should employ an extra unit of labour. The firm is a price-taker in both the product market and labour market. It can therefore calculate the value of the marginal physical product of the extra unit of labour as being the product of the price it is taking for its good and the marginal physical product of labour. If this total exceeds the money wage it must pay to attract the additional unit of labour, its profits will rise by an expansion of employment. Where the monetary value of the marginal physical product of labour falls short of the going money wage rate then it can increase profits by reducing the input of labour. The optimal input of labour will be when the value of the marginal physical product of labour is equal to the going wage rate. The firm will have applied the profit-maximising rule of equating marginal revenue with marginal cost. It follows, other factors remaining unchanged, that a higher money wage rate must lead to a reduction in the desired level of employment, given diminishing marginal physical productivity. An alternative specification of the equi-marginal rule is that the firm should equate the marginal physical product of labour with the ratio of the price of labour to the price it is taking for its product, that is the real wage it is paying. Once again, as the marginal physical product falls as the firm hires additional labour, it will only wish to hire more if the real wage is also falling. The demand curve for labour is downward sloping with respect to the real wage.

If we extend this analysis to the long run firms can now alter their production techniques as relative factor prices change, suggesting that the demand for labour becomes more sensitive to the level of real wages, the demand curve becoming flatter. More generally the price elasticity of the demand for labour for a given change in the wage rate will depend upon:

1. How sensitive the demand for the firm's product is to changes in price. The more elastic is the demand for the product the more elastic is the firm's demand for labour.
2. The ease of substitution of capital for labour. The greater the ability to substitute capital for labour, the greater the elasticity of demand for labour.
3. The contribution of labour costs to total costs. If labour costs are a small proportion of total costs, the effects of higher wages on total costs and therefore sales and employment will be small.

4. The elasticity of supply of substitute factors of production. The more inelastic are the supply of non-labour factors the more inelastic is the demand for labour.

If we aggregate this analysis to the industry or economy level then we can no longer maintain the assumption that product price remains unchanged as firms adjust to different wage rates. However, if we maintain the assumption that the final level of demand is independent of the wage rate, then we can conclude that, as the scale of aggregation increases, the price elasticity will tend to increase. As employment in an industry rises in the short run, now both the marginal product of labour and the price of the product fall. This makes demand more elastic for a given change in the wage rate, or in other words, the demand for labour curve becomes flatter.

The neoclassical marginal productivity theory is purely a theory of profit-maximising firms' desired demand for labour. By itself it tells us nothing about the levels of employment and wages in the economy unless we combine it with a theory of labour supply. Contrary to the beliefs of some early exponents of the theory, because the value of the marginal product of a unit of labour depends upon how much capital it can utilise, wage levels in accordance with marginal productivity have no normative implications. Marginal productivity cannot resolve the issue of what constitutes a 'fair' wage.

2.1.2 The supply of labour

Before we can summarise the neoclassical theory of labour supply we need to make one clarification and one modification to our earlier discussion. We have so far been reluctant to specify the units of measurement for the demand and supply of labour. The quantity of labour is two-dimensional: the quantity of workers and the hours worked per worker. Any analysis must therefore examine both the participation rates of the population and hours supplied per participant. The modification is to the earlier statement that neoclassical labour market analysis is concerned with individual decision-making. Such analysis is particularly inappropriate when we discuss the supply of labour where decisions are typically taken by households. Thus family, not personal, utility maximisation becomes the goal of rational decision-makers.

The model assumes that participants are free to vary their hours of work. In deciding the appropriate supply of labour the household has to decide the optimal combination of market work and non-market activities. Market work generates income which enables the household to purchase goods and services, but utility is also obtained from leisure and home production of goods and services. The opportunity cost of market work is forgone leisure and home production. The optimal supply of labour will be that which maximises utility subject to the constraint of an exogenously determined wage rate. Unfortunately for the purposes of testing, the model gives us an ambiguous response of labour supply to changes in the real wage rate. A change in the real wage rate represents a change in the relative price of work and non-market activities, and as such must generate both substitution and income effects. Any rise in the wage rate increases the opportunity cost of non-market activities and will generate a substitution of income-generating time for the more expensive non-market activities. However, the rise in the wage rate has altered the household's income from its existing supply of market labour and it is unlikely that the income elasticity of income time and non-income time are equal. If, for example, the household has already achieved their target income then the income effect of a rise in the real wage rate would be to reduce their market labour supply. The net impact of the wage rise therefore depends upon the relative size of the substitution and income effects, and labour supply may rise or fall as a consequence. For the multi-person household the analysis is even more complex with a rise in a wife's wage rate causing changes in both the quantity and composition of her family's labour supply. It is not therefore clear whether the labour supply curve with respect to real wages has a positive slope. Conventionally and without any obvious justification, neoclassical economics proceeds by assuming that over the relevant wage range the substitution effect dominates during the short run, giving us an upward-sloping supply curve of labour.

2.1.3 The interaction of labour demand and supply

Consider a single labour market where individual firms' and households' decisions have been aggregated to generate market demand and supply curves for labour; such a market is shown in Fig. 2.1. The assumptions of perfect competition, particularly homogeneity of workers and jobs, allow most of the problems of aggregation to be avoided.

Assume initially that the prevailing real wage level is w_1; at this wage firms wish to hire n_1 units of labour while households wish to supply a greater quantity, n_2. At a wage of w_1 the market is experiencing an excess supply of labour. The adjustment mechanism

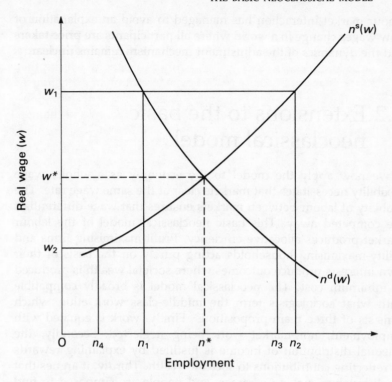

Fig. 2.1   A perfectly competitive labour market

in this model is that those workers without jobs, or underemployed in their present jobs, offer themselves to firms at lower wages. This downward movement in wages has two effects: households withdraw marginal units of labour from the market and firms are stimulated to increase employment. Given the assumptions of the model, the downwards movement of wages will eventually be sufficient to restore the market to equilibrium, where employers' and households' plans can both be fulfilled, that is at w^* and n^*. Consider the alternative case of disequilibrium: w_2. At this wage rate employers plan to hire n_3 units of labour while households only wish to supply n_4. In this case the market has an excess of demand for labour. Here the model stresses that profit-maximising firms in their desire to fulfil production plans will bid up wages. Rising real wages will encourage households to supply more labour and also discourage firms from some of their expansion plans, once again pushing the market towards equilibrium. This neoclassical description of labour market interaction has managed to avoid an explanation of how wages change in a world where all participants are price-takers and the dynamics of the adjustment mechanism remains unclear.

2.2 Extensions to the basic neoclassical model

If we now apply the model to the economy as a whole, wage flexibility necessitates that markets clear at the same wage rate. The mobility of labour between markets ensures that wage differentials are competed away. This basic neoclassical model of the labour market produces allocative efficiency. Profit-maximising firms and utility-maximising households acting purely on the basis of their own interests produce outcomes where societal wealth is produced at minimum cost. The neoclassical model is broadly compatible with what sociologists term the middle-class work ethic, which consists of three main propositions. Firstly, work is equated with employment, non-market work being neglected. Secondly, the unequal distribution of income is justified by explaining rewards as reflecting contributions to societal wealth. Thirdly, it argues that work involves making a career, and people are supposed to find self-fulfilment through their work. Opportunities for advancement are available for all, a harmony of interests between employers and employees is assumed and disutilities of employment apart from lost leisure are largely ignored. Such a set of beliefs may not make sense for major groups in society such as unskilled workers, housewives and ethnic minorities. While radical critiques are considered later, initially we develop refinements to the analysis within the existing approach. To explain these refinements we gradually relax some of the restrictive assumptions of the basic model. The development of neoclassical labour economics has been the result of a gradual realisation that many real-world labour market characteristics are inconsistent with the perfectly competitive model.

2.2.1 Heterogeneity of workers and jobs

Early in the development of neoclassical labour market analysis, Adam Smith's explanation of wage differentials was incorporated into the approach. Once we relax the assumptions of homogeneous workers and jobs then wage differentials will persist in the long run. Workers now have different tastes regarding conditions, responsibilities and regularity of work, and utility maximisation is no longer synonymous with income maximisation. Workers maximise the sum of pecuniary and non-pecuniary returns from employment. Even with all workers having the same productivity characteristics, it is the 'net advantages' of employment which are equalised by competition, not wage rates. Workers, however, do not have the same productivity characteristics, and the main explanation of wage differentials in this approach is in terms of differences in education, training and experience. Workers can invest in costly, productivity-augmenting activities and so gain increased future labour market income. Such investment decisions can be treated akin to fixed investment decisions, and competition ensures that in the long run rates of return on investments of equal risk are equalised. Wage differentials in the long run will therefore reflect the costs of acquiring the required skill and experience to enter the market, as well as different rates of time preference and attitudes to risk-taking. Implicit in this human capital approach to wage differentials is the view that productivity is worker, not job, determined and that labour market opportunities are unaffected by characteristics of workers unrelated to productivity, such as sex and race. Where firms have unique production processes then training will have to be firm-financed. Such firm-specific training encourages the adoption of employment practices which reduce labour turnover and therefore lower training costs.

In the short run any shortages of skills in an expanding market should cause an increase in the relative wage of that market. The rate of return from investment in that skill is now higher and that should induce an increase of labour supply to that market. This adjustment mechanism is not instantaneous and disequilibrium wage differentials may persist for long periods. Human capital theory is more fully examined in Chapter 4, together with competing theories which reject the notion that education enhances earnings through augmenting worker productivity. Modern neoclassical analysis can therefore accommodate certain aspects of real-world heterogeneity. The labour market now consists of a collection of perfect sub-markets, classified by occupation and location, in each of which a single wage rate prevails and within which employees are perfectly mobile. There are fundamental theoretical problems introduced by factor heterogeneity, particularly concerned with whether factors can be aggregated and marginal products identified. Cambridge critics doubt whether the underlying production function can be specified in such a neoclassical world.

2.2.2 Monopsony and organised labour

The basic model outlined above assumed firms faced perfectly competitive product and labour markets. If the assumption of perfectly competitive product markets is initially relaxed, the market now consists of firms with downward-sloping demand curves for their products. As they hire more labour they not only face diminishing marginal productivity but also a lower price for their product. The main conclusion is that wage and employment levels will be lower with the introduction of imperfectly competitive product markets, assuming the rate of innovation is independent of market structure. If, alternatively, dominant employers in a labour market are introduced the behaviour of monopsonistic labour markets can be studied. As the monopsonist wishes to hire more labour, because the firm faces the market's upward-sloping supply curve for labour, it has to offer a higher wage to induce additional supply of labour. Compared to a perfectly competitive market, employment and wage levels will again be lower in equilibrium.

More problematic to neoclassical theory is how to model a market where labour is organised. Trade unions must face a downward-sloping demand curve for their members' labour supply: they face a trade-off between wage and employment levels. Early attempts to integrate trade unions into the model relied upon the treatment of unions as being equivalent to monopolists in product markets. Models of bilateral monopoly were developed but had the fundamental weaknesses that they provided no justification for their particular assumptions regarding the union's wage–employment preference or explanation for prevalence of collective bargaining. The efficient bargain model attempts to rectify these objections by allowing unions and firms to bargain about wage rates and employment. As relative strength determines outcomes there is no unique relationship between employment and wage levels. However, outside of Japan unions rarely seem to bargain about employment. To explain such behaviour it appears that we have to move away from the notion of unions as monopolists and consider union bargaining behaviour as reflecting the interests of the majority of their members. These models, where trade unions merely want to push wages as high as possible, are discussed in Chapter 7 where the contribution of wage rigidity to unemployment is considered.

2.2.3 Imperfect and costly information

The competitive model of labour market behaviour relies upon labour mobility to adjust wages to market-clearing levels. Typically the model emphasises supply-side forces dominating the adjustment mechanism: workers move from low-paying to higher-paying firms so equalising wage rates in the market. For this adjustment mechanism to operate speedily workers and firms must be aware of labour market conditions. Where workers and jobs are not identical, information is not fully and freely available and search will be a basic feature of the market. Markets will therefore take time to adjust to environmental changes, and in the short run imperfect information gives all firms an element of monopsony power. The mobility of labour no longer instantaneously eliminates disequilibrium wage differentials. Neoclassical search theory tames some of the problems of imperfect information by the application of the standard tools of constrained maximisation decision-making. Facing costly search, decision-makers on both sides of the labour market adopt optimal strategies where the costs and benefits of further search are equalised at the margin. Such analysis can be utilised to explain the existence of inter-firm wage differentials within local labour markets. Market clearing is no longer instantaneous and persisting inter-firm differentials may reflect different solutions to optimal recruitment strategy. To an extent, wage costs and search costs are substitutes for a firm, and firms can pay lower wage rates if they search more intensively.

Firms wishing to fill a vacancy no longer hire the first applicant and workers no longer accept the first job offer. The existence of unfilled vacancies and unemployed workers is now consistent with efficient labour markets. Firms and workers are investing in productive search prior to job-matching. Job and worker search theories are more closely examined in Chapter 5. Where workers and firms have different attitudes to risk-taking it is possible that they can find mutually beneficial solutions to coping with shocks. The implicit contract theories to be discussed in Chapter 7 have developed from this proposition.

2.2.4 Costly turnover and job-changing

In the basic model developed, labour mobility is assumed costless to firms and workers, yet in the real world firms do not view turnover benignly nor do workers view involuntary redundancy with indifference. The reason for the model's failure to explain this feature of labour markets is that so far we have equated firms' costs and workers' benefits with the prevailing wage rate. For firms the critical variable is labour costs per unit of output, not wage costs per unit of labour. There are fixed costs of employing labour as well as the variable wage costs. These fixed costs are, in part, comprised of turnover costs, such as firm-specific training and recruitment costs. To replace existing employees is expensive to firms because of the hiring costs and the lower productivity of new workers during training. Where these costs are significant firms will adopt personnel policies which attempt to minimise turnover. Compulsory redundancies are avoided where possible, and firms rely on natural wastage. In temporary downturns firms will tend to hoard labour, especially skilled labour. The observed pro-cyclical movements in labour productivity are consistent with this behaviour, generating a slow adjustment of employment levels to changes in output over the business cycle.

The personnel policies which firms introduce to encourage worker loyalty generate rents for their employees. They are earning higher wages than their labour could command elsewhere in the market. Wage and non-wage benefits based upon seniority, such as holiday and sick pay entitlement, reduce labour mobility. The benefits which workers receive from employment are not purely financial; socialisation has produced consumption benefits. This psychological gratification obtained reflects the social interaction and status which a stable work environment generates. Involuntary separation requires costly search and the non-wage characteristics of job offers cannot easily be discovered. Risk-averting workers and cost-minimising firms are therefore likely to produce low mobility in those sections of the labour market, where the fixed costs of employing labour are high. Implicit in the contracts between workers and firms in these sectors will be employee tenure.

2.2.5 Contemporary neoclassical labour economics

We have tried to summarise the 'central core' of the neoclassical approach to labour market behaviour, and in its basic form this model has a coherence and elegance unapproached by its predecessors and competitors. The major refinements made to the basic model have been examined and the approach can now reconcile many of the features of contemporary labour markets which are outlined in Chapter 3. The existence of widespread inertia, imperfect information and unemployment is consistent with the competitive approach. Modern neoclassical analysis is still supply dominated, ignoring intra-firm decision-making and assuming that production is the outcome of a purely technical relationship between inputs, but it is not monolithic. It is indeed so malleable and robust that it is difficult to find testable propositions unique to the approach or to identify its distinctiveness. The uniqueness of neoclassical theory appears to rest on the belief that marginal analysis applied to individual decision-making in competitive markets can explain labour market behaviour. The remainder of this chapter considers analysis which seeks to replace traditional theory rather than refine it.

2.3 Alternative approaches to the analysis of the labour market

2.3.1 Segmentation

Prior to the neoclassical model being formally developed, John Stuart Mill introduced the concept of non-competing groups. He argued that to treat the labour market as competitive was erroneous and would generate false policy pronouncements. This century the apparent failure of policies based on conventional theory to improve the position of the low paid, led to a resurgence of interest in segmented labour markets. In this approach, auction or open labour markets are only found in labour-intensive, low technology industries; these 'bad' jobs are collectively termed the secondary labour market. Elsewhere there are substantial barriers to labour mobility. In the 'good' jobs, or primary, sector firms operate a structured, internal labour market, largely independent of competitive forces in the wider market. The emergence of these structured internal labour markets is explained by the increased technological demands of production which makes each firm's skill requirements unique. In this approach, associated with Doeringer and Piore, each firm has to finance its own training programme and therefore has an interest in reducing labour turnover. The reliance on set procedures in internal pricing and allocation decisions is a result of this concern. Wage structure will reflect custom, rather than worker productivity or external market forces. Firm-specific training makes current employees or 'insiders' more valuable to employers than similar workers in the external labour market or 'outsiders'. Vertical job ladders and age- or tenure-related remuneration policies designed to retain 'insiders' are a feature of high-wage, primary labour markets.

In Okun's (1981) version, turnover is postulated to impose a 'toll' on employers, which is the sum of their search, screening and training costs. Given these turnover costs firms must make a long-term arrangement which is attractive to workers, hence the development of 'career' or internal labour markets. Since there are turnover costs for both workers and employers, exploitation could occur on either side, depending on relative costs and conditions in the external market. These problems can be avoided if employers and employees can agree on 'fair' conditions of employment. Hence the emergence of implicit contracts which feature agreed responses to environmental changes. As we shall discuss in our consideration of unemployment (Ch. 7), these contracts are likely to produce employment adjustments rather than wage adjustment in the face of product demand contractions.

Internal labour markets take two main forms: firm internal labour markets and occupational internal labour markets. Firm internal labour markets are operated by 'good' employers who recruit predominantly at the lowest grades, the higher grades being filled internally, often on the basis of seniority. Because firms' presumption is that hired workers will be given tenure and progress up the job ladder, the screening process for recruits is extensive and applicants with characteristics similar to existing employees are likely to be favoured. According to the segmented labour market approach 'good' jobs make 'good' workers, not vice versa. Wages in jobs are therefore set by the technology-constrained productivity, not by the productivity potential of the particular employee. Written agreements will specify wage rates for different employments rather than employees and specify firing and redundancy procedures. The idea that wages are attached to jobs, not people, becomes particularly important when we discuss education and training in Chapter 4 and labour market discrimination in Chapter 6. Firms who operate internal labour markets are reluctant to adjust wages, when faced with specific labour shortages or changed product market conditions. This reluctance stems from the disruption which would be caused in established wage differentials and relativities. They fear that this disruption would produce disenchanted employees and turnover would increase. Preferred adjustment takes place through overtime, shift-working or short-time working according to established rules.

Occupational internal labour markets transcend particular employers. Movements between firms follows established rules unique to the occupation. The higher professions such as medicine and law illustrate such behaviour. Occupational licensing and entry requirements are controlled by a professional body such as the British Medical Association which also specifies a procedure for promotion. Membership of the professional association almost guarantees employment, since entrance is restricted. Withdrawal of membership is only countenanced when specific rules have been violated. In certain periods and countries craft workers have managed to maintain an occupational internal labour market.

The composition and form of labour market segments will change over time. Bluestone and Stevenson (1981) present the example of the changing employment strategy in the retail trade. Until recently the department store was commonly a locally based family firm with an internal labour market, which recruited school-leavers as full-time sales assistants and provided a job ladder to management posts not filled by the family. Since the 1960s nationally based chain stores have replaced these stores and changed the nature of the labour market. The greater firm size has created a need for professional managers, extended internal labour markets have been developed for this section of employees. At the same time electronic cash tills, pre-packaging and self-service have deskilled sales jobs. Firms have replaced many full-time employees by unskilled and part-time or casual workers, who work the tills or fill the shelves at peak sales times only. Different and changing environments will cause employment structures to differ both within firms' sub-markets and over time; primary labour market firms are neither monolithic nor sacrosanct.

2.3.2 Employer–employee relationships

Recently the segmented labour market theory has been linked more directly with approaches which examine the impact of industrial relations on labour market behaviour. Orthodox theory pays little attention to the importance of industrial relations in the labour market. It assumes that production of goods and services is purely the consequence of a technological relationship between labour input and output. Hours of work are assumed to have unique productivity for a given worker in a given job: the motivation of the worker is treated as irrelevant to the outcome and conflicts of interest between workers and employers ignored. An alternative approach is to adopt Leibenstein's suggestion that, rather than operating on their production function, firms inevitably suffer from inefficiencies, and their task is to minimise this X-inefficiency. Unlike capital, firms are restricted in the way they can use labour, by health and safety legislation for example, and therefore have to generate a spirit of co-operation. Employers and workers can usually agree on an appropriate wage per hour worked but it is difficult to specify an agreed outlay of employee effort per hour worked. In Marxian terms there is a distinction between labour and labour power; firms hire and workers lease only the human potential to work. There is accordingly a basic conflict of interest between employers and employees: the former wish to maximise effort supplied per hour of work, workers to minimise it. To an extent supervisors and quality inspectors can monitor workers' effort and limit shirking, but employers need to get workers' co-operation if they are to generate potential profits. Firms adopt systems of labour control to minimise these tensions and conflicts and reduce worker solidarity. The efficiency wage approach emphasises that paying above competitive market wages may be effective as a means of producing high productivity and low turnover and therefore low labour costs per unit of output. Alternatively employers may widen divisions among their workforce, reducing their bargaining power, by rigid grading structures and discriminatory hiring and promotion practices.

In Williamson's *et al* (1975) model, because workers hold a short-term monopoly in the knowledge of how to perform their job and due to the need for co-operation between employees in production, internal labour markets develop. The task of these internal labour markets is to encourage employees not to exploit their short-run bargaining power. The offer of more stable employment and a 'fair' contract, encourage workers to view their own self-interests as compatible with the long-term prospects of the firm. Job evaluation and work study are means firms adopt to gauge 'fair', that is acceptable, relativities. Firms implement a single unified pay structure, where wage rates are specified by job, not by individual workers. Labour management is therefore bureaucratised, elaborate rules and job criteria are specified to fragment the workforce and encourage individual worker commitment and loyalty. A hierarchically organised internal labour market promises to reward workers with increases in income and status if they are prepared to identify with, and accept, the discipline of the firm. Once again the firm will be very reluctant to change wage levels and structures, and these will be largely independent of labour and product market forces.

Alternatively Akerlof (1982) attempts to integrate the arguments of Okun and Leibenstein discussed above, with the work of sociologists and Marxists. In his model concentrating on team production, workers have sentiment for their fellow workers and cannot be treated individually by their employer. Sociologists argue that the determinants of workers' effort will be the norm of the work group. The giving of gifts is determined by the norms of behaviour, workers acquiring utility from an exchange of gifts with employers. Workers exchange their gift, effort in excess of minimum standards, for that of employers, wages above external market levels. Wages and effort are therefore mutually reciprocal gifts. To integrate with the segmented labour market approach, Akerlof suggests that primary labour markets are those where the gift components of the labour input and wage levels are sizeable. Secondary labour markets in contrast are where the wage level reflects market-clearing requirements.

2.4 Competitive v. structural models of the labour market

In some ways the arguments of the last two sections are reminiscent of the neoclassical approach with imperfect information, heterogeneous workers and fixed costs of employing labour. All of these arguments lead to the conclusion that firms view turnover as costly, that wage costs are a poor proxy for unit labour costs and that wages may be slow to reflect changes in market conditions. The possibility that through incentive or selection effects labour productivity depends upon wage and not vice versa, repeals the laws of supply and demand and single price (Stiglitz 1987). The segmented labour market approach has yet to be fully integrated with the efficiency wage approach, at present it lacks the elegance and coherence of orthodox theory, and questions have been raised about what additional insights are gained by rejecting the competitive approach. Perhaps this is the wrong question to be asked at this time. There are two main reasons for this suggestion; firstly, competition and segmentation are not absolute concepts and an either/or choice is not required. Secondly, both approaches are at present so amorphous that almost any labour market behaviour appears consistent with at least some part of their paradigms. The wide use of terms such as 'segmentation', 'duality', 'insider–outsider' and 'internal labour markets' has not been accompanied by agreement on the meaning of these terms (Ryan 1981), while in the neoclassical approach conventional competitive influences appear to have become less important and labour mobility no longer viewed as desirable. For example, the presence of imperfect information can induce firms to use wages to manipulate productivity. A higher wage raises productivity by attracting better qualified applicants, and inducing present employees to increase effort. Such theories completely reverse the traditional causation between wages and productivity of neoclassical analysis. Within the neoclassical approach there is such an enormous range of opinions and theories, that the label 'neoclassical' appears no longer to be useful as a means of specifying a particular belief or approach. A better dichotomy for our consideration of manpower policy in this study is between competitive, and structural or segmented models of the labour market. While any simple division is somewhat arbitrary, and to an extent produces 'straw men', our dichotomy will illuminate many of the key differences in contemporary debates.

The competitive approach can be summarised as follows: the emphasis is on labour markets responding to market forces. While the auction market is recognised as an over-simplification, wages do move to equilibrium levels and do produce market-clearing adjustments in labour supply. Though there is some rigidity of absolute and relative wage levels in the very short run, for policy purposes labour markets can be viewed as flexible price markets. The long-run movement towards equalising wage differentials means that any persisting differentials reflect differences in employee productivity, due to uneven investments in education, training and experience. Because of the quantity and variety of sub-labour markets, information is costly, and firms and workers search prior to job-matching. Unemployment and unfilled vacancies are therefore consistent with labour market equilibrium. Labour market efficiency in this approach can be proxied by long-run employment levels, or unemployment levels, since the allocative mechanism eventually operates and firms are always making best use of their workforce.

The structuralist approach pays much more attention to custom and practice in the labour market. Collective rather than individual decision-making is dominant, the labour market cannot be insulated from society as a whole. Enterprise-specific rents are paid to workers, and this together with their individual bargaining power leads to highly stable work groups. These stable groups develop norms concerning the fairness of work effort and distribution of those rents. It is social cohesion, rather than efficiency, which underlies the development of relative wage rigidity and seniority-determined pay scales in internal labour markets (Doeringer 1986). Firms in many sectors of the economy have structured their labour markets in order in produce motivated and loyal employees. This primary sector comprises of career labour markets where there are long-term job-matchings. Firms are reluctant to change wages when labour and product market conditions alter, and any adjustment is slow and largely through previously determined rules for changes in working patterns. Primary labour markets are therefore fix-price markets and only secondary markets are flex-price. Education and training can assist workers' acceptance into internal labour markets but luck is important; wages reflect the jobs', not workers', characteristics. Underemployment and unemployment are partly a consequence of this quantity adjustment, rather than price adjustment in the labour market. Much greater emphasis is placed on the determinants of labour demand in this approach, with employers usually being the dominant decision-makers in the hiring process. Because the productivity characteristics of the worker no longer determine their present employment, and X-inefficiency is always present, employment levels no longer proxy efficiency in the economy. Efficiency is no longer an absolute concept and can only be assessed once the social welfare function has been specified.

While competitive forces dominate the secondary labour market they are not completely absent from the primary sector. These labour markets are subject to the entry of new work groups and firms themselves face competition in the product market. These forces may be weak in the short run but cannot be ignored in the long run. Also the sharp dichotomy between 'good' and 'bad' jobs in the dual labour market model appears too simple, and the distribution of the quality of jobs is more likely to be multimodal rather than bimodal. However, the emphasis upon the social foundations of internal labour markets, as opposed to human capital, price incentives and technical efficiency foundations, has produced fruitful insights into labour market behaviour. Critically the two approaches are not really substitutes for each other since both types of labour markets exist in the economy. The important question concerns the relative importance, location and permanence of these two types of market.

2.5 Policy implications

It is in the area of policy proposals and assessments that the emergence of structured labour market models has produced the most significant debates. In the neoclassical approach, the presumption that competition promotes efficiency dominates policy-making, and inefficient firms and institutional arrangements are automatically displaced. It is the correction of market imperfections or adjustment for market failure that should motivate labour market policy. Unemployment, above that resulting from imperfect information, is seen as primarily reflecting the imperfections produced by trade unions and the system of unemployment compensation. Poverty is the result of low investments in human capital, reflecting failures in the capital market. Discrimination in the labour market is continually being undermined by competitive forces.

In the segmented labour market approach the efficiency of unregulated markets cannot be assumed. Competition cannot be relied upon to produce acceptable levels or distributions of employment and income, and institutional arrangements may be slow to change even when they have outlived their economic rationale. The policy emphasis is here upon structural and environmental changes in the market. Unemployment now reflects quantity adjustment in the market-place, and the self-correcting mechanism of real wage adjustments is ineffective in all but the longest time period. The required policy is to stimulate demand by expansionary macroeconomic policies or use tax/subsidies to alter the desired worker and hours input of given output levels. Discrimination here reflects the inability of certain groups to gain access to 'good' jobs. Poverty is due to an inadequate supply of 'good' jobs. Again policy needs to be directed at the demand side of the market or at fundamental social and political reforms. Policies based upon positive discrimination, together with the extension of the spread of ownership and control of resources, are what are required to combat these problems. We have thus the classic confrontation between an approach which generally limits governments to protecting and creating competitive markets, and an approach which can sanction widespread government intervention in the labour market.

Minimum wage laws provide a vehicle to explore the differences between the two approaches to labour market policy. The competitive approach believes that either such laws have no influence since the minimum wage is fixed below the market-clearing level or that employment of unskilled workers must fall significantly as substitution occurs. According to the structuralist approach these allocative distortions may be offset by potential benefits. Since unemployment is created the costs of being displaced from the primary sector are greater and this should lead to lower wages and greater employment in the primary sector. For those firms directly affected by the minimum wage there should be productivity gains and benefits from less supervision of workers. Hence without considering equity issues minimum wage legislation could enhance social welfare.

In these concluding sections we have attempted to identify two broad approaches to analysing the behaviour of labour markets. These approaches are much less rigid than may have been suggested and, of course, overlap. Each approach recognises, though not publicly, the existence of the other type of market in some sectors of the economy. This partial complementarity gives rise to, and is reinforced by, a lack of empirical studies in labour economics which directly test competing theories. However, most contemporary disputes in labour economics can be traced back to differences of opinion about the relative importance of competitive and structured labour markets. More commonly these disputes actually surface as disagreements about whether labour markets are price or quantity adjusting in the period of time under consideration. Such a dispute transcends labour economics and constitutes the central issue of contemporary economic debate. In Chapter 3 we outline the operation of a modern economy's labour market and compare that operation with that predicted by the models discussed above. In the succeeding chapters we will repeatedly find that underlying economists' differences on policy proposals and assessments of existing policy are caused by either differences in value judgements, or a fundamental disagreement about how labour markets operate. We trust that these two causes are independent!

Further reading

This chapter has not attempted a complete survey of contemporary labour economics; those who require such treatment should consult some of the following texts before continuing. Comprehensive and competent introductory reviews of neoclassical theory are contained in Fleisher and Kniesner (1984), Joll et al. (1983) and Reynolds, Masters and Moser (1987). The collection of surveys edited by Ashenfelter and Layard (1986) represents a comprehensive, graduate-level review of labour economics. Carline et al. (1985) offer a more specialist survey of certain areas of contemporary labour economics. Robinson's (1986) book includes an original and stimulating introduction to labour economics in the first half of his assessment of UK monetarism. Doeringer (1986) provides a concise summary of the present position of the structuralist approach. The survey by Stiglitz (1987) examines the efficiency wage models and considers their fundamental implications for economics. For stimulating insights into labour economics try Akerlof's (1984) exploration of the contribution which anthropologists, sociologists and social psychologists can make to the investigation of labour market behaviour. Marsden (1986) also makes an interesting contribution to the development of a broader, social science approach to labour economic phenomena.

Chapter 3

THE LABOUR MARKET

The present methodological basis of most social science is that analytical developments reflect the consensus of empirical studies. This implies that the popularity of any economic theory should in principle reflect empirical support rather than analytical elegance or consistency with widely held political or philosophical viewpoints. In practice the immaturity and inadequacy of economic analysis and the strong normative elements inherent in investigations of economic phenomena prevent such purity. Moreover there are long lags in the interaction between theory and evidence, with economic theories often reflecting institutional frameworks of the past rather than present. Neoclassical labour market theory, for example, was initially developed for an economy dominated by a male workforce heavily employed in small and predominantly manufacturing establishments. In this chapter we attempt to summarise the key characteristics of contemporary Western labour markets; discussion concentrates on long-term trends and on British experience, although when this is different from other Western experience this is noted. Detailed discussion of education and training, search, discrimination and unemployment are contained in the specialised chapters and here we largely emphasise other characteristics.

In the first part of the chapter we concentrate upon three features of the labour market: employment, wages and institutional forces. The survey shows that modern economies offer employment predominantly in the service sector, with future growth of full-time employment likely to benefit the high skill or knowledge occupations. Small firms, self-employment, part-time and temporary employment are becoming increasingly important areas of the UK labour market. The majority of the workforce experience low inter-firm mobility and many appear to be rewarded for seniority by higher pay or promotion. Wage differentials tend to be broadly stable, though recently there are indications of an increased dispersion of wages. Unions bargain predominantly about wages rather than employment, establishments appear to pay more to union employees than they would to a non-organised workforce. In comparison with other developed economies the UK lies somewhere in the middle of the range covering employment and hours worked flexibility, but at the bottom of the range in real wage flexibility. In the latter part of the chapter we examine more directly the interrelationships between the current behaviour of the labour market and the various attempts to model that behaviour discussed in the previous chapter. Detailed analysis brings out the diversity of behaviour found in individual labour markets; it is therefore concluded that it is appropriate to analyse policy issues in the succeeding chapters within an economic framework which includes both competitive and structured labour markets.

3.1 The structure of the UK labour market

3.1.1 Employment

The working population of the UK towards the end of the 1980s was around 27 million, about half the total private household population. The size of the workforce depends upon two influences, the size of the population and the proportion of that population available for work, the latter being termed the activity or participation rate. In recent years the population of working age has been rising fairly rapidly, partly offset by a lower overall activity rate. About 60 per cent of the male and 38 per cent of the female population are economically active in the UK, rates only surpassed by Denmark in the EEC. Over the last twenty years in particular, changes in patterns of consumption, international comparative advantage and family role specialisations have produced fairly dramatic changes in the composition of this workforce. The growth of the service sector and institutional forces favouring part-time employees has generated demand pressures for female workers which together with supply-side forces have caused a steady increase in female participation rates. The most significant changes have occurred among married women; in 1951 only 22 per cent of wives were economically active, but that figure had risen to 53 per cent by 1986.

Females now account for about 45 per cent of all employees, though almost half of women work part-time (less than thirty hours per week). In aggregate females have a low but rising activity rate, while males have a relatively high but slowly falling activity rate, the latter largely reflecting the growth of further and higher education and earlier retirement. Britons appear to have a relatively long working life compared to other developed economies, with higher participation rates for males and females in the ten years before British state retirement pension is payable (though the UK has a relatively low proportion of adult males and females in full-time employment).

The recent changes in the industrial and occupational patterns of employment may have been as significant as the more often noted growth of the female workforce. Thirty years ago about 42 per cent of employees worked in both the service and manufacturing sectors. Since that time the absolute decline of manufacturing means that currently about 67 per cent of employees now work in the service sector. Within this growth sector the most rapid increases in employment in the 1980s have been in the financial services, wholesale distribution, repairs and health sectors. As Table 3.1 illustrates, these trends have been replicated in all Western developed economies,

Table 3.1   Composition of employment by sector

	Percentages of total employment			
	1974	1979	1984	1987
UK				
Agriculture	2.8	2.6	2.7	2.4
Industry*	42.2	38.7	32.9	30.8
Services	55.1	58.6	64.4	66.8
EEC				
Agriculture	11.8	10.0	8.9	—
Industry*	40.5	38.2	34.3	—
Services	47.8	51.8	56.7	—
USA				
Agriculture	4.2	3.6	3.3	2.7
Industry*	32.5	31.3	28.5	26.8
Services	63.4	65.2	68.2	70.4
Japan				
Agriculture	12.9	11.2	8.9	7.0
Industry*	37.0	34.9	34.8	34.6
Services	50.1	53.9	56.3	58.4

Source: OECD *Labour Force Statistics*
* Industry includes mining, utilities and construction.

and the growth of employment in the service sector reflects both the faster growth of demand for its products and the faster growth of labour productivity in the manufacturing sector. Manufacturing has a slightly higher proportion of full-time employees, though its economic prominence is due to about two-thirds of British exports of goods and services originating in this sector.

Non-service sector employment is more cyclically unstable and therefore the impact of recession is to speed up this structural change; between 1979 and 1985 the number of manufacturing employees fell by 1 838 000. Over the same period the number of employees in the service sector increased by 575 000 while the numbers of self-employed, predominantly in the service sector, rose by 708 000. The contractions of employment within manufacturing since 1971 have been dramatic: employment in textiles, leather footwear and clothing has fallen by 49 per cent, while in motor vehicles and parts it has fallen by 44 per cent. The heterogeneity of the service sector has been increasing with half of the growth in the service industries' employment being in the business services areas, which includes accountants, advertising and public relations and computer personnel. In part this change reflects the direct transfer of jobs from manufacturing to the service industries as professional services become more specialised and are subcontracted (Rajan and Pearson 1986). About 15 per cent of service jobs now directly depend upon manufacturing companies, and these particular service sector jobs are cyclically sensitive.

The interaction of structural change and technical progress has produced quantitative and qualitative changes in the workforce with a decline in the importance of manual skills and the automation of inspection and quality control tasks. Rajan and Pearson's survey together with the medium-term forecasts of the Institute for Employment Research (1987) allows a more detailed investigation of these trends. In 1985 about 45 per cent of employees in the production industries (energy, construction and manufacturing) were operatives, about 20 per cent craftsmen and a further 15 per cent in professional or managerial occupations. Employers and forecasters expect recent trends, which have seen increases in the importance of occupations with a high skill or knowledge content, to continue for the remainder of this decade. In the service sector, about 32 per cent of employees were technicians, craftsmen and operatives; 25 per cent clerical and sales; 23 per cent personal services (cooks, waiters, cleaners, porters, etc.) and just 16 per cent managerial and professional. Recent expansion has particularly benefited occupations of low skill intensity in clerical, sales and personal services, and these trends are likely to continue but with part-time workers displacing full-time ones in these occupations. Overall a significant decline is expected in full-time unskilled employment with increases anticipated in professional, technical and multi-skilled craft occupations. In general qualitative improvements are seen as being required across the whole range of occupations, with more flexible managerial and technical workers required and better social skills for support and personal service workers. Where technical change is most rapid home-working will increase, perhaps up to a fifth of the workforce in these sectors by 2010 will be 'teleworking' from home.

The important roles played by small firms and self-employment have featured prominently in recent British Government labour market pronouncements. The Bolton Committee reporting in 1971 concluded that the decline in the small firm sector appeared to be more severe in the UK than elsewhere. Compared to other major developed economies the UK had a higher proportion of workers in medium and large-sized firms in 1981; over 51 per cent of British workers were employed in establishments with at least 100 employees compared to 45 per cent in the USA, 40 per cent in France, 26 per cent in Italy and just 22 per cent in Japan. Some recent studies on job generation have suggested that small firms have a greater importance than their overall share of employment would indicate. Gallagher and Stewart (1986) claim that over the period 1971–81 small firms with under twenty employees were the only group which created net new jobs, results reproduced for the period 1982–84. This trend partly reflects the concentration of about two-thirds of small firms in the expanding service sector, with especially large proportions in the catering and retailing sectors. The Gallagher and Stewart results appear to rest crucially on their proposition that firms' death rates are independent of firm size, and Hart (1987) provides a critique of their analysis and doubts whether the importance of small firms has been established. Given the overall unimportance of small firms in the composition of total employment and their high death rate, the permanence of present emphasis upon their relative importance may be questioned, especially if stability returns to the economy.

It is widely believed that one impact of the recent recession has been to stimulate new and more flexible patterns of work in the UK, though Hakim (1987b) shows that this restructuring trend dates back to the 1950s. There are three dimensions to this concept of flexibility: flexibility of numbers, of time and of function. Most emphasised has been the flexibility of numbers; Atkinson and Meager (1986) find that firms have been reducing their 'permanent' or 'core' workforce of full-time permanent employees and increasing their 'peripheral' or 'flexible' employees. The latter offer greater flexibility in labour input and consist of self-employed, temporary and part-time workers of whom about a quarter are home-based (Hakim 1987a), and are supplemented by subcontracted workers. By the mid 1980s the UK labour force was divided into two-thirds permanent and one-third flexible, and similar ratios are found in all major Western economies. In the UK about one-quarter of all employed males and half of all employed females are in flexible employment. The expansion of shift-working particularly among manufacturing employees has also increased the flexibility of time of permanent employees; the 1985 *Labour Force Survey* found that about 12 per cent of the workforce work shifts and 44 per cent worked at some point over some weekends. Flexibility of function requires the development of multi-skilled workers and increased mobility between production and maintenance tasks; it appears the least developed by British employers. Hakim (1987b) shows that the flexible workforce is concentrated in construction, hotel and catering, distribution, repairs and professional and business service. As Standing (1986) has argued, the term 'flexibility' should be used with care since it conjures up positive images; however, what is flexibility to employers may be perceived as insecurity by some affected employees.

Recent changes in the traditional structure of the UK labour market are indicated by the rapid growth in part-time employment, which accounts for about half of the flexible workforce. In 1971 only 15 per cent of employees were in part-time jobs (thirty hours or less per week) compared to present figures of around 22 per cent. Married women, specifically those returning after childbirth, account for about three-quarters of all part-time employment, and three-quarters of these work in the service sector predominantly in low-status jobs. In the mid-1980s increases in part-time jobs accounted for all the growth in employment, hence contributing to the poor correlation between the growth of employment and decline of unemployment. Most part-time workers do so through choice; the 1986 *Labour Force Survey* found that only 8 per cent of females and 26 per cent of males are in part-time employment because they could not gain full-time employment. Only the Netherlands, Denmark and Sweden have a greater proportion of part-time workers than the UK among major Western economies (Neubourg 1985), though in North America students form a much higher proportion of this group of workers. In part this high ratio of part-time workers in the UK reflects supply considerations, but the large relative size of the service sector and the operation of the National Insurance Scheme appear contributory factors (Schoer 1987).

Greater numerical flexibility has been obtained in the service sector by the expansion of part-time working, but in the manufacturing sector temporary working is relatively more important (Atkinson and Meager 1986). Indeed the most dramatic overall increase has been in the number of temporary workers; around 6 per cent of employees are now in this category. Temporarily employed workers on fixed-term contracts are more likely to be seeking full-time permanent employment than those in part-time or casual employment (King, 1988).

Until recent years self-employment appears to have no long-term trend, with the level fluctuating around 1.9 million since 1949, notwithstanding the demise of agricultural employment; however, it has risen rapidly in the UK in the last decade. Most of this growth is due to single-person businesses with self-employment now accounting for 12 per cent of the employed workforce. Two-thirds of the self-employed are now in the service sector, predominantly in professional and managerial occupations. Almost a third of the nearly 1 million workers with two jobs were self-employed in their second job.

The extent of labour mobility and tenure in the labour market has become an important issue in recent years. The 1986 *Labour Force Survey* discovered that about 10 per cent of those who remained in full-time employment changed jobs during the previous year, while 7 per cent of those remaining in part-time employment did so. The average current job tenure at the end of the 1970s was nearly nine years, comparable (as Table 3.2 illustrates) to that in most Western European countries, though for Japan the figure was nearly twelve years. In all countries female workers have a shorter tenure of ongoing jobs, usually about two-thirds of male duration. In part these international differences in tenure reflect age composition of the workforce and methods of human capital formation. Japan and the USA are at opposite ends of the league table. The US workforce appears significantly more mobile than the British workforce especially for workers with short tenure, though the recent changes in patterns of work discussed above have reduced these differences. Job-changing appears to be highly concentrated in the workforce, tenure of the mean UK employee being surprisingly high. Main (1982) estimated that for those currently in full-time employment, males would on average be in their jobs for twenty years and females for twelve years. The figures for females were similar to those for the USA but those for males slightly longer.

Table 3.2   Employment tenure in developed economies

| Country | Year | Uncompleted duration of jobs currently held | | All job tenure (years) | |
		Under 2 years (%)	10 years and over (%)	Males	All
Australia	1985	36	20	7.0*	6.3*
France	1978	18	35	9.7	8.8
Germany	1978	19	38	8.9†	8.5†
Italy	1978	13	37	7.4†	7.1†
Japan	1982	21	48	13.5	11.7
UK	1984	28	31	9.6‡	8.6‡
USA	1983	39	27	8.4	7.2

Source: OECD (1986) Table II–1 and OECD *Employment outlook*
* Data refer to 1982.
† Data refer to 1972.
‡ Data refer to 1979.

While engagements in the UK move pro-cyclically the leaving rate has historically been cyclically insensitive. The relationship between involuntary and voluntary separations altered over the cycle, with redundancies rising in recessions and voluntary quits rising in tight labour markets. Firms have therefore predominantly adjusted employment during the downswing of the cycle by relying upon natural wastage, with redundancies seen as the last resort. However, the recent recession saw the total movement out of employment rise as redundancies increased by more than the decline in voluntary quits (Jones and Martin 1986).

Official statistics, when adjusted for definitional changes, indicate that male unemployment in the UK quadrupled between 1970 and 1986, from 4 to 17 per cent of the working population. This rise largely occurred in two huge surges, one in 1974–76 and the second in 1979–82. Unfilled vacancies fell but not to the same extent as the rise in unemployment. By the mid-1980s using OECD's standardised definitions male unemployment in the UK was nearly twice as high as in France, West Germany and the USA. The rise in unemployment up to 1986 was largely due to the unemployed remaining unemployed for longer rather than any large increases in the inflow to unemployment. Over 40 per cent of claimants have been unemployed for over a year, yet nearly 40 per cent of those becoming unemployed will have left the count within two months. The incidence and impact of unemployment are highly concentrated in the workforce. The characteristics of the unemployed are more fully discussed in Chapter 7.

So far employment has implicitly been used to indicate labour input, but labour input is the product of the number of workers and the hours worked per worker. During this century actual hours worked have fallen from an average of sixty hours per week to just over forty hours at present, an average annual decrease of about 1 per cent since the Second World War. Over 70 per cent of males were working between thirty-six and fifty hours per week in their main job in 1986, while over 50 per cent of females were working less than thirty-six hours. The hours of work for which normal rates of wages are paid to full-time manual workers has remained around forty hours per week for the last decade; actual hours worked has varied more significantly, with by the middle of the 1980s about a quarter of all people in employment working regular overtime. About a half of those working regular overtime received additional payments for doing so and they averaged nine hours per week. Male average hours of work have fallen in line with the long-run growth of productivity, a 4 per cent rise in productivity being associated with a 1 per cent fall in hours. Cyclical changes distort this relationship as hours worked fall with the growth of unemployment, firms generally avoiding reducing their workforce proportionate to the fall in output. Average holiday entitlements are around twenty-two days for manual workers with seniority entitlements common. Annual working hours in the UK are broadly similar to the rest of Western Europe, but significantly lower than those in the USA, in Japan annual hours are almost a third higher.

3.1.2 Wages and labour costs

Wages and salaries constitute about 60 per cent of gross domestic product (GDP) at factor cost and 85 per cent of total non-training labour costs in the UK; both these proportions are high compared to other developed economies. Statutory National Insurance costs are about 7 per cent of labour costs, private social welfare payments about 5 per cent and the remaining 3 per cent represents subsidised services and payments in kind. Labour productivity has typically grown between 2 and 3 per cent per annum in recent decades with strong pro-cyclical swings due to the slow adjustment of employment. A sustained 3 per cent increase in labour productivity doubles per capita output every twenty-five years. Productivity grows faster in the manufacturing sector which saw an international slow-down in growth in the mid-1970s. Unusually in the recent recession, British productivity grew from 1980 at the abnormally rapid rate of 4 per cent per annum, although UK manufacturing output fell between 1978 and 1987.

In the previous chapter it was stressed that the crucial labour cost variable for employers was not the real or money wage rate but labour costs per unit of output. Productivity changes and non-wage labour costs prevent a close correlation between the two series. International comparisons of manufacturing labour costs (Ray 1987) suggest that in 1986 using current exchange rates, only Austria, France and Ireland had lower hourly earnings in manufacturing than the UK in a sample of sixteen OECD countries. After allowing for social charges, the UK had the lowest hourly labour costs with the sole exception of Ireland. Hourly labour costs were almost 50 per cent higher in Western Europe, 30 per cent in Japan and 60 per cent in North America. Although labour productivity in British manufacturing grew faster in the first half of the 1980s than in the other seven largest OECD countries, the UK's low labour costs are offset by her low overall level of labour productivity. Ray's estimates indicated that unit labour costs may be highest in the UK, perhaps 50 per cent higher than the costs in the USA and Japan. Productivity levels are exceedingly difficult to compare because of the international differences in hours worked, relative prices and continually changing exchange rates, but Maddison (1987) and Rossi et al. (1986) reach similar conclusions about the low level of GDP per hour worked in the UK. Notwithstanding this problem the main point appears well established: wage costs are a very poor indicator of unit labour costs due primarily to differences in turnover costs, social charges and productivity levels. Low wages often tend to indicate unproductive labour rather than cheap labour.

In the UK as elsewhere in Western Europe, wages are largely stipulated for the length of the agreement independently of market conditions and firm profitability. About 14 per cent of UK manual workers' earnings are overtime payments, 8 per cent PBR (payments by results) and incentive payments and 3 per cent shift premium payments. These components are generally unimportant for non-manual workers where basic wage rates are much more closely linked to actual earnings. About half of production workers are on PBR schemes, which are more common the greater the size and unionisation of the establishments' manual workforce (Elliott and Murphy 1986a). Even by the end of the 1970s over half of UK manufacturing establishments had adopted work study techniques, and job evaluation schemes covered over half of their employees.

Fringe benefits account for about 20 per cent of pre-tax remuneration and are especially important for high-income earners (Green, Hadjimatheou and Smail 1985). Surveys suggest that profit-sharing schemes are becoming more popular, with Blanchflower and Oswald (1987b) reporting that 43 per cent of private sector establishments had some form of income-sharing scheme in 1984.

There appears to be a surprising degree of stability in the dispersion of the distribution of earnings and a similarity of wage differentials over time and between countries, though the variation of gross weekly earnings in the UK is considerable. The *New Earnings Survey* for 1987 showed that the average gross weekly earnings of a male worker was about £224, yet the median level of earnings was £198, and that 10 per cent of employees earned over £350 per week. Mean hourly earnings are significantly higher for non-manual workers and the dispersion is greater than for manual workers. The distribution of earnings has widened significantly since 1979, partly it appears due to the recession and partly due to growth in the numbers in the top occupational groups (Adams, Maybury & Smith 1988). Women have both a low mean hourly earnings and also a low dispersion, with average gross hourly earnings for full-time women being less than 74 per cent of male earnings. To understand the composition of these differences it is necessary to consider age–earnings profiles and the nature of industrial and occupational wage differentials. Figure 3.1 shows that for full-time non-manual workers the earnings profiles for both sexes rise over a longer period of their working life than for manual workers. This reflects the greater incidence of incremental salary structures for non-manual workers as well as promotion by seniority; this issue is considered in more detail later in this and the following chapter.

The causes of the starkly flatter age–earnings profiles for all groups of female workers are investigated in the discussion of labour market discrimination in Chapter 6. The profiles illustrated in Fig. 3.1 compare the earnings of different individuals of various ages in these five groups. They are not earnings histories for specific individuals; since earnings increase secularly, studies using longitudinal data indicate much steeper age–earnings profiles for individuals, with maximum earnings reached typically in their mid-fifties (Creedy and Hart 1979).

Any further investigation of pay structure in the UK requires more disaggregation of the data. Consider initially industrial wage differentials: although hourly earnings increased fivefold in monetary terms between 1970 and 1981, seven of the top ten and eight of the bottom ten industries in terms of male gross

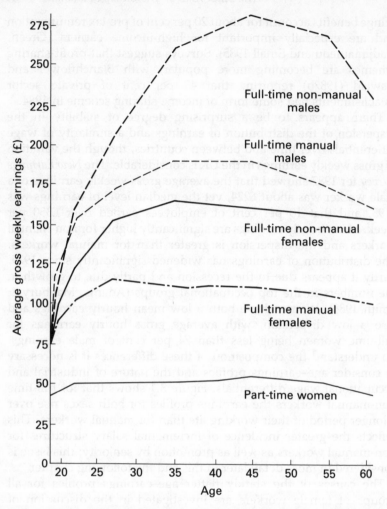

Fig. 3.1   Age–earnings profiles: UK 1986: (— — —) full-time non-manual males; (– – –) full-time manual males; (——) full-time non-manual females; (– · – · –·) full-time manual females; (—) part-time women. *Source: New Earnings Survey 1986*, Part E Table 124, Part F Table 129

hourly earnings were the same (Marsden 1983). This picture of broad stability over time together with different industries paying substantially different wages to apparently similar workers is also accurate for the USA and the rest of Western Europe (Dickens and Katz 1987). The ranking of industries depends in part upon the level of skill, working conditions, levels of concentration and unionisation together with the age and sex composition of the workforce. In the long run there seems little relationship between changes in pay and employment or between productivity gains and real wage growth (Leslie 1987). In the shorter period the anticipated positive relationship between these variables has been observed, suggesting that custom and comparability restrict longer-term adjustments of relative industrial wages.

Gross pay differentials between occupations are bigger in percentage terms than are those for industries. The role of education and training in explaining these differentials is discussed in Chapter 4. The differential between the highest paid occupations, managerial and professional workers, and the lowest paid, unskilled manual workers, have narrowed this century, though this may have been offset by changes in the importance and size of fringe benefits. At the beginning of the century higher professional males earned something like five times the average earnings of unskilled manual workers; this ratio had fallen to about two and a half times by the end of the 1970s. The skilled manual to semi-skilled worker differential has also narrowed in developed Western economies, especially since the 1950s. More recently there is some indication that wage differentials have widened in the UK, with a large relative fall in the pay of male unskilled workers. The differentials between managerial and other occupations are similar to those in the USA, larger than those in West Germany but smaller than the differential in France and Italy. Wage differentials by sex and race are discussed in Chapter 6.

Studies of intra-industry wage differentials in the UK have generally found evidence of substantial intra-occupational wage dispersion in local labour markets. Average earnings of manufacturing workers with apparently similar job descriptions could be over 50 per cent higher in the highest-paying firms compared to the lowest-paying ones in the same local labour market (Nolan 1983). These differences tend to persist over time and suggest that individual firms have much discretion in the fixing of their wage levels. For a typical firm the wage bill is about four to five times profits, hence even a firm paying 10 per cent above the going wage would appear to be reducing profits by 40 per cent. However, such an inference ignores the existence of product market monopolies and countervailing reductions in non-wage labour costs and productivity gains.

Since about 80 per cent of total personal income comes from employment and self-employment, the standard of living of the majority of families will be largely dependent upon their members' labour market incomes. If we wish to consider the distribution of income and the extent of income inequality then the distribution of labour market earnings appears a good place to start. However, there is a poor correlation between low labour market earnings and low total income. The bottom 20 per cent of UK households receive about 7 per cent of total income after adjustments for taxes and benefits in cash and kind, but relatively little from employment, their share being just 0.3 per cent of the total pre-tax, pre-benefit income (Central Statistical Office 1987). This is not to say that poverty is unrelated to the labour market since the unemployed and retired people represent large sections of the poor. At the other extreme the top 20 per cent of households receive about 40 per cent of total incomes after adjustment and receive an above-average proportion of their income from the labour market. However, for the richest 1 per cent who receive more than 5 per cent of total income, investment income and self-employment are disproportionally important. The social security budget is now about 12 per cent of the gross national product (GNP) and about 30 per cent of all public expenditure, and proposals for reform of the originally insurance-based system are discussed in Chapter 8. Wealth is more unequally distributed with the wealthiest 1 per cent owning about 20 per cent of UK marketable wealth and the most wealthy 25 per cent of the population owning about 80 per cent (Board of Inland Revenue 1987). Post-war trends have been towards greater equality of income and wealth in the UK and in other developed economies, but since the end of the 1970s the widening of pay differentials in the UK together with a less egalitarian tax and benefit system has halted this trend and indeed reversed it for income distribution.

3.1.3 Institutions

In recent years about 44 per cent of UK workers have been members of trade unions, down from over 52 per cent at the end of the 1970s. This percentage compares to between 70 and 90 per cent in Scandinavia and Belgium and 20–30 per cent in the USA and Japan. Union density in the UK has fallen during the recession due to the high incidence of closures among large manufacturing plants with high union density, redundant workers tending to let their membership lapse. Unionisation rates are about 80 per cent for manual workers and 40 per cent for white-collar workers in manufacturing. Only about 15 per cent of workers in the private service sector are union members with other low rates in agriculture, the distributive trades and generally among smaller firms (Bain 1983). In recent years about 70 per cent of UK full-time workers have been covered by a collectively bargained agreement. It is thus negotiations not the impersonal yet supposedly individualistic movements of the competitive market which determine wages. Single-employer agreements now dominate much of the labour market, with Oswald and Turnbull (1985) reporting that such agreements determine pay and conditions for two-thirds of manual and three-quarters of non-manual employees in manufacturing establishments with over fifty employees. The majority of single-employer collective bargaining takes place at the plant level, so although 80 per cent of trade unionists are members of the largest twenty-two unions, bargaining is highly decentralised in the UK. The 1980 Workplace Industrial Relations Survey (Daniel and Millward 1983) found that 27 per cent of the workforce were covered by closed shops, overwhelmingly of the post-entry form. The 1984 Workplace Industrial Relations Survey (Millward and Stevens 1986) found a significant decline in the extent and importance of closed shops; new legislation meant that many of the remaining closed shops were not legally enforceable. Although the traditional role of shop stewards as union members' representatives has continued there has been a rapid growth of joint consultative committees, and formal consultation is becoming more common especially in larger plants. About 41 per cent of workplaces had formal consultative machinery in 1984, though company boards were only inclined to discuss employee relations when particular crises occurred. Personnel management is becoming more professionalised (Marsh 1982), with plants owned abroad being much more likely to employ personnel specialists.

The frequency of collective bargaining would be expected to reflect the costs and benefits of bargaining, information-gathering costs may be substantial for both parties and more frequent bargaining may increase the incidence of strikes if the latter are really inevitable 'accidents'. Evidence from the USA suggests that in non-union sectors wages are revised more frequently which supports the previous proposition. As in Japan, UK collective agreements typically fix wage rates for only twelve months though longer ones are becoming more common, compared to the normal three-year US contract, and hence UK 'contracts' rarely contain indexing. While British unions do not regularly bargain directly about the level of employment, manning levels are often specified in agreements (Oswald 1987). Collective agreements also usually contain agreed procedure for reducing employment levels with natural wastage and voluntary redundancies preceding last in first out (LIFO) involuntary redundancies.

The impact of trade unions on relative wages and labour productivity has been the source of much dispute among labour economists. Since Freeman and Medoff (1984) it has become common to consider not only the monopoly role of unions, which may cause wages to rise above competitive levels, but also their role in providing a collective voice and thereby assisting the more efficient utilisation of labour. Unfortunately for the UK no studies have been conducted on the extent of unions' contribution to efficient production; only studies on their impact upon relative wages are available. Until the early 1980s most studies suggested a union/non-union differential of the order of 20 per cent or so (see the survey by Carline 1985). More recent studies have used more disaggregated data allowing for heterogeneous workers and jobs (Stewart 1983b; Blanchflower 1984) and have yielded much smaller, single-figure estimates of the differential. Blanchflower (1986) and Stewart (1987) provide estimates for 1980 which suggest that the differential is subject to large variation between industries and establishments. Significant and widespread union differentials only appear to be found among smaller establishments, the public sector and in firms with a pre-entry closed shop. Only a minority of establishments appear to pay significantly more to union labour than they would to non-union labour. Layard and Nickell (1987) suggest that the union mark-up has tended to rise over time, even during the recession. These issues are considered in more detail in Chapter 8.

Although the present government has been against any direct interference in private sector wage-fixing, as a major employer and through its industrial relations legislation it has a major indirect role; we specifically consider Wages Councils in Chapter 7 and incomes policies in Chapter 8. Ignoring public corporations, public sector employees peaked at around 5.5 million at the end of the 1970s; about 55 per cent are employed by local authorities; and nearly 60 per cent female. The recent slight fall in public sector employment occurred at a time when there was a significant rise in the real cost of general government consumption (Britton 1986). Weekly earnings figures suggest that relative pay of non-manual public sector workers has remained fairly stable, with changes in public sector wages apparently being strongly influenced by private sector pay and existing relativity (Zabalza and Kong 1984). In contrast Elliott and Murphy (1987) analyse hourly rates of pay and find a significant deterioration in the relative pay of non-manual, and especially female, workers in the public sector since 1970.

Institutional wage-fixing is relatively rare in the UK, with no universal minimum wage laws and the selective operation of Wages Councils covering few workers.

3.2 Theory and practice in the labour market

The above discussion has attempted to describe some of the key characteristics of the UK labour market. It is now necessary to attempt to relate these characteristics to the competitive and structuralist models developed previously. The outline above suggested relatively long tenure and stable wage differentials in the UK labour market, all consistent with the broad structuralist approach. However, this inference ignores the qualification that a significant minority of workers experience a high degree of mobility and wage instability and also ignores the question concerning the extent of wage and employment adjustment predicted by competitive theory. To draw any firm conclusions we need to consider empirical work, both econometric and case study. At this stage we limit discussion to three crucial labour market issues: aggregate adjustment and flexibility; inter-market adjustment, and the significance of structured internal labour markets.

3.2.1 Adjustment in the labour market – the issue of labour market flexibility

In Chapter 1 it was noted that one of the fundamental issues dividing economists concerns whether markets are best viewed as predominantly price or quantity adjusting. Here we are interested to discover how the UK labour market adjusts to changes in market conditions, an issue which reappears in our discussion of the causes of unemployment in Chapter 7. We wish to discover the relative importance of wage and employment adjustments and whether UK labour market adjustments differ from those in other developed economies. Specifically is it true that the lack of flexibility in British and other European labour markets explains their high levels of unemployment compared to North America and Japan? This question is illustrated in Fig. 3.2, where n_1 and w_1 represent the initial levels of employment and real wages for the given level of demand for labour, n^d. Consider the impact of a recession which

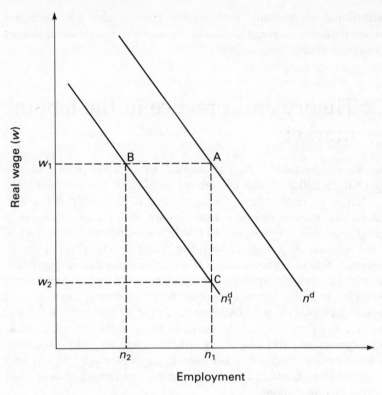

Fig. 3.2   Labour market adjustment to a contractionary shock

causes the demand for labour to fall to n_1^d; if real wages fall to w_2 then employment levels need not initially fall; at the other extreme, if real wages remain at w_1 then employment has to take all the initial burden of adjustment and contracts to n_2. If we ignore any supply adjustments, whether the economy moves from A to B or from A to C is therefore the critical issue.

The cyclical stability of employment will therefore be dependent upon the flexibility of wages; if demand fluctuations are absorbed through wage adjustments then employment levels will be cyclically stable. To estimate this flexibility we need to relate the variability of real wages to the size and frequency of labour market shocks and the elasticity of demand and supply of labour. Considering elasticity first, the recent survey by Pencavel (1986) concludes that men's choice between work and leisure is only weakly affected by wages, though for married women the influence is stronger. Hamermesh (1986) reports that estimates of the long-run, constant-output labour-demand elasticity lie in the range 0.15–0.50. Given such low estimates of elasticity, Knieser and Goldsmith's 1987 survey of models of the aggregate US labour market concludes that the auction model is particularly unsatisfactory in explaining the stylised facts of a typical recession; real wages do not fall and quits do not rise yet unemployment rises faster than the auction model predicts. In comparative terms, Grubb, Jackman and Layard (1983) have suggested that the UK 'suffers' from high real wage rigidity, the USA from high money wage rigidity, while in Japan both real and money wages are flexible by international standards. These results were broadly supported by an OECD study (Klau and Mittelstädt 1986) where short-term wage rigidity seemed positively correlated with the rise in unemployment since the mid-1970s.

The response of the UK and Japan to OPEC II in 1978–79 is a useful illustration of these differences. In the UK despite this major disturbance money wages grew rapidly and real wages rose, partially stimulated by the international appreciation of sterling, yet profits fell rapidly. In Japan real wages fell sharply and the consequence was that in the next couple of years unemployment rose fifteen times more rapidly in the UK. The greater flexibility of Japanese wages partly reflects the importance of 'bonus' payments, about 25 per cent of earnings, and the previously discussed flexibility of hours worked. In addition the weakness and bargaining behaviour of trade unions may be a significant source of this flexibility. Specifically the absence of LIFO in Japan means that those who control unions are not immune from the employment consequences of the bargained wage, hence there is more concern with employment levels that in British unions. This may also be encouraged by the higher degree of synchronisation of wage bargaining in Japan.

So far we have assumed that labour input in Fig. 3.2 is directly related to numbers employed; however, if hours per worker are flexible then labour input can change without requiring any adjustment of employed labour force. As the demand for labour is a derived demand, aggregate employment changes will partly reflect cyclical changes in output; however, the turning-points in employment occur in the UK around two to three quarters behind output. It appears that employers faced with the fixed costs of hiring and firing workers initially react to increases in demand by inventory disinvestment and/or increasing overtime working rather than adjusting the size of their workforce. Similarly in the recession phase of the cycle employment reductions lag behind contractions of output. This relationship between output and employment changes is the subject of Okun's law (Okun 1970); Paldam (1987) estimates that a 1 per cent growth in GDP lowers unemployment by about a quarter of a percentage point in OECD countries. In international terms the UK ranks somewhere between the case of Japan where hours worked are much more flexible than employment, and the USA where long-term contracts cause adjustment to demand changes to be primarily through employment adjustments such as temporary lay-offs (Tachibanaki 1987). The supposed greater flexibility of the Japanese labour market is reflected in their composition of labour force with permanent employees accounting for only about 40 per cent of the non-agricultural workforce, with 30 per cent self-employed and the remaining 30 per cent in temporary employment. In recessions unemployment rises comparatively little in Japan because hours worked per worker fall among the permanent workforce and self-employed, while discouraged temporary workers leave the labour force.

Whether a high degree of wage or working hours flexibility is necessarily preferable to employment flexibility is an important, yet neglected issue involving consideration of the associated social and political institutions. It does not follow that the British system is inevitably inferior to the Japanese system where much of the adjustment to demand changes in the latter country is borne by peripheral workers or to the US system which compensates for the prevalence of long-term contracts by having to rely upon temporary lay-offs as a major adjustment mechanism.

Given that money wages do not adjust instantly to price changes UK real wages cannot be rigid in an absolute sense. Robinson (1987) reports that almost a third of occupational groups in his study were worse off in 1984 than in 1979. However, most studies suggest that real wages are insensitive to demand shocks and hence the relative rigidity of UK real wages (Carruth and Oswald 1987). Gregory, Lobban and Thompson (1987) find that apart from during 1980/81 the risk of redundancy failed to exert any appreciable downward pressure on pay settlements in the UK, though profitability was a significant determinant of the outcome of the bargaining process. The apparent failure of absolute wage rates to clear UK labour markets leads directly to a consideration of whether relative wages are any more effective in reducing imbalances between labour markets.

3.2.2 Wage differentials

Wage differentials are supposed in the competitive model to play a key role in the allocation of labour. Notwithstanding the rigidity of wage differentials discussed above, some economists have also argued that on closer examination behaviour is consistent with the competitive model of equalising net advantages. We now consider the available UK evidence in more detail; given the international differences in labour market adjustments discovered above, it appears inappropriate to use results from outside the UK. (Rosen (1986) provides a survey of US studies.) Pissarides and McMaster (1984a) allowed firms to adjust both relative wages and vacancies in order to adjust employment levels in an industry. They concluded that both changes in relative wages and vacancies were linked to sectoral changes in employment, but that wages responded to aggregate rather than sector vacancies. Layard and Nickell (1987) concluded that relative wages are relatively unimportant in the adjustment to demand and supply shocks.

Some studies of inter-occupational and inter-industry wage differentials have supported the competitive model of equalising net advantages. Marin and Psacharopoulos (1982) concluded that data on occupational earnings and risk of death at place of work, supported the proposition that the labour market does compensate for the dangers associated with a given occupation. Elliott and Murphy (1986b) in a more comprehensive examination of industrial wage differentials also found evidence to support the equalising differences hypothesis. Workers who had to work overtime, in large plants or expend greater effort because of the operation of PBR systems appeared to be rewarded by higher weekly gross earnings, though the influence of risk of accidents was more uncertain.

The existence of large and stable intra-industry wage differentials has also been explained within neoclassical orthodoxy. Addison (1975) has pointed out that competitive theory postulates the equalisation of net advantages not wage rates, and heterogeneity of workers and working conditions means that the former does not imply the latter. The presence of systematic inter- and intra-industry wage differentials for similar workers requires some explanation of why high-wage industries and firms do not cut their wages. Either firms find that reducing wages would lower profits or firms do not maximise profits. A neoclassical interpretation is to point to the existence of search and firm-specific training which prevent the equalisation of inter-firm wage rates. Nolan and Brown (1983) in their study of occupational wage movements questioned the adequacy of the competitive model's explanation of UK wage differentials. Their main criticism was that conventional analysis paid too little attention to the demand side of the market. Competitive theory expects occupationally specific factors to dominate firm-specific factors in the movement of wages, but the Nolan and Brown study suggested the reverse ranking. They interpreted these results as showing the importance of efficiency wage considerations in internal labour markets. Firms require a coherent internal pay structure, independent of external labour market considerations, to reduce X-inefficiency. High-paying firms maintain this strategy and contrary to the net advantages approach the limited evidence suggests that wage and non-wage benefits tend to be positively correlated. The movement towards single-employer bargaining, the spread of job evaluation schemes and of work-study techniques all contributed to and reflected, Nolan and Brown argued, the adoption of a stable internal wage structure. Their arguments take us into a discussion of the relative importance of structured internal labour markets in the UK to which we now turn.

3.2.3 The importance of structured internal labour markets

A key characteristic of the structuralist approach is that employers adopt a set of rules and procedures in their pricing and allocation of labour. These rules are applied rigidly to decision-making, independent of external labour and product market conditions. The approach suggests that labour allocation and wage determination by compliance to social rules and custom are aimed at producing a stable and motivated workforce. The benefits of lower transaction monitoring and training costs outweigh any harmful effects which greater employment security has on work incentives. The previously noted variety of models within this broad approach together with a lack of suitable data have hindered empirical assessments of the importance of structured internal labour markets. Most labour market data consist of aggregate or cross-sectional observations, while what is required to assess this model is individual worker and firm evidence. Once data problems are overcome, researchers face a further problem in trying to find testable propositions unique to this approach. For example, the early concentration in the literature on worker mobility seems on reflection to have been misplaced. The structured internal labour market approach suggests workers will have low inter-firm mobility, with seniority being rewarded by higher pay. The inter-firm mobility which occurs will be highly concentrated among those workers with little labour market experience, and external mobility will decline with age. The human capital approach predicts exactly the same behaviour where firms have a production process which is unique. Here training will have to be provided which is firm-specific, and in order to reduce training costs the firm will adopt policies which restrict labour turnover among their trained workforce. This difficulty in distinguishing between alternative theories has caused problems in all studies; Taubman and Wachter (1986) survey US studies and we concentrate on British studies.

The initial attempt to test the segmentation hypothesis in the UK labour market was made by Bosanquet and Doeringer (1973) who searched for a bimodal distribution of the 'goodness' of jobs, reflecting the simple dual labour market division. They presented fairly weak and inconclusive evidence indicating higher job instability among unskilled workers and flat age–earnings functions for black and female workers, which they interpreted as supportive of duality in the market. Such statistics fail to standardise for the characteristics of different groups of workers and give no insight into the causes of the differences in earnings profiles. Psacharopoulos (1978) suggested that since age is so important in explaining occupational attainment and inter-generational mobility among secondary workers so high, then it followed that segmentation was too weak to be a useful model of labour market behaviour. However, his study relied primarily on cross-sectional occupational data which were arbitrarily broken down into primary and secondary segments. This problem of acquiring time-series data on occupational mobility and then finding some meaningful way to test duality has caused many problems for researchers, though Mayhew and Rosewell (1979) discovered mobility at every point on the occupational distribution. They rejected the dual labour hypothesis on this basis, although their study also indicated a low downwards mobility of workers from what they defined as the primary sector. Metcalf and Nickell (1982) also tested for mobility within UK occupational groups, finding that about two-thirds of individuals were in the same occupational band in 1965 and 1975. They find some evidence that workers without education and training can get trapped in the secondary sector of the labour market. There are many difficulties in using occupational data to assess alternative theories since it is not clear what degree of mobility is anticipated by orthodox and segmented theory.

An alternative approach to the assessment of the importance of segmentation is to consider whether wages are determined by the same criteria in different sectors of the market. Structuralist approaches suggest that schooling and training investments should be more profitable for workers who gain access to the primary sector. McNabb and Psacharopoulos (1981a) attempted such an examination, estimating earnings functions, of the type explained in the following chapter, for primary and secondary workers. They found that although human capital factors had a weaker impact upon earnings among secondary occupations, experience and schooling were still rewarded in this sector. McNabb (1987) attempts to divide the workforce by industry as well as occupation. The secondary sector is here defined as the female-intensive and weakly unionised industries rather than on occupational lines. Segmentation is rejected since earnings functions are similar for both sectors, and industry-specific factors are less important than education and experience in determining individual earnings. Contrary to earlier findings, McNabb does find that education and experience have very different effects on earnings by occupation when industry is controlled, though he prefers a specific human capital interpretation of these results. The use of occupational or industrial data in such studies remains problematic since recent segmented theory concentrates on 'bad' employers, not 'bad' occupations or industries. Vertical job ladders or seniority pay systems in 'good' firms mean that workers can gain advancement from 'bad' jobs in the primary labour market. If this is the case then aggregate studies are incapable of assessing the importance of segmentation and it is more detailed individual firm and worker data which are required to investigate this issue.

The recent recession has stimulated interest in a closely related issue: the relative importance of internal and external influences on wage determination in the UK. Researchers have begun to adopt a more eclectic approach to wage determination and allowed both external labour market forces, such as unemployment, as well as internal factors, such as profitability, to influence wage outcomes. Time-series and cross-sectional studies find that external labour market pressures do influence wage levels, though most estimates suggest that the elasticity of wages with respect to unemployment is quite low at -0.10 (Oswald 1986b). Blanchflower, Oswald and Garrett's (1987) analysis leads them tentatively to suggest that internal factors are more important in determining an individual worker's pay. We return to this issue in our examination of unemployment in Chapter 7.

Many recent investigations have tried a case study rather than econometric approach to the issue of the importance of segmented labour markets in the UK economy. Mace (1979) examined the operation of the market for professional engineers and developed criteria for identifying structured internal labour markets. His consideration of turnover, entry ports, promotion ladders, training, adjustment mechanisms and salaries within twelve firms provided strong evidence of structured internal labour markets. The firms recruited primarily to junior jobs with lengthy firm-specific training induction, relying on internal promotion for higher-level appointments. They experienced low turnover and maintained a rigid salary structure even in the presence of labour shortages in particular occupations. Job evaluation was initially used to legitimise the structure of salaries, and the need to avoid frictions and maintain employee morale prevented any widespread adaptation of that structure to reflect external market pressures. Creedy and Whitfield (1986) in their investigation of the market for professional chemists in the UK found a high incidence of specific training. Inter-firm mobility is concentrated among junior workers, searching for the most suitable job ladder. The majority of upward job mobility occurs without change of employer and is a continuous process of moving up the job ladder.

For manual and clerical workers the findings are slightly different; Kaufman (1984) surveyed twenty-six small and largely non-union firms and found evidence that efficiency wage arguments underlie the development of structured internal labour markets. Although most employers believed they could find qualified workers at lower wages than their present employees, they did not even consider nominal wage reductions and were reluctant to adjust their real wages. Firms argued that X-efficiency would be damaged as morale fell, and two-tier wage systems, where new recruits were paid at lower rates, were dismissed as unrealistic due to associated workplace frictions. Kaufman's study also suggests that firms whose activities might have suggested that they would operate in the secondary labour market, can have structured labour markets. Nolan (1983) pointed out that the reverse is also true, with many large firms supposedly in the primary sector actually offering terms and conditions of employment more common in the secondary sector. It is this diversity of firm behaviour in the labour market which generates the inter-firm wage differentials discussed above and gives rise to a rejection of the simplistic versions of the dual labour market hypothesis.

George and Shorey (1985) surveyed employment practices at eighteen engineering establishments at the end of the 1970s. Once again voluntary turnover was low and firms were found to have a rigid and formalised pay structure across all jobs. However for semi-skilled and skilled workers internal promotion was rare, occupational mobility for these groups in the firm being horizontal rather than vertical. Once again employers stated a preference for a stable wage structure and internal promotion for X-efficiency reasons. They preferred to adjust labour input through altering hours worked rather than the number of employees because they feared that a reputation as a hirer and firer would reduce the quality of future applicants. George and Shorey concluded that structured internal labour markets may reflect efficient solutions to resource allocation. The specificity of skill requirements often makes internal training schemes profitable if turnover can be limited; this need together with the importance of worker motivation in determining actual productivity, makes a stable wage structure with seniority rules an efficient policy. It appears common for firms to recruit workers through their existing workforce, hence giving rise to the extended internal labour market discussed in Chapter 5.

All of these findings are broadly compatible with the segmented labour market approach; however, for manual workers even in the primary labour market the job ladder appears to have few rungs. Studies in the UK at present suggest that internal promotion is much more relevant to the career labour market faced by technical, professional and managerial workers than it is for manual workers. In other words for manual workers the 'good' jobs are better than secondary labour market jobs but not that much better, and many manual workers in 'good' jobs are still employed in tasks which underutilise their talents. Few unskilled and semi-skilled workers can ever cross the manual–technician/supervisory–management divide. Recent technological developments have reduced the number of inspection and quality control jobs and reduced even further opportunities for advancement. Promotion of workers with manual backgrounds into managerial posts has also become even rarer with the professionalisation of managers. These findings are consistent with the arguments of Osterman (1982, 1987) who suggests that several sub-markets, both primary and secondary, may exist within a single firm. Moreover the form of the various sub-markets may change over time as technological and labour market conditions change.

Another characteristic of structured internal labour markets which appears well documented in UK labour markets is seniority pay. Shorey (1980) found that quits vary inversely with mean wages and non-linearly to age. One reason why firms reward tenure is to reduce voluntary quits and therefore the costs of internal training; alternatively learning-by-doing may cause productivity to be linked to tenure. A minority of non-manual workers outside of the public sector have incremental pay scales and these are very rare for manual workers; it follows that any observed positive seniority premium for manual workers must largely reflect job promotion which is related to seniority in the internal labour market. Collier and Knight (1985) report significant payments for seniority which they suggest are independent of age. Among full-time male employees in their forties, manual workers with at least ten years of completed service earned 15 per cent and non-manual 22 per cent more than similarly aged employees with less than a year of service. The greater reward to seniority for non-manual workers is consistent with the arguments developed in the previous paragraph. A comparison with Japan suggests that the British seniority premium is only about half the Japanese level, and turnover is accordingly much lower in that country than in the UK for prime-age adults. In the UK we have concluded that the seniority premium largely takes the form of promotion to higher-paying jobs; in Japan the emphasis is on incremental pay scales, where tenure is directly rewarded. The likely decline of promotion opportunities for manual workers consequential on the adoption of new technology suggests that the Japanese seniority payment system is more likely to produce the desired combination of high morale, low turnover and low training costs in the future. Caution in emphasising the importance of seniority payments is, however, suggested by two recent US studies (Abraham and Farber 1987; Altonji and Shakotko 1987) which suggest that the correlation between earnings and seniority is ambiguous – it may result from better workers having both longer seniority and higher wages.

3.3 Conclusions

There is insufficient UK evidence to reach firm conclusions concerning the relative importance of competitive and structured internal labour markets. It appears that many technical, professional and managerial workers will experience a working environment close to that predicted by the structuralist approach. For manual workers and lower-level non-manual workers the evidence is less emphatic. The distinction between competitive and non-competitive markets is itself less clear, firms appear to change their behaviour over time and apparently similar firms can adopt very different employment policies. Gregory, Lobban and Thomson (1987) have suggested that the recent increased dispersion of manual wages in the UK indicates a dichotomy between the behaviour of profitable and marginal firms. Those at the top end of pay distribution practise

internal labour market behaviour, while those at the bottom react
to external product and labour market conditions. This argument
represents a major dilution of the structuralist view, since it implies
that structured internal labour markets are transitory. Firms can
choose what mix of sub-markets they wish. In periods of difficult
product market conditions they can increase the relative importance
of secondary sub-markets. Such an explanation is consistent with
the recent rise in the importance of part-time and temporary
workers, the growth of subcontracting and the fall in the relative
wage of unskilled workers. A tightening of the labour market could
slow or even reverse these trends as labour markets become more
sensitive to supply-side preferences. Such arguments suggest that
the diversity and instability of labour market structures are much
greater than existing models predict.

Oswald has argued that 'The view that pay is determined
by the interaction of supply and demand within some kind of
competitive market has almost certainly gone forever' (1986b: 190).
We find such conclusions premature; within sizeable sectors of the
UK labour market behaviour approximates to that predicted by the
competitive model. At the same time it appears that significant
components of the labour market behave as if structured internal
labour markets dominated. We do not know the relative size of
these components but have suggested that importance will vary in
the short and long run. Given this uncertainty, we adopt a heterodox
approach in the following policy chapters. More prominence is given
to non-competitive theories than is conventional, but approximately
equal weight is given to applying modern competitive models which
recognise market imperfections. This and the following chapters
repeatedly indicate that it is wrong to consider competitive and
structural models as alternative and competing explanations of
labour market behaviour. Manpower policy will be more firmly
based when it is fully appreciated that both models can provide
important insights into UK labour market behaviour.

Further reading

A slightly more comprehensive examination of the UK labour
market is in the chapter by Metcalf in Prest and Coppock (1986).
Unfortunately the other excellent introduction to the UK economy
(Morris 1985) is weak on labour market behaviour. A read through
Bain (1983) with its regrettably rare blend of industrial relations and
labour economics is still worthwhile. The chapter by Layard and

Nickell in Dornbusch and Layard (1987) presents a more technical review of recent British labour market performance. The Annual Report of the MSC contains a useful summary of labour market developments as does the monthly *Employment Gazette* and the *Quarterly Labour Market Report* of the MSC.

Sources of labour market information

Always start any search for official statistics with the *Guide to Official Statistics* (CSO 1986). The Institute of Manpower Studies published a comprehensive guide to statistical sources entitled *The UK Labour Market* in 1980 and much of this is still useful. Most major British labour market statistics are published in the *Employment Gazette* as a statistical supplement. The supplement has its own index giving frequency, issue and page or table number of the various series. Care should be taken to read the small print as labour market statistics have a penchant for being redefined. The *Employment Gazette* contains articles summarising the major findings of other important official sources of labour market information. The *British Journal of Industrial Relations* features a section which provides a helpful commentary on labour market developments and relevant legislative initiatives. The annual *Labour Force Survey* provides the most comprehensive information on labour market behaviour, but care should be taken to ensure that definitions are compatible with other published data. The annual *General Household Survey* contains information on labour supply, search and unemployment. The annual *New Earnings Survey* provides the most comprehensive information on wages and hours, though *Incomes Data Report and Study* give good occupational pay data. *Social Trends* provides a particularly informative review of UK income and wealth distribution. The 1980 and 1984 Workplace Industrial Relations Surveys (Daniel and Millward 1983; Millward and Stevens 1986) provide detailed information on the nature of British industrial relations. Medium-term forecasts of the British labour market are published annually by the Institute for Employment Research in their *Review of the Economy and Employment*. The OECD's *Labour Force Statistics* provides quarterly comparative labour market statistics of member countries, and the ILO publishes a mammoth *Yearbook of Labour Statistics* covering nearly 200 countries.

Chapter 4

EDUCATION AND TRAINING

Since the middle of the last century there has been a debate in the UK concerning the importance of developing vocational skills within the school system. It became evident after the Great Exhibition of 1851 that the UK lagged behind other European countries in manufacturing technologies, and this led to calls for state intervention to improve the rudimentary system of technical education. The discovery of another case of market failure added new dimensions to previous economic debates about state financing of elementary education. The conclusion of the classical economists, that government should finance popular education, rested largely on the benefits of moral education rather than any direct productivity gains. Only towards the end of the nineteenth century did economists emphasise education and training as a significant source of economic growth, though human capital theory itself can be traced back to Adam Smith. These early debates had many of the characteristics of contemporary ones. Employers bemoaned the failure of the educational system to serve the needs of industry. Usually this was interpreted to mean a failure to provide basic literate and numerate skills, but also failure to stress the 'unique' wealth-creation powers of industry. Governments and educationalists responded by stressing the selfish and short-sighted behaviour of many employers in providing inadequate access to industrial on-the-job training.

This debate was given new impetus by the results of early growth accounting studies, such as those by Denison. The studies conducted in the 1950s and early 1960s discovered large 'residuals', that is growth not due to inputs of homogeneous factors of production. These results were often interpreted as showing the importance of education as a major determinant of economic growth, and the economics of education became an established branch of economics. This development was reflected by Western governments paying much greater attention to the quality of their workforce. The 1960s saw widespread reforms of state educational and training systems, and concern with the supposed failure of private sector training as evinced by widespread skill shortages in cyclical upturns. By the late 1970s there was, in many of these Western countries, disillusionment with these activist policies, and a retreat towards a more voluntarist or passive approach to industrial on-the-job training. However, the appropriate duration and composition of initial education have remained controversial, and in the UK with the emergence of the MSC and its recent concentration on the school-to-work transition, policy has entered a new stage.

Economic theory may aid an understanding of this education versus training debate and of the contribution of education to economic growth, but it is important to stress the limitations of conventional theories. Human capital theory emphasises that education and training increase worker productivity, and through that channel earning power in the labour market. The consumption benefits of education are often neglected, as are the social and political positive externalities produced by having an educated population. Conventional economic theory is directed at a narrower issue: the quality of the match between the knowledge and skills of the supply and demand for labour. Even as a theory of the link between education and earnings, human capital theory has been increasingly attacked in recent years by economists extending the segmented labour market approach. In this chapter the discussion starts with an examination of some of the key characteristics of education and training in contemporary Western economies. Conventional competitive analysis is then considered, its human capital approach emphasising adjustment on the supply of labour side of the market. Technology is usually assumed to be fairly fixed and thus it is predominantly the supply, not demand of labour, which responds to changes in relative wages. Evidence concerning the operation of this adjustment mechanism is considered and the policy implications of this approach outlined. Structuralist models of the labour market are then related to these issues. These models suggest an alternative relation between education and productivity and predict that increasing workers' potential productivity may not improve employment prospects, unless entrance into structured labour markets can be gained. This discussion leads to a consideration of recent educational and training policy, initially considering the school-to-work transition. The chapter ends with a critical study of the present role of the state in both on- and off-the-job training in the UK.

4.1 Current patterns of education and training

In the UK just over half of the young people leave full-time education at minimum school-leaving age, a slightly higher proportion of girls staying on. The education and labour market status of young people has changed dramatically since the late 1970s due to the recession and the introduction of the Youth Training Scheme (YTS). Recent trends are illustrated in Table 4.1; the 'in employment' category which measures predominantly the employed has been derived as a residual and is therefore subject to greater uncertainty than the other estimates.

Table 4.1   Education and labour market status of sixteen- and eighteen-year-olds: UK

Status	Percentage of age-group (January each year)							
	16-year-olds				18-year-olds			
	1974		1987		1974		1987	
	Males	Females	Males	Females	Males	Females	Males	Females
In full-time education:								
School	26.5	26.7	29.6	31.7	2.1	1.9	2.7	2.1
Further education	7.2	10.2	11.6	18.0	13.1	13.8	15.4	15.5
All	33.7	36.9	41.2	50.0	15.1	15.7	17.9	17.6
On YTS	—	—	30.6	23.4	—	—	0.2	0.2
Unemployed	4.2	2.6	11.8	9.5	3.7	1.7	18.3	14.1
In employment*	62.1	60.5	16.4	17.1	81.2	82.6	62.3	68.1

Source: Table 2, p. 462, Table 3, p. 464 Employment Gazette, Sept. 1987. Terms are fully explained in footnotes in these tables.
* Includes those unemployed and not claiming benefit and those neither unemployed nor seeking work.

The decline in the proportion of sixteen-year-olds in employment is the most striking feature of the table, though an increased participation in full-time education occurred in all groups. About 14 per cent of the age-group start full-time higher education at polytechnics and universities or their equivalent, though if higher education is interpreted broadly and part-time professional courses are included then the proportion rises to nearly a third.

Given the differences between developed nations, any comparison of educational and training statistics is problematic. After compulsory schooling some countries such as the USA have a predominantly college-based system for both academic and vocational learning, while others such as West Germany prefer an apprenticeship system for the generation of vocational skills. Thus in the early 1980s 35 per cent of the US labour force had experienced higher education, but only 8.4 per cent in France and 13.5 per cent in West Germany (Psacharopoulos and Arriagada 1986). At the end of the 1970s the average Briton had eleven years of full-time education compared with a US average of over twelve years. The median student leaves full-time education in his sixteenth year in the UK and in their nineteenth year in the USA, and this means that given their later commencement present American students have something over an extra year of schooling. Some of these international differences in the destination of school-leavers are illustrated in Table 4.2, which indicates the relatively low participation rates in the UK especially in full-time education and training. More recent data suggest that 95 per cent of Japanese students stay in full-time schooling till they are eighteen years of age. In West Germany the wide spread of apprenticeships through all sectors of the economy makes them especially important while in France full-time vocational education is particularly emphasised. Before the YTS about 30 per

Table 4.2 Participation in education and training: international comparisons*

| | Percentage of 16–18-year-olds (1981) | | | |
| | Full time | | Part time | Total |
	School	Other		
UK	18	14	32	63
France	33	25	8	66
West Germany	31	14	40	84
Italy	16	31	18	65
Japan	58	11	3	73
Netherlands	50	21	8	79
USA	65	14	—	79

Source: Table 3.11 Social Trends 1987 HMSO, London
* Includes apprentices and those on government training schemes.

cent of boys and 40 per cent of girls who left school at sixteen or seventeen in the UK and entered jobs received no formal training.

In recent years of those who enter the British labour market at sixteen, about half were on the YTS by the following January, and two-thirds in full-time employment by the spring. The instability of young entrants' employment status makes it dangerous to use any single data series to summarise their experience. The Youth Cohort Study shows that the young unemployed came disproportionately from large families with a manual background and were poorly qualified. Young people's jobs are significantly concentrated; over 70 per cent of those in employment or on YTS were in just five occupational groups: clerical work, selling, catering and personal services and the two processing, making and repairing occupational groups. Marsden and Ryan (1986) have shown that the distribution of youth employment across industries appears similar across Western European countries. However, there are large differences in the form of that employment, with a lower training element in British employment. These differences in entrant experience are reflected in the present stocks of employees; whereas two-thirds of the West German labour force had vocational qualifications at the end of the 1970s, only one-third of the British workforce had such qualifications.

Earlier a distinction was made between countries such as West Germany and Switzerland, who rely upon an apprenticeship system for industrial skills, and those such as France, Italy, the USA and the Benelux countries who have a full-time system of vocational education. When the UK is compared with countries where vocational training is school- or college-based then different apparent shortcomings appear; Table 4.2 indicates that a low proportion of sixteen- to eighteen-year-olds in the UK were participating in full-time education. Overall about 14.5 per cent of males and 12 per cent of females enter British higher education, that is about nine-tenths of males who are qualified to do so and three-quarters of qualified females. In contrast, about 72 per cent of US school-leavers were qualified to enter higher education and 58 per cent of US high-school graduates did so in 1985. About 18 per cent of US workers have completed university degrees, three times the British proportion. A quarter of undergraduate American students major in business studies and the same proportion of postgraduate degrees are MBAs, much higher than British proportions (Daly 1986). In part this difference reflects the greater range of degree courses in the

USA, but less than a quarter of US employees have no schooling qualifications compared to over half of British employees.

If we turn from entrants to a consideration of the provision of training for the workforce as a whole, then although there is no comprehensive measure of training financed by individuals and employers a 1984 survey suggested that British manufacturing employers spent about £1015m. on training in that year. Even with apprentice wages included this level of spending represents around 1.3 per cent of the total labour costs (Department of Employment, 1988). The 1986 *Labour Force Survey* indicates that one-third of British employees have no schooling or training qualifications and about another third have A level or higher academic qualifications. Although the USA relies much more heavily than the UK on the educational system for work preparation, American employers still spend at least 3 per cent of their annual turnover on training compared to less than 0.5 per cent in Britain (NEDO 1984). In France legislation requires companies employing 10 or more workers to contribute at least 1.2% of the total wage bill on training and the average expenditure is twice this percentage. In 1986 about 5 per cent of British full-time employees were in training, and double that proportion had received some job-related training in the four weeks prior to survey. This training was mostly off the job and was heavily concentrated among employees with educational qualifications, recent recruits and among those in higher-level occupations in the service sectors. In 1967, just after manufacturing employment began to fall in absolute terms, about 450 000 young people were in apprenticeships or other similar training, equivalent to about 5.5 per cent of all employees, by 1987 only about 95 000 were being so trained, just under 2 per cent of employees. Similar contractions have occurred in the numbers on day or block release to colleges of further education, though these reductions are partly offset by the introduction of the YTS and reduction in length of the apprenticeships. This contraction has caused the MSC's training schemes, which contribute about 600 000 starts per year, to assume great importance. In summary, the British workforce has neither the high proportion of university graduates of the school-based training system of the USA, nor the high proportion of intermediate skills which the European work-based schemes have produced. Finally the provision of on-the-job training by British employers does not appear to compensate for these international differences and may compound them.

4.2 The competitive approach to education and training: human capital theory

4.2.1 Human capital theory

Human capital theory makes no fundamental distinction between education and training: individuals, or more recently households, are concerned with maximising lifetime income and it is assumed that each educational/training level is uniquely related to an earnings stream. This latter relationship reflects causal relationships from education to skills, between skills and marginal productivity, and finally from productivity to earnings. The latter link is the marginal productivity theory of labour demand and thus human capital interacts with this theory to provide an explanation of wage differentials. The decision-taker is viewed as following conventional investment appraisal methods. The student or worker compares the benefits of further investment in education and training with the costs. The benefits are expected higher future labour market income, the costs are of two forms: the direct costs of undertaking the education or training course and the indirect opportunity costs of forgone earnings while studying. These benefits and costs extend over time and the individual will have to compare the present value of the expected benefits with the present value of the expected costs. The rational investor in human capital will therefore invest up to that level of education and training where marginal benefits just exceed marginal costs. In equilibrium the rate of return on this marginal investment should just equal the rate of return on fixed investments of comparable risk and uncertainty.

To model the investment strategy of a wealth-maximising individual, consider the decision of whether to undertake an additional year of schooling or training. Let C be the cost of undertaking the extra year, largely forgone earnings. This has to be compared to the anticipated benefits of higher labour market earnings. Let the present value of these returns be R, then

$$R = \sum_{t=1}^{N} k_t (1 + i)^{-t} \qquad [4.1]$$

where k_t =   expected extra annual earnings in the tth year;
     i =   market rate of return on investments of comparable risk and uncertainty;
   N =   length of remaining working life.

If $R > C$ then the net present value of the investment is positive and the individual should invest in the extra human capital. An alternative formulation is to calculate the internal rate of return r, which equates the R and C of the marginal investment, here

$$C = \sum_{t=1}^{N} k_t (1 + r)^{-t} \qquad [4.2]$$

The individual should invest as long as $r > i$. Investment in human capital formation is therefore encouraged by a low C and i and high k and N. The theory of human capital accumulation can explain the observed concavity of the age–earnings profile discovered in Chapter 3. During the formal schooling period individuals specialise in the accumulation of human capital as the returns are high due to the length of future employment, N, and opportunity costs of forgone earnings, C, are low or even approach zero where there are legal constraints on child labour. Post-compulsory schooling investments are more costly and as retirement approaches N falls and the shorter pay-off period makes most investments unprofitable and the stock of human capital, and with it earning capacity, falls as depreciation dominates. This depreciation will take the form of outdated knowledge and skills which have been displaced by new technical processes and products.

It is usual to assume that the marginal rate of return to human capital investment declines as the quantity of human capital acquired by the individual increases. One supportive argument is that an individual may have a fixed capacity to benefit from human capital and therefore the principle of diminishing marginal returns to ability applies. This assumption leads to individuals having a negatively sloped demand for human capital investments; r falls as investments increase. On the supply side as funds to finance investments are obtained by borrowing or selling assets, extra funds are only likely to be available to individuals at a higher rate of interest, and the supply curve of funds for investment in human capital will be positively sloped. The supply and demand for investment in human capital are illustrated in Fig. 4.1.

Wealth maximisation requires that the individual invests in all

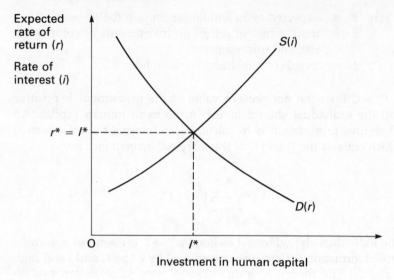

Fig. 4.1   Investment in human capital

schooling and training that yields a rate of return (r) greater than the rate of interest (i), hence I^* represents the optimal level of investment where $r = i$. Factors making it easier to finance investments in human capital such as increased family wealth and cheap government loans to students, shift the supply curve to the right and raise I^* and lower the equilibrium rate of return. Factors which raise the rate of return such as increased wage differentials for educated workers or the provision of cheaper training facilities, shift the demand curve to the right and raise both I^* and r^*.

Consider extending this analysis to a competitive economy where government and unions have no influence on the supply of education and training resources. Skill shortages cause a rise in relative earnings, raising the rate of return to those training for the occupation. If we view Fig. 4.1 as the demand and supply curves for this particular occupation then the demand curve has shifted outwards. The higher rate of return induces a higher inflow to training and the shortage is gradually eliminated by newly qualified workers. In the long run in a competitive economy differences in earnings across individuals should be related to differences in education and training investments. The equilibrium wage differentials should just compensate for the costs of these differences.

Attempts to test these propositions of the simple human capital approach, suggest that interpersonal differences in human capital investments appear to be capable of explaining substantial proportions of actual income variability. Such variations appear to account for about a third of actual income differentials. To explain a greater proportion of these differentials, some of the assumptions of the basic model need to be relaxed. The simple model assumes perfect knowledge and a perfect capital market, and imperfections will in practice prevent people of the same ability achieving the same educational level. Human capital investments are not homogeneous and quality as well as quantity measurements of investments are required to refine the model. Dispersions in the rates of return on investments will also be caused by non-pecuniary returns from employment and these may be linked to educational attainment. In addition the model ignores other sources of income variations such as scarcity of natural abilities, nepotism, discrimination and luck, which lead to people with the same educational attainments receiving different compensations. While the model can be modified to include many of these refinements its central proposition remains that the human capital element dominates earnings differentials. Its usefulness rests upon the empirical issue of whether workers can and do respond to the signals of relative wages when making their supply decisions in the labour market. Do occupational labour markets actually adjust through future and present workers making educational and training decisions on the basis of wage differentials?

One further assumption of the model so far developed is that individuals pay their own education and training costs; Becker's (1975) variation was to argue that a further cause of wage differences was the sharing of investment costs by firms. Investment in human capital has one major difference from investment in physical investment: the property rights of the enhanced human capital reside in the worker regardless of the source of the finance for that investment. Outside of a slave or feudal society, the worker retains the right to sell his labour to any employer with whom he can negotiate mutually favourable terms. Becker analyses the question of who pays for training given this characteristic of the labour market, and to answer it makes a distinction between general and specific training. General training (transferable skill training) enhances a worker's productivity both within his present firm and in other firms and accordingly has a market value. The increase in potential earnings which such training produces, irrespective of employer, provides the worker with a direct incentive to invest. It follows that workers will pay the costs of general training undertaken voluntarily. This outlay reflects their expectation that such investment will be profitable. The low pay of trainee accountants, law clerks and student doctors is consistent with investment in general training. As in the simple human capital approach, the adjustment mechanism is a change in relative wage rates. Firms facing skill bottlenecks raise the relative wage of that occupation, thereby increasing the anticipated rate of return from investment in that skill and inducing would-be investors (workers) to enter the occupation.

Some training, Becker argued, has no outside market value. Learning the organisational structure of a particular firm or its stores procedure would not increase the value of the worker to outside employers. The worker, therefore, has no incentive to forgo current earnings to undertake such specific training. The firm must decide itself on the optimal level of specific training; it will invest in such training until the rate of return is equal to the rates of return on other investment opportunities of comparable risk and uncertainty. The adjustment mechanism to any imbalance is more direct in this case and requires only information internal to the firm to be communicated to decision-makers. The optimal investment policy for the firm in specific training is made more complex because the ownership of the training belongs to the worker. A critical input into the investment decision will be the expected turnover of labour. Quits and other involuntary terminations of present employees represent forgone returns on specific training and firms will want to reduce such investment 'losses' by increasing worker loyalty. One mechanism may be to share the benefits of specific training with employees and, accordingly, the costs. Therefore employers will encourage workers to accept lower wages during specific training by promising higher wage levels after completion. Workers' post-training wages will be above their earning capacity with alternative employers, and this rent will promote low turnover.

In either of the above cases the adjustment mechanism is not instantaneous and short-term skill shortages will emerge. 'Poaching', the bidding away of workers from the firms who trained them, is here viewed benignly; it has no effect on the quantity of training since poaching can only concern general training and such training is costless to firms. Competitive market advocates thus prefer to view poaching as part of the normal mobility of labour, necessary to adjust to changes in the product and labour markets. Certain imperfections in the market are acknowledged in recent literature. Under-investment in general training may occur if workers cannot finance desired training due to imperfections in the capital market. Specifically human assets, unlike physical assets, are not acceptable as collateral for loans, and the poor may have less ability to finance potentially profitable human capital investments. Training may also be constrained because workers are more risk-averse than firms. Any losses fall directly upon workers themselves, whereas firms have limited liability and any losses are borne by shareholders whose portfolios of assets are already diversified. A further imperfection in the training market may arise because firms and workers adopt a short time horizon to training decisions, perhaps because of the absence of a futures market in labour services. One final source of imbalance may be that institutional forces prevent the flexibility of relative wages necessary to signal market changes to investors in human capital. Trade union bargaining behaviour is seen as a potentially major impediment to the workings of the market, to the extent that unions bargain to resist changes in established wage differentials and relativities. Those competitive economists who are prepared to argue that costly turnover induces firms to share the costs of specific training, develop this argument further. They argue that trade unions have 'artificially' increased apprentice wages above market-clearing levels, reducing the profitability and hence the supply of general training by firms.

4.2.2 Policy implications of the competitive model

Proponents of the human capital approach view educational and training markets as potentially efficient. Market forces should be strengthened and then allowed to operate with minimal government interference. Individuals can obtain sufficient information to make optimal investment decisions, which determine their demand for education and therefore their supply of labour. If social benefits and informational externalities can be internalised, and imperfect capital markets compensated for, say by the provision of educational vouchers and provision of manpower forecasts of labour demand, then the supply of educational places can also be market determined. Similarly, imperfections in the training market are independent of firms' behaviour and are correctable by institutional reform. In general firms can be relied upon to generate the desirable level of specific training and respond to workers' demand for general training. There is therefore no rationale, at least on economic grounds, for long-term government supervision or any direct training provision.

An illustration of this belief was the adoption by Western economies in the 1960s of educational and training programmes for anti-poverty purposes. At that time it was common to interpret

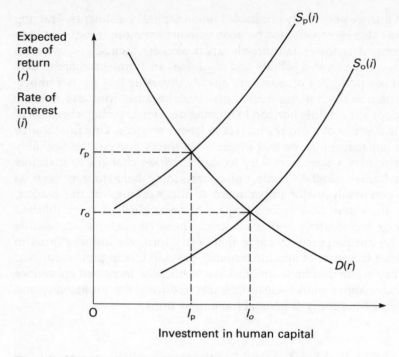

Fig. 4.2   Human capital, supply differences and earnings

poverty as being the consequence of low labour market earnings. The appropriate response to poverty was to raise those earnings. According to the human capital theory a major cause of low earnings is low investment in education and training. This lack of investment may be a reflection of attitude to risk-taking or an inability to finance desired investments. This latter factor may reflect the unwillingness of the capital market to lend on the basis of human assets rather than property. In terms of our simple diagrammatic representation of the model, the supply curve of the poor, S_p, lies above that of the rest of society, S_o, as Fig. 4.2 illustrates.

Since S_p lies above S_o applying optimal investment policy results in the poor investing less in education and training (I_p) than other groups (I_o), although they experience a higher marginal rate of return, $r_p > r_o$. A solution is to provide subsidised education and training for these groups, shifting, S_p to S_o, thereby removing the constraint on the demand for human capital among the poor. Notice that this argument implies that the poor face the same demand curve as the rest of society, in particular that the labour market rewards for investing are the same. The alphabet of programmes which constituted President Johnson's War on Poverty in the USA during the mid-1960s had the philosophical base illustrated in Fig. 4.2. Help towards doing without help, was the message underlying the introduction of the Job Corps and the reform of the Manpower Training and Development Act programmes. The impact of such policies remains controversial as the discussion on labour market discrimination in Chapter 6 illustrates.

4.2.3 Human capital theory: an assessment

The usefulness of the competitive market theory's approach to the demand for education and training appears to depend upon the relative importance of education and training, together with other competitive factors, in the explanation of labour market outcomes. Casual observation indicates that higher levels of education are associated with a lower incidence of unemployment. The 1986 *Labour Force Survey* found an unemployment rate of 4.5 per cent for people with degrees, 8.4 per cent for those with A levels, 10.1 per cent for those with O levels and a steep rise to 17.4 per cent for those whose highest qualifications is a CSE below grade 1. The pattern of earnings is likewise compatible with human capital theory; the 1984 *General Household Survey* showed that the mean gross weekly earnings of graduates was about 50 per cent higher than those workers just with A levels and 90 per cent higher than those with no qualifications. However, a proper assessment requires a multivariate analysis. There are two stages to the human capital explanation of earnings differentials: accumulated human capital determines worker productivity and the latter determines relative wages. Initially empirical studies did not separate these two relationships and instead directly tested the impact of education and training on earnings levels. The early emphasis was on the performance of earnings equations of the type first popularised by Mincer (1962).

Rates of return to education and training are usually estimated by a regression equation. Following Mincer's studies, a typical human capital based earnings function looks as follows:

$$\ln Y = \alpha + \beta S + \gamma e + \delta e^2 + \sum_{t=1}^{N} \theta_i D_i + u \qquad [4.3]$$

wherein $Y =$ the natural log of some earnings measure;
$S =$ the number of years of schooling;
$e =$ years of experience, a proxy for post-school investments;
$e^2 =$ included to proxy the depreciation of human capital;
$D_i =$ dummy variables to allow for personal characteristics such as health, sex, location and union membership;
$u =$ the error term.

The influence of e and e^2 are expected to give the function the parabolic shape with respect to age seen in Fig. 3.1. If it is assumed that the rate of return is independent of the number of years of schooling then β is an estimate of the rate of return on schooling, γ gives an estimate of the rate of return from on-the-job training only when the fraction of working time devoted to training is known. Siebert's (1985) survey of estimates for the private rate of return indicated a range around 10 per cent, that is above the returns on physical investments and the market rate of interest. Recent studies adopting this approach suggest widespread international under-investment at all levels of education (Psacharopoulos 1985), and declining rates of return by level of education and across levels of national income. Specification problems abound with the Mincer approach: allowance needs to be made for ability, interaction between education and experience, and quality adjustments made to jobs and schooling. Ability will tend to be related to level of schooling achieved and attempts to distinguish the two influences are problematic. If heredity or environmental factors affect the ability of individuals to benefit from education then 'family' influences are difficult to separate from human capital ones. In contrast with Fig. 4.2, it is the demand curve which differs and individuals from 'better' families invest more and get higher rates of return. Famous studies by Jencks et al. (1979) and Taubman (1976) attempted to resolve the problem by studying, respectively, brothers and identical twins; their estimates for the returns on schooling are much lower than reported above. This would suggest over-investment in education, though the neglect of consumption benefits could explain this discrepancy. Returns appear greater if adjustment is made for the quality of jobs, some of the returns to education apparently being taken in the form of better working conditions and more stable employment.

It is the goodness of fit of these earnings functions which we earlier suggested could be crucial to the assessment of the importance of human capital theory. A common size for the explanatory power of the Mincer equation is about 30 per cent, but as the number of independent variables is increased this figure will rise. For example, Wilson (1987) manages to 'explain' about 39 per cent of the variation in the log of annual earnings of his sample of professional engineers with the unaugmented Mincer earnings function without dummies, the average return to a year of schooling being 5.7 per cent. Explanatory power increases if dummies are introduced for personal characteristics such as: industry, occupation, location, membership of professional institution, collectively bargained salary, trade union membership and form of training. Wilson manages to achieve an R^2 of 0.55, with the implied rate of return on a year of schooling reduced to 4.2 per cent. Increasing the number of dummy variables increases estimation problems and it does not resolve many of the fundamental problems with the approach; in particular the effects of education and ability can rarely be separated.

An alternative approach to testing is to consider directly whether the demand for education is responsive to economic forces and whether structural and other environmental changes have the predicted impact. Freeman's 1986 survey finds that the demand for higher education appears sensitive to wage incentives and to tuition costs. In the UK early work by Blaug, Dougherty and Psacharapoulos (1982) reached tentative conclusions consistent with the human capital model. Raising the British school-leaving age to sixteen did tend to make age–earnings profiles steeper and raise mean earnings of the lower paid. In human capital terms the increase in school-leavers' human capital due to the extra year of investment raised productivity and therefore earnings, a result reinforced by the one-time contraction of supply of school-leavers. Pissarides in two associated studies (1981, 1982) found some evidence that the staying-on rate at school was sensitive to economic incentives, though the relationship was weak for girls and he ignored social factors important in decision-taking. The depression of male applicants to university in the early and mid-1970s was, he claimed, related to declines in the rate of return on university education, together with an economic recession which reduced family investment in education and offset the stimulating influence of rising unemployment on applications. Rice (1987) estimated a model of investment in post-compulsory education which did allow the socio-economic background of the family to influence investment decisions. Family background was found to be an important determinant of participation, a factor not stressed in the human capital model. Attempts to test directly whether family background influences the accuracy of labour market information have been scarce, but low-ability and working-class pupils appear to have a poorer awareness of the economic returns from educational investments.

Bosworth and Wilson (1980) found relative earnings elasticities for scientists and engineers of 0.6 and 1.3 respectively, and interpreted contemporary reductions in the relative earnings as the cause of the proportional fall in science and engineering graduates in the late 1960s and 1970s. An alternative but potentially complementary hypothesis is that the apparent decline in the rate of return from undertaking degree courses in science and engineering in the early 1970s reflected an equalising demand-side adjustment to the rapid rise in higher education. Attempts to explain apprentice recruitment in terms of the supply of apprentice recruits have been less successful. Lindley (1975) prefers a labour demand explanation of this general training, though this is inconsistent with the Becker model where firms passively respond to the demand for general training. Nissim (1984) found evidence that the demand for skilled labour in the British mechanical engineering industry was less responsive to wage movements and cyclical changes in output when compared to less skilled workers, results consistent with greater hiring and firing costs associated with higher on-the-job specific training.

The results summarised above have been broadly consistent with the competitive approach, while also suggesting that non-competitive forces have a significant impact on earnings differences. The problem with these studies is that they rarely confront the individual components of the model: by directly considering the relation between education and earnings they fail to address the nature of the causal link between the two variables. To equate the apparent private profitability of most educational investments with social profitability it is necessary to establish how the accumulation of human capital enhances earnings. With human capital theory the higher earnings of educated and trained workers reflect higher output and therefore both private and social benefits from such investments. It may not be the case that education raises earnings through the mechanism of enhancing worker productivity; if instead education largely acts as a signalling device to employers about the employability of applicants then private returns are a poor proxy of social returns, and human capital theory is fundamentally flawed. A further problem stems from our discovery in Chapter 3 that structured internal labour markets were common in the UK. Here wage and salary adjustment are not the principal adjustment mechanism and internal labour markets prevent the required signals being sent to human capital investors. In which case the human capital theory is not a helpful explanation of supply decisions in such labour markets, and we now turn to alternative approaches.

4.3 Structuralist approaches to education and training: screening hypothesis

In Chapter 2 the structuralist approach to labour market behaviour was outlined. The main conclusions of the model are that firms design internal employment policies largely independent of external competitive forces. These policies will be characterised by internal job ladders and wage rates specified by job, rather than by individual workers. How does this model explain the role and determinants of education and training? On-the-job training will be concentrated in the primary labour market and the strength of these internal labour markets makes all such training essentially firm-specific. Given the long-term attachment between workers and firms the distinction between general and specific training is in practice redundant. Any on-the-job training, even in a transferable skill, will have a content unique to the firm such as work organisation, or a particular machine and product specification. Firms are therefore not indifferent between current employees and applicants from the external labour market with supposedly the same transferable skill. The former have higher productivity due to their firm-specific knowledge and are of known and acceptable quality and reliability. The quantity of on-the-job training will be determined by the firm, and it will be insensitive to the demand for training among workers. Any shortages of labour will not be countered by wage changes, that would distort existing agreed relativities; instead firms will initially respond by restructuring existing work schedules and subcontracting.

For the individual worker the key to obtaining on-the-job training is therefore to gain entrance into the primary labour market; in part this reflects luck and can explain why earnings functions explain so little of earnings differences. Education and pre-entry training have the function of assisting access to good jobs in the structuralist model. Recruitment occurs by firms choosing between applicants to fill positions usually at the bottom of the job ladder. The observed high 'wastage' of skilled workers to promotion is here interpreted as a consequence of the dominance of internal labour markets. It is not workers' short-term productivity which employers are interested in, since all recruits require firm-specific training and are offered, implicitly, long-term contracts. Here the emphasis is upon employers' hiring policy and firms choose between applicants on the basis of the 'employability' and 'trainability'; employers cannot directly discern these characteristics and therefore applicants need to signal their quality. The 'screening' hypothesis argues that education can perform this task. Workers in the same occupation differ in their productive performance due to differences in reliability, intelligence and social skills. Firms wish to hire the best-quality applicants and require some means of distinguishing the quality of applicants. High-quality applicants may therefore find it profitable to invest in acquiring a characteristic which signals their quality to employers. A good signal will be one which lower-quality applicants will have difficulty in achieving due to ability or cost. Educational qualifications meet such requirements and high-quality applicants will have relatively high investments in education in order to produce their signal. Thus employers exercise 'statistical discrimination' on the basis of educational attainment; it is too expensive to identify atypical members of a given group and 'employable' members of a low educational achievement group suffer discrimination. A further advantage of education as a screen is that it is legal to exercise discrimination on this basis while using other stereotypes such as race or sex is not; moreover it is at present socially acceptable. All elements of society view educational achievement as reflecting individual effort and accept their 'fairness' as criteria for recruitment. Its use therefore promotes good working relations and avoids conflicts which threaten to constrain productivity.

The structuralist view of the role and effects of education and training in the labour market is often linked with radical arguments about the objectives of education in a capitalist economy. Bowles and Gintis (1976) argue that most jobs require non-cognitive personality characteristics such as: concentration, compliance, industry punctuality and co-operation. These characteristics rather than cognitive knowledge dictate productivity for the bulk of the labour force. It is therefore the role of compulsory schooling to generate these valued behavioural characteristics. The emphasis upon discipline is just one example of their proposition that the social relations of schools in capitalist economies reflect the realities of the social division of labour. The sociologists' emphasis upon the socialising role of education has its origins in the work of Adam Smith and other classical economists. They argued that moral re-education of the masses was required if factory-based production was to be promoted. However, until Bowles and Gintis this argument had been neglected by modern economists. If employers care more about how school-leavers behave than about what they know, then the traditional arguments for vocational education for the majority of the population dissolve. At higher levels of occupations different individual characteristics are required and leadership ability and self-reliance become more important. In many professional occupations cognitive skills do become important to job performance, though often these are fairly general numerical and communication skills such as those required by accountants and lawyers. Thus employers take educational credentials as proxies for the qualities which they require in their workforce. Hence the poor match between specific educational qualifications and actual occupation.

The term 'screening hypothesis' has also been used to describe the view of education as a non-competitive barrier to entry rather than as a signal. Here education is a means of transmitting privilege and maintaining inequality over time. Employers discriminate on the basis of education, education being a proxy for preferred characteristics, such as class or race, which are unrelated to potential productivity. This is a more radical version than the above view that since employers cannot identify individual potential productivity they require a low-cost screen; here potential productivity is not the target of employers. Implicit is the argument that productivity and profitability are almost independent of worker qualities, otherwise competition, however weak, would ultimately eliminate such firms. Credentialism has sometimes been used to categorise this approach, but both this term and screening are ambiguously used in the literature.

In some respects the screening hypothesis is similar to the human capital approach. Both view the benefits of education as being higher lifetime earnings and generate similar determinants of the individual's optimal investment strategy. Statistical discrimination and internal labour markets can explain why educated workers on average earn more, although their potential labour market productivity remains unaffected by their investments. It is when the social, as opposed to private returns to education are considered that the crucial difference of the approaches is identified. The screening approach identifies the benefits to society from education in terms of the quality of the signal it provides to employers about the pre-existing characteristics of applicants. The socially optimum level of education thus depends upon the relative cost and effectiveness of this signal and the output gains from a better allocation of workers between jobs. These gains are illustrated by Akerlof's analogy of jobs as dam sites (1981). A dam which is too small for a particular site permanently underutilises that site, similarly employers must fill vacancies by the best available workers if they are to produce efficiently. The screening approach thus rejects any general application of manpower planning, outside of a few professional labour markets. Generally the required characteristics which education should promote are universal to employment and therefore the educational system cannot cause labour market bottlenecks. The emphasis on vocational education in current policies to reduce youth unemployment and promote higher growth paths is, according to this view, misplaced. Economic growth has deskilled many jobs and technical innovations like electronic calculators and word processing have reduced the importance of traditional numerate and literate skills in the majority of the labour market. Required manual and cognitive skills are best acquired on the job where firms can impart their particular requirements. Hence radically different policy implications follow from the structuralist viewpoint.

Whether the established link between education and earnings reflects the influence of education on productivity, recruitment probabilities or discrimination has yet to be empirically established. There are severe problems in finding tests which distinguish between these views, and beliefs about the current weight of the evidence concerning the relative importance of competitive and non-competitive influences, differ between commentators. Siebert (1985) believes that there is little deviation of the social from the private benefits, whereas a British study (Shah 1985) found evidence supporting the screening hypothesis. He reached this conclusion by examining earnings differentials between employed and self-employed, where education should have little impact upon earnings, and screened and non-screened employment. This leaves great uncertainty concerning the relationship between the private rate of return and social rate of return, making assessment of educational policy issues problematic.

4.4 Policy issues

4.4.1 General comments on educational and training policy

Both of the above approaches can agree that an appropriate

objective for public policy can, in principle, be framed in terms of social benefits and costs. Calculations will differ from those covering the private rate of return as there is a wider definition of costs and benefits, and a different rate of discount. Society will favour individual investments in education and training as long as social benefits exceed social costs. Where individuals are under-investing in education and training on the basis of calculations using social benefits and costs, governments should intervene to ensure efficient levels of investment. Since these social benefits and costs are spread over time, society will have to discount according to its preference for present consumption over future consumption. This is measured by the social rate of time preference and it is often proxied by the rate of interest on long-term government bonds. The social rate of time preference is usually assumed lower than individuals' rates of time preference as the government is less myopic than individuals and more concerned with the needs of future generations. Though where governments are subjected to regular elections it is not so obvious that they will be more far-sighted than the electorate. The appropriate measure of costs is forgone output plus the resource costs of the education or training. A far greater problem concerns the specification and measurement of social benefits. Leaving aside for the moment the true nature of the private benefits, any calculation of social benefits of education and training requires calculations of the size of the externalities produced. Few estimates of these have been produced; Haveman and Wolfe (1984) review these externalities, from the impact on the quality of leisure and non-market work, through effects on health and fertility to social cohesion, crime reduction and consumer and search efficiency. In addition there are the potential contributions to economic growth from greater mobility, elimination of skill bottlenecks and technological and organisational improvements. The inability to measure these non-market externalities together with the screening–human capital debate have limited social cost–benefit studies. These problems are often assumed to be slightly less severe in the case of higher education and training; Wilson (1981) and Ziderman (1975) have estimated social rates of return for British Government expenditure on higher education and direct training which exceed the Treasury test discount rate. The 1986 White Paper on higher education, utilising relative wages and allowing for the direct costs of teaching, estimated the social rate of return to be around 8 per cent, about equal to the test discount rate though double the long-term yield on financial assets. Given these problems with cost–benefit analysis, in practice Western educational policy was much more influenced by studies purporting to measure the contribution of education and training to economic growth.

The early attempts of Denison to estimate the sources of growth, although lacking a consistent theoretical framework, popularised the belief that education was a major source of growth. The inability to aggregate heterogeneous labour and capital inputs and the problem of specifying a production function which allows different forms of technical progress, led to the adoption of rules of thumb in these studies. With the increasing rigour of empirical studies, growth accounting has inevitably failed to live up to its 1960s popularity. An alternative approach also popular at this time held that there were fixed input coefficients for education groups of workers specific to each industry, hence shortages of a particular level of educated workers can constrain growth. Accurate manpower forecasts could therefore identify labour bottlenecks and educational needs. This approach depends critically upon a low elasticity of substitution between different levels of educated labour and between educated labour and capital. Freeman (1986) reports elasticities between more and less educated labour of between 1.0 and 2.0, suggesting that the manpower planning approach to the allocation of educational provision is too rigid.

More recent attempts to examine the contribution of education to economic growth are less ambitious. The evidence does not support any simple relationship between the size of educational investment and differences in economic growth rates and, as Daly (1982) has argued, more emphasis should be placed on the type and quality of educational and training expenditure. The large, and persisting, productivity differences between manufacturing industries in the USA, West Germany and the UK have been the source of many investigations. Prais (1981) and Daly (1986) have attempted to compare international productivity differences with differences in workforce education and training. Daly, Hitchens and Wagner (1985) argue that productivity differences between West German and British manufacturing plants cannot be explained by differences in the age of machinery but by differences in the efficiency with which the machines are operated. These studies provide tentative evidence that productivity differences are biggest in those industries where the differences in educational attainment of the workforces are greatest. This can be combined with the earlier suggestion of Caves (1980) that the UK performs badly in management-intensive industries, another area of training where the UK under-invests in comparison with other developed economies. Whether one interprets such tentative evidence in terms of the human capital or screening approach remains a neglected issue.

The above discussion illustrates how far economists are from offering guidelines for educational and training policy. Given that economic objectives may not dominate such decision-making, this is in part inevitable and even desirable. However, training and higher education policies have been changed on the basis of perceived economic advantages and it should be stressed how little evidence exists to support many common beliefs in this area. The present government's belief in the supremacy of vocational over more academic schooling, and of work-based training schemes over school-based ones, are not backed by any systematic empirical studies. Among the supposed successful, high-productivity national economies there are examples of both systems. Why the West German system of vocational training should be taken as the model to follow in much of the literature and policy rather than American, Japanese or French systems, remains a mystery. The West German system provides apprenticeships for about 85 per cent of minimum-age school-leavers, high-school graduates often preferring this path to university entrance, and apprenticeships are the traditional access to work in all sectors of the economy. The syllabus is determined at the federal level and examinations organised at the local industry level. This means that the training is 'general' and may explain the low relative level of training allowances in West Germany (Casey 1986).

If one considers the report of a 1984 conference organised by the National Institute of Economic and Social Research (NIESR) on the subject of education and economic performance (Worswick 1985), the implicit assumption of virtually all participants was that the British system failed to provide an adequate supply of cognitive and manual skills, hence more vocational schooling was required. Only occasionally did discussants question the lack of evidence for such assumptions and raise the issue of the supply of social and behavioural skills. As Williams commented, perhaps to start an investigation of deficiencies of the British economy with the educational system is misplaced, and a better starting-point would be to consider managerial decision-making. He argued that in practice employers remain unimpressed by vocational qualifications obtained by school-leavers and are really impressed by 'conventional modes of dress, speech and behaviour and a critical attitude that none the less accepts the basic ethos of the firm' (Worswick 1985: 133). Surveys of recruitment practices for manual and clerical workers reviewed in the next chapter indicate the unimportance of task-specific skills in present hiring decisions. Moreover given their lack of any systematic evaluation of the efficiency of hiring practices, which is also discovered in Chapter 5, we cannot even accept that employers know what they should be looking for in recruits. Until employers can identify what qualities they require in recruits and in particular the relative importance of behavioural and cognitive skills, then appropriate educational and training policies cannot be decided by this group of decision-makers any better than other groups who may be further removed from production.

In addition much of recent British policy discussion fails to reflect the realities of modern production technology and the historical decline in manufacturing employment examined in Chapter 3. Vocational education and industrial training initiatives have often emphasised manual skills, rather than skills relevant to a service- and information-based economy. Even within manufacturing, technical progress has altered the educational and technical requirements of the workforce. Although historically mechanisation increased the demand for semi-skilled machine minders, the present trend towards automation has reduced the demand for technically unqualified and inexperienced labour. Workers displaced by the automation of feeding, operating and unloading machines, often do not have the qualifications to fill the increased demand for supervisors of automated machinery. We now consider in more detail two contemporary important policy issues: the school-to-work transition and provision of industrial training.

4.4.2 School-to-work transition

In the mid-1980s eighteen- to twenty-four-year-olds accounted for about 20 per cent of the British workforce, yet they constituted a third of the unemployed and a quarter of the long-term unemployed. This indicates one of the origins of present debates on the school-to-work transition. Two of the most common criticisms of the present British system of schooling are inadequate standards of achievement and the irrelevance of the curriculum to employment. Postlethwaite (1985) and Prais (1985, 1987) attempt to provide some much needed international comparisons of scientific knowledge, reading comprehension and performance in mathematical tests. Unfortunately much of their data refers to the performance of students before the introduction of comprehensive secondary education, though the results of the 1981 survey conducted by the International Association for the Evaluation of Education appears consistent with their argument. Their conclusion is that the UK performs especially poorly in the education of pupils in the bottom half of academic achievement. Only about a quarter of British pupils get O level mathematics, while the average West German and Japanese achieve this level and at an earlier age. These conclusions are consistent with the present policy emphasis on training on the YTS and implementation of a common national core curriculum in schools, though evidence is lacking to support their contention that this is the most crucial weakness of the British system. As Williams (1985) and Peston (1985) note, there are other unique characteristics of the British system of education, which may be associated with poor economic growth performance. Few other advanced economies have such a sharp distinction between the private and public sectors in secondary education; none allow the universities to require able school pupils to make early decisions about narrow subject specialisation; few have such an emphasis on pure as opposed to applied science and technology or have such a tendency to recruit the best graduates into academic, Civil Service or money market employment. The mid-1980s concentration of policy on the education and training of the least academically able school-leavers, in essence delaying their entry into the labour market, may have reflected political pressures for preventing further rises in measured unemployment as much as beliefs about the economic benefits of cheap imitations of West Germany.

Surveys of employers suggest that they are unimpressed by school-leavers who have pursued vocational courses (Gordon 1983) and prefer applicants who are good at English and mathematics. Achievement at O level appears to be the crucial yardstick by which employers judge applicants and they appear reluctant to lower entry thresholds which are unattainable to the majority of school-leavers (Roberts, Dench and Richardson 1986). Such preferences do not appear to indicate the importance of such skills to employment, but reflect a belief that ability to master English and mathematics indicate trainability. A recent survey of 1000 firms (Donaldson *et al.* 1987) exploring the links between education and employment in the information technology field produced similar findings. Employers were virtually unanimous in placing little emphasis upon specific vocational skills in their selection criteria. Employers instead favoured a sound general education; however, for recruits from further and higher education academic achievement is the single most important criteria in selection. Personal qualities and appearance dominate recruitment criteria for those leaving school at sixteen and for YTS trainees. What firms appear to look for is the 'right' attitude to work, willingness to accept workplace discipline, regularity of attendance and ability to 'fit in' with their work group. In the absence of previous work experience employers look for indications of such qualities in the appearance and attitudes exhibited in interviews. Partly reflecting employers' additional desire for recruits to be sympathetic to the firm's ethos, schemes which encourage positive attitudes to private enterprise have been financed by the MSC. The pilot schemes in the Certificate of Pre-Vocational Education, the Technical and Vocational Education Initiative (TVEI) and pilot schemes in higher education were small in scale, and much less ambitious than current schemes in France, West Germany and Japan. From 1987 TVEI has been introduced nationally although evaluation is at an early stage; the importance of such schemes is that they represent cracks in what Steedman calls the apartheid of academic and vocational education in the UK. The Higginson Committee's investigation into the future of A levels together with the introduction of GCSE and AS level examinations may ultimately represent further weakenings in this divide.

The YTS began in September 1983, replacing the Youth Opportunities Scheme which had been criticised for its neglect of training. The voluntary YTS initially guaranteed twelve months' training, including at least thirteen weeks off the job, for all minimum-age school-leavers and where available for those aged seventeen. In essence the scheme adopts a down-market version of the West German strategy rather than the full-time vocational education system of the French and Japanese. Practical skills dominate rather than theoretical work, though TVEI and city technical colleges represent small-scale British imitations of the latter approach. Employers and trainees at first interpreted the YTS as specifically vocational job preparation, and although it contains elements which stress literacy, social and life skills, only about a quarter of participants in the first two years gained any qualification. The government hoped to keep this foundation training in a 'real' work environment by encouraging employers to design the programmes and employer-based schemes account for nearly three-quarters of entrants, over two-thirds of work experience occurring in the service sector. Around two-thirds of YTS leavers were in employment three months after leaving the course, the overwhelming majority with their placement firms, apparently a higher ratio than for non-participants. The net cost per filled place was estimated at just under £1500 to the exchequer and £130 to employers in 1985/86 (Gray and King 1986). Estimates of displacement effects, where trainees fill jobs that would have been filled by other workers, have been as high as 90 per cent (Chapman and Tooze 1987). A survey of providers by Sako and Dore (1986) indicated that employers view the present scheme as low-cost screening, rather than as being a direct contribution to their own training programmes. This could indicate that internal labour markets make training highly firm-specific and that firms look for trainability rather than particular vocational skills. It also suggests that the YTS is a substitute for secondary education for entrants and employers in many areas of the labour market.

The most comprehensive study is Deakin and Pratten's (1987) survey of managers' opinion of the operation of YTS. Their collation of management responses suggested a 'deadweight' effect, YTS places replacing jobs for young workers, of about 30 per cent and 'substitution' effects, where YTS places displace adult workers, of about 5 per cent. The total displacement effects were bigger by a factor of two in small companies, which may explain the discrepancy between these and earlier estimates. Managers' estimates of the contribution of trainees to output, adjusted for the displacement effects, suggested that a first-year trainee produced the equivalent of two-thirds of their pay in the service sector and smaller proportions in other industries. Other surveys have suggested that employer's experience a net gain from providing work experience and training. About two-thirds of trainees completing YTS were retained by their placement firm and all but 5 per cent found employment, a much lower rate than that of other studies. For most providers YTS trainees were a relatively small proportion of their workforce, though in the personal services sector the YTS could be subsidising up to 10 per cent of total labour costs.

With the launch of the two-year YTS in April 1986, employers were required to pay more of the training costs, as the second year of training became more occupational and employer-specific. A review of the fragmented system of vocational qualifications led to the establishment of the National Council for Vocational Qualifications in 1986 with responsibility for supervising a new national framework. This emphasis is reflected in the achieving of standards of competence and the gaining of vocational qualifications on the two-year YTS. Quality as well as cost per filled placement and wastage rates has become a criterion for evaluation, though Steedman (1987), in making a comparison with France, questions whether the target levels of training are sufficiently ambitious. Far too little is known about the short- and longer-term progress of YTS leavers to make any strong conclusions as to the efficiency of the scheme. The introduction of quality as well as quantity objectives is generally welcomed, but the neglect of any long-term planning of national manpower needs and allocation by short-term availability of training places seems inconsistent with this change. Perhaps questions about the efficiency of the YTS can only be properly answered when the screening as well as the training efficiency of the scheme are addressed. The distorting influence which YTS allowances have on staying-on at school decisions also needs to be examined.

Present evidence suggests that only at the higher levels of education were employers concerned about the adequacy of supply of job-specific skills. Such findings question the underlying rationale for the YTS as presently operating, as well as the emphasis upon the need for more 'relevant' schooling and pre-entry training. Strengthening links between employers and schools is to be welcomed, but as a two-way process where both educators and managers question present practices. If compulsory education is being supplemented or even displaced as a screen by near-compulsory YTS for many school-leavers then the role of the former is unclear. The weakness of the training element in many placements suggests that for many employers the YTS is little more than a targeted employment subsidy. Hence the conclusion of most commentators is that the YTS needs to concentrate placements on training relevant to the elimination of skill shortages, and this leads to our next topic.

4.4.3 Government and skill shortages

Until the 1960s most Western governments made only minor intervention into the training market and these were largely on social grounds, not economic ones. In the UK the government's direct vocational training services had their origin in the 'instructional factories' established in 1917 to train disabled ex-servicemen. Government Training Centres, similar to the Skill-centres functioning today, were introduced to combat the depressed labour market of the mid-1920s. During the next forty years there was a gradual shift towards providing training in scarce skills for the disabled, unemployed and ex-servicemen. However, by 1962 the service had been so contracted that only 2500 training places remained. As a consequence of apparent shortages of certain types of labour in the 'booms' of the 1950s and especially 1959–60, the government became increasingly concerned with the private sector's provision of training. This concern manifested itself in an expansion programme for Government Training Centres begun in 1963 and the 1964 Industrial Training Act establishing Industrial Training Boards. These measures were justified by the poor quality and cyclical instability of the quantity of training provision in the private sector. This supposed market failure had caused skill bottlenecks, which constrained expansion and added to the inflationary pressures in the labour market. Other Western economies, such as Australia, have maintained a 'voluntarist' approach to industrial training and avoided any large-scale government intervention. The effectiveness of these alternative policies will be considered later, but it is first necessary to consider how we should measure the extent of market failure and even more fundamentally, what constitutes a skill shortage.

Studies by Hunter (1978) and Thomas and Deaton (1977) of labour shortages, drew attention to the differing usage of this term. To the neoclassical labour economist a labour shortage means the existence in a well-defined market of ex-ante excess demand at the current relative wage. The anticipated adjustment mechanism is through changes in that relative wage. Employers interviewed in these studies considered a labour shortage as occurring when they had difficulty in recruiting and retaining staff at their offered wage and working conditions. Their adjustment to the shortage was by overtime working, subcontracting and improvement in non-pecuniary benefits, behaviour consistent with the structuralist view of the market. The competitive approach suggests that persisting shortages must reflect market imperfections and would consider whether trade unions or governments were preventing wage adjustments; the structuralist interprets these shortages as reflecting ineffective personnel policies. In neither case is it obvious that an appropriate measure of a shortage is the ratio of registered unemployment to vacancies in an occupation which was commonly used until occupational unemployment data ceased to be available in 1982. An alternative is the manpower requirements approach which compares actual or forecasted demand for labour with supply in a specific occupation. Meager (1986) considers some of the problems of reconciling the manpower requirements and economic approaches to estimating skill shortages.

At present there are three main regular sources of information concerning skill shortages in British industry. The Confederation of British Industry conducts monthly surveys of employers in manu-facturing industries. Respondents are asked whether their output is likely to be constrained by a shortage of skilled labour. In recent times about 15 per cent of respondents expect such shortages and identify specific shortage occupations as: professional engineers, machinists, technicians, assembly and inspection occupations, welders, computer and management services, and electrical and electronic fitters. The Professional and Executive Recruitment offices of the MSC conduct twice-yearly surveys identifying occupational and regional shortages. In recent years the main skill shortages identified have been for: computer programmers/systems analysts, accountants, and electronic and electrical engineers. The MSC also carries out a quarterly analysis of Jobcentre vacancies. Those vacancies unfilled for two months are identified and the reasons for them remaining open considered. Recently about one-eighth of the total stock of vacancies are long-duration, about a quarter of these are indicative of skill shortages and of these about a half are located in the south-east and London. About 80 per cent of recent skill shortage vacancies are within the making and repairing, personal services and professional occupations within education, health and welfare groups. The reason why only one-quarter of these long-duration vacancies are treated as a consequence of skill shortages is that the survey recognises that in many cases the employer is making wage, or conditions of employment, offers to applicants which are unrealistic given current market conditions. We discuss present levels of occupational mismatch again in the examination of recent British unemployment in Chapter 7.

The problem of identifying skill shortages becomes even more problematic when the screening hypothesis is raised; do shortages reflect a lack of specific job-related skills or in reality do they often reflect a shortage of social skills among applicants? The study by Oliver and Turton (1982) emphasises a key consequence of structured labour markets, that managers have adopted a behavioural concept of skill. They argue from responses of firms interviewed, that managers seem to operate on a basis that skill refers to trainability and socially acceptable behaviour. Thus although technical skills and work experience are important in the hiring of skilled workers, skill shortages are often a reflection of shortages of certain types of temperament and social characteristics, rather than shortages of specific levels of cognitive and manual dexterity among applicants. It is often 'good blokes' which firms cannot recruit, not electrical fitters or other trades. Skill shortages of this type are not solvable by market forces or training policy and have implications for labour market discrimination discussed in Chapter 6. The discussion of the last few paragraphs suggests caution in interpreting firms' complaints about labour shortages as a reflection of training market failures.

4.4.4 Government and on-the-job training

There was general belief in the early 1960s that the amount of in-service training in the UK was inadequate, of poor quality and unfairly distributed between firms. Shortages were thought to be exacerbated by 'poaching', where firms avoided training costs by bidding newly trained workers away from their employers. This 'free riding' raised training costs and supposedly encouraged firms who did train to reduce quality or quantity. The 1964 Industrial Training Act was an attempt to confront this perceived problem. The Industrial Training Boards established by the Act were to operate a levy–grant system is order to expand and modernise training provision while ensuring a fairer distribution of the costs. A 1973 Act modified the levy–grant system, noticeably by limiting the levy to a maximum of 1 per cent of payroll and by exempting small firms and those who could show they were adequately training to meet their own requirements. Economists at this time were heavily influenced by the Becker model and were generally critical of the initiative. For example Hartley (1982) argued that poaching could only occur among workers with general training, that is training which raises productivity in all firms, and such training is therefore worker-financed. Firms cannot lose from the mobility of generally trained workers, and poaching cannot occur with specific training since the higher productivity is unique to the training firm. The initiative was therefore misconceived and grants paid to firms for general training were wrongly assigned, since trainees paid the costs of such training. No grants were required for specific training since the profit motive was sufficient to generate optimal provision. Competitive economists favoured intervention but only to correct imperfections on the other side of the market, such as the lack of loan capital for trainees, or measures to promote wage flexibility by curbing trade unions.

Such criticisms make a very rigorous distinction between general and specific training which does not appear to be warranted in real world labour markets. Moreover such views fail to explain why the quantity of initial skill training appears to be supply and not demand constrained. Merrilees (1983) summarises British engineering employers as initially deciding upon the desired intake of apprentices and then adjusting the quality of applicants to reach this level. Firms therefore do not respond to the demand for apparently general training. The reason appears to be that although apprenticeships may consist of large amounts of general training, during the period of training workers are immobile and also learn firm-specific skills. Typically therefore the costs of apprenticeship training may be shared between trainees and firms, with firms also sharing in the benefits. Jones (1986) estimates, though from a very small sample, that the net costs of training an apprentice in 1984 was about £14 600 in non-engineering and £8900 in engineering trades.

About 70 per cent of these costs were trainee wages and other payroll costs. The difference between sectors Jones ascribes to the greater specificity of skills in the non-engineering sector. Poaching now is costly to firms, though avoidable by employment policies which reward length of service. Inefficient employee compensation policies and inadequate internal decision-making may now cause under-investment in training.

Jones (1985) speculates that British training deficiencies may be due to relatively high trainee wages. In comparison with Swiss and German trainees, British apprentices earn a much higher wage relative to skilled adult workers. Moreover British apprentices earn a much higher proportion of the wage of non-apprentices of the same age, yet earn comparable returns in terms of post-training earnings. Thus Jones concludes that the structure of pay produced by collective bargaining is seriously out of line with that required by a workplace-based industrial training system. It is not clear why this should be so. He has no data on post-training worker productivity, tenure or earnings and therefore has not established that training is unprofitable for firms once longer-term benefits are included. If the lack of testing makes British training more firm-specific then this would also explain his findings. If his conjecture is correct then why do firms not adjust wages down for trainees? The existence of an excess supply of applicants would seem to indicate such behaviour would be profitable in a competitive market. It is as yet premature to conclude that the deficiencies in private sector training are the consequence of the unprofitability of on-the-job training.

The cyclical instability of training appears to result from the illiquidity of training investments; cash-flow viability rather than long-term profitability appears to underlie firm behaviour in recessions. An important further source of under-investment may be the result of British firms satisficing rather than optimising; the persistence of such behaviour may be due to its low 'costs' in the past. Thompson and Walford (1986) surveyed employers and found widespread neglect of training and a failure to apply any techniques of investment appraisal to training decisions. If under-investment is widespread, this low level of X-efficiency will cause external competitors to gain markets, and domestic firms move 'down market' in world trading terms. That is, the self-correcting mechanism by which under-investors are displaced works but via increased import penetration. Katrak (1982) has suggested that the relatively slow growth of the British skilled workforce has been associated with a decrease in the skill intensity of her exports and an increase in that of her imports. Training deficiencies in this case lead to the adoption of techniques and products which have low training needs. British firms have generally moved down market into the more competitive, lower value added per unit products. It is just this sector which has experienced slow growth, especially during the world-wide recession of the 1980s. If one accepts this more structuralist view of the training market, then subsidies and the professionalisation of training associated with the introduction of Industrial Training Boards may improve private training performance.

The MSC's 1980 review of the 1964 Act publicised widespread employer hostility to the Industrial Training Boards. Managers often acknowledged that the boards had improved training standards and improved managerial attitudes to training; however, they resented the bureaucracy and 'paper' training promoted by the boards. There was no evidence that the Act had any significant long-term impact on the quantity of training, though given the emphasis on training for firms' own, rather than the industry's long-term needs this may not be surprising. The previous 1976 review had recognised this problem, and suggested collective funding of transferable skill training and increased public subsidy of training at the margin, only the latter policy eventually being adopted. Instead of these policies, the 1981 Employment and Training Act and a White Paper of that year, launched a New Training Initiative which in the case of in-service training heralded a return to the 'voluntarist' approach of the pre-1964 Act era. When employers were faced with the prospect of financing the full costs of the training boards two-thirds were quickly abolished, responsibility for determining the socially optimal level of training again returning to the market. The move towards certified standards of training and a more flexible entrance age, and away from time-serving is still to be encouraged. Comparative studies considered earlier (Prais 1981; Prais and Wagner 1983; Prais and Steedman 1986) have illustrated the quantity and quality inadequacies of the British system, and it seems unlikely that the present reliance on the 'voluntarist' approach and the YTS will improve this poor relative performance.

Australia introduced a wage subsidy scheme for apprentices in 1973. The scheme provided a tax-exempt rebate on day-release training for eligible employers and at times this has been supplemented by a marginal employment subsidy element. The latter providing additional financial support for employers increasing their apprentice recruitment, Merrilees (1984) investigated the impact of the scheme. Testing the form of the demand function for apprentice labour he found that output effects dominated, though he also found, like Nissim (1984) for the UK, significant wage elasticities.

That is, Australian employers did adjust training places to trainee wage levels; accordingly he concluded that the wage subsidy scheme had increased apprentice intake and that reallocation of the rebate towards high elasticity sectors would maximise recruitment effects. Implicit in the scheme and this assessment is the assumption that apprentice intake is a suitable policy objective and that displacement of other workers is minimal.

4.4.5 Government direct training schemes

An alternative to government attempts to influence private sector training is for it to provide training opportunities itself. The government may provide training facilities to further a variety of objectives: promote economic growth; relieve poverty or reduce registered unemployment. These objectives will change over time; the pioneering 1962 Manpower Training and Development Act (MTDA) in the USA initially stressed unemployed among the primary workforce, but developed by the end of that decade into an alphabet of programmes targeting the poor. The main criticism of the 1962 MTDA Act was the weak link between the training provided and employment prospects in the labour market. Under the 1973 Comprehensive Employment and Training Act (CETA) these schemes were consolidated and new emphasis was given to decentralisation of decision-taking and job creation in the public sector. At the programme's height under the Carter administration, 3 million individuals were enrolled in some type of training programme. Studies into the effectiveness of the CETA programme led to the abolition of the scheme by the Reagan administration in 1982, to be replaced the following year by the Job Training and Partnership Act which places much greater emphasis upon private sector training and job creation.

In the UK in the early 1960s there was a general belief that the government was under-investing in its Vocational Training Scheme. By the end of the 1970s 15 000 new training places had been created in Government Training Centres, since renamed Skillcentres. The type of training offered in these centres is accelerated skill training, still predominantly in traditional manual crafts. The duration of most courses is six months, training hopefully being completed in employment. The limitations of the then existing scheme were again highlighted in the Department of Employment's 1972 publication *Training for the Future*. The inadequate quantity of training was again referred to, but also the limited range of courses offered and the failure to co-ordinate plans with the private sector. The Training

Opportunities Scheme was launched in 1972 and rapidly expanded to 100 000 completions by the end of the 1970s. The emphasis initially was on trainees choosing their own courses, with business, clerical and personal services rather than traditional crafts becoming popular. The onset of recession encouraged a further expansion of the scheme; however, disillusionment with direct training as a counter-cyclical device followed, partly reflecting the high cost of the schemes, and low post-training employment rates. Gross exchequer costs of Skillcentre training were £4820 per unit at 1984/85 prices, more than double the unit costs of training provided by employers and colleges under the scheme. In addition in the early 1980s only around 30 per cent of Skillcentre trainees were finding initial employment utilising their acquired skills, 10 per cent lower than the percentage of non-Skillcentre trainees.

By the mid-1980s government in the UK had retreated from concern with training needs of the individual to the training needs of industry. The New Training Initiative stressed the need to rethink education and training policy; no longer should they be viewed as a once and for all investment prior to employment, instead they should be viewed as a continuing process. Hence the PICKUP scheme to provide mid-career training and the launch of the Open Tech Programme. However, the problem of opening up 'widespread opportunities for adults' remained unsolved, though the Job Training Scheme was relaunched in 1988. This provides 'high quality', six months' training for up for 110 000 long-term unemployed, and is aimed at achieving recognised qualifications. The scheme attracted only about a quarter of that number initially and experienced drop-out rates of around 45 per cent. The previous lack of any financial incentives for unemployed eighteen- to twenty-five-year-olds to join the scheme and trade union resistance appear to have been the main causes for the low take-up of places. Skillcentres now account for only about a tenth of the training now provided under the Adult Training Programmes, with training in employers' establishments accounting for about 55 per cent of the total provision. In 1986/87 the percentage of those completing training who found work using their skills learnt rose to 56 per cent, reflecting better occupational targeting of training, but probably more significantly the economic recovery. The New Training Initiative also transferred financing responsibility for certain parts of work-related NAFE from the Rates Support Grant to the MSC. The MSC has sought to match provision to local labour market needs, particularly by increasing employer involvement in local education authorities' decision-making. The testing of the Career Development

Loans in 1987 represented another new initiative, this time aimed at capital market imperfections; the scheme provides some assistance to individuals for the securing and repaying loans used to finance vocational training.

One recent area of concern has been the provision of management training in the UK. A National Economic Development Council study (NEDC 1987) pointed out that compared to other developed economies few of top managers in the UK had degrees; only a fifth of all managers had degrees or professional qualifications of any sort. The report estimates that 90 000 new managers are required per year to renew the existing stock, yet current output from the educational system of business and management students is less than a tenth of this level. By default accountancy training in the UK has become an established route for career development for managers, with the stock of qualified accountants in the UK being thirty times the West German and twenty times the Japanese stocks. The suitability of an accountancy training for a managerial career may be questioned and the dearth of engineers and surfeit of accountants among top managers in the UK makes a striking contrast with West German practice.

There have been a large number of studies, especially American, which attempt to measure the effectiveness of this 'merit good' training. The absence of data on social and political benefits leads to the benefits being treated in most studies as largely output gains. Traditionally it has been argued that the social benefits are likely to exceed private benefits because of the net effect of externalities. The replacement effect is likely to reduce the output opportunity costs of the training, as there will be direct or indirect substitution of the trainee's labour by previously unemployed labour. Complementary effects will raise the benefits of training above those to the trainee if they eliminate a labour bottleneck and so cause an increase in the employment of auxiliary and ancillary workers. Competitive markets should internalise some of these benefits in the post-training earnings of trainees. The displacement effect will partially offset these positive externalities as trainees will displace some existing or potential employees, especially when placed outside their training trade. To the extent that the training acts as a screen, social benefits will again be lower than the private benefits.

The consensus of American studies is that the MDTA and CETA programmes produced benefit–cost ratios of around unity (Congressional Budget Office 1982). Though the Job Corps Programme aimed at the most disadvantaged groups, high-school drop-outs, it appeared to produce greater proportionate returns.

The relatively low returns generated by these schemes partly reflects the targeting of resources to the employment-handicapped. For individual participants, Barnow's (1987) survey reports positive and significant effects on earnings, especially for women, though problems of adjusting for selection bias in the control group give rise to a wide range of estimates. The major cause of this positive earnings effect was that CETA trainees had higher post-training labour force participation rates and worked longer hours (Bassi 1983), rather than any increase in their hourly wage rate. This suggests that it is employability which increases with the training, rather than the specific cognitive training, embodied in the skills being taught, raising post-training earnings. On-the-job training and public service employment were generally more effective in increasing earnings than either classroom training or work experience.

Such screening interpretations have not been tested in the studies of British Government direct training schemes. Typically much more attention has been paid to estimating the size of the externalities than in identifying the source of the benefits. Ziderman (1975) concluded that expenditure on such training passed Treasury targets for appropriate rates of return. Experience of recent years has suggested that the British off-the-job manpower training schemes may be ineffective as counter-cyclical devices. The nature of accelerated skill training requires immediate placement of the trainee after completion of the course, if the benefits of the training are not to be lost. In practice, as previously indicated, the placement rate of trainees falls to very low levels in a recession. The training programme is thus largely redistributing unemployment, rather than making any major contribution to the reduction of any skill bottlenecks. Training in a recession to produce a pool of skilled labour for the recovery is illusory, unless that training is long term, addressed at immediate shortage occupations or combined with measures to stimulate aggregate demand. In Sweden the longer-term training which the authorities encourage has to be started in the recession. In the 1970s and early 1980s any recession was met by paying firms to expand their training, so that up to 5 per cent of the labour force may be covered by the various training schemes.

4.5 Conclusions

Given the above discussion it should not be surprising to find such diverse opinions being expressed in current debates. For example, some commentators have criticised the YTS for including large elements of social and life skills in initial training, while others encourage such components. Present debates on educational and training policy contain a dearth of evidence and an excess of opinion. Thus initiatives such as city technology schools may reflect the prejudices of politicians and high-level industrialists rather than labour market realities. The evolution of human capital theory and early growth accounting studies led to a burst of policy initiatives in the 1960s and early 1970s. Gradual recognition of the practical limitations of educational and training policies in influencing poverty and discrimination, has recently been combined with fundamental theoretical questioning of the whole human capital foundations of those policies. The link from mental attainments to productivity in the workplace and therefore to labour market income has been seriously challenged by the screening approach. If schooling predominantly enhances employability and hence earnings, by encouraging the adoption of desired behavioural patterns among students, then much contemporary policy is misconceived. This alternative approach starts from the presumption that employers find it expensive to discover the actual characteristics of applicants and require an efficient low-cost screen. Education is just such a screen, it also has the great advantage that it is socially acceptable to recruit on the basis of educational attainments. Use of such a screen therefore promotes the mutual co-operation of workers which is so crucial to the level of production and profits in the firm. Economic growth according to this view requires no particular educational structure; such skills that are required will be acquired predominantly on the job because the specificity of individual firms makes their production requirements unique.

Even if we remain unimpressed by the screening critique there is a further reason for uncertainty over optimum educational policy. To design appropriate policy requires an appreciation of the benefits and costs, and at present we have no indications of the size of externalities produced by different systems of education. It could be true that a more selective and streamed system of schooling would raise overall potential labour market production, but the personal and social divisiveness of such policies may prevent such gains from occurring or cause unacceptable increases in inequality. Thus participants in current policy debates need to come clean about not only their underlying economic model, but also their perception of the externalities and preferred social welfare function. While present evidence is incomplete the screening hypothesis is now sufficiently well established to suggest that it is a necessary complement to human capital theory. Our consideration of recruitment strategies in Chapter 5 indicates that while human capital theory may have relevance to many professional and higher-manual skilled occupations, for lower skilled occupations the screening approach appears more appropriate.

If we turn to consider training policy then the early certainty based upon the distinction between general and specific training has disappeared. The strength of internal labour markets, in particular the long-term relationship between many employees and their employer, suggests that on-the-job training dominates the market. However, there is widespread belief that individual companies' training policies are often inadequate and that equity requires an increase in training provision for adult workers. It may be that British firms have adjusted to too low standards among both present employees and entrants and that UK employment is not so technically demanding as in Japan and West Germany. It is unlikely that the persistence of such behaviour will sustain desired national growth rates. In addition with externalities, compressed wage differentials and capital market imperfections it is unlikely that a *laissez-faire* policy towards private sector training is optimal, hence recent proposals for a non-bureaucratic system of intervention.

If we anticipate a finding of Chapter 7 that unemployment is concentrated among unskilled and semi-skilled labour, then it can be argued (Layard and Nickell 1987) that the social returns to training exceed the private returns. If skilled workers are fully employed whereas some unskilled workers are unemployed, then by training up the unskilled worker, societal returns are at the least their marginal product and the opportunity cost is merely the direct training costs (though society may also gain from complementary effects on the demand for unskilled labour and from reduced wage pressure in skilled labour markets). The private returns to the firm and worker combined are the difference between the skilled and unskilled workers' productivity after compensating for increased probability of employment. Given this argument for state subsidy of training then Layard (1986) argues that a marginal tax subsidy on 'deficient/excess' training expenditure is the appropriate response. This requires a computation of training expenditure per wages paid, probably on an industry basis, and the ratio to form the basis for firms' self-assessment of their liability in the following year. Firms who spent above that average would have a rebate on their excess expenditure financed largely from a tax on firms with relatively low training outlays per wage payment. Over time this system would encourage an increase in training expenditure as a proportion of an industry's wage bill, in 1988 the French introduced a similar scheme providing tax rebates for increased training expenditure.

The main problem with the Layard proposal is that as with current policy it concentrates upon the wrong level of training. Existing data and forecasts indicate that the present and future labour shortages are concentrated in certain intermediate-level occupations such as technicians and multi-skilled craftsmen and among more highly qualified managers and technologists. It is these shortages which constrain technological development and cause low-skill options to be taken (Institute for Employment Research 1987). Demographic trends as well as the bias of current policy indicate that adult training at intermediate and higher levels is likely to emerge as the next high priority area. This chapter illustrates how little guidance can be given to the appropriate response to this need.

Further reading

Psacharapoulos (1987) edits a comprehensive reference book in the economics of education. A good place to begin a study of theory in this area is the paper by Sobel (1982) comparing human capital and institutionalist theories, and a more detailed introduction to human capital theory is provided in Chapter 3 of Joll, *et al.* (1983) and by Freeman (1986). Lindley's chapter in Creedy and Thomas (1982) provides another useful but more applied introduction which can be supplemented by his contribution to Bain (1983). Blaug's two surveys of the economics of education (1976, 1985) provide a stimulating introduction into contemporary debates and plot the startling rise and gradual demise of human capital theory. As an antidote, Siebert (1985) provides a comprehensive review of human capital theory; the emphasis is upon empirical studies and his conclusions are sympathetic to human capital theory, whereas Willis (1986) concentrates upon US human capital earnings functions. The NIESR conference proceedings edited by Worswick (1985) are a good place to start policy consideration. Make sure you read the discussants' attempts to uncover the implicit assumptions of the presented papers, all of which assert that education has a major influence on economic performance.

Chapter 5

SEARCH AND MOBILITY IN THE LABOUR MARKET

The productivity of the total labour force and thus the standard of living in any economy, will depend upon the speed and quality of the job-matching process and the extent of mismatch in the labour market. Time which workers spend searching for suitable vacancies represents time not spent producing. Unfilled vacancies which reflect employers' search for suitable workers, similarly represent lost output. The quality as well as the speed of the hiring process is also important; to maximise output and maintain incentives for human capital investments employers must make efficient use of workers' productive potential. Mismatch in the labour market produces wage pressure at relatively high levels of unemployment and this also constrains employment and output levels. In this chapter we initially discuss the way in which workers and firms search in the labour market and then consider the appropriate role of government in facilitating search. In particular we consider why most developed economies have a state-financed placing agency and how such agencies should operate to promote efficient and equitable hiring practices. In the previous chapter we discussed occupational mismatch and here in the second part of the chapter we concentrate upon geographical mismatch. Our main interest is in policies to encourage migration as a means of reducing spatial differences in employment opportunities.

In the first part of the chapter we initially consider the current nature and extent of job search in modern economies. Conventional neoclassical search theory is then examined and some of its limitations exposed. A discussion of how employers actually recruit leads to the introduction of the concept of the extended internal labour market. The rationale for state employment agencies is then reconsidered and their current operation reviewed. We conclude the first section with a consideration of the appropriate role of the government in the job-matching process, concentrating on a labour market in recession.

5.1 Job search: theory and evidence

5.1.1 Origins

The origins of labour market search must first be examined. In a feudal society workers had no right to choose their workplace, but in modern societies they have freedom to enter into an employment contract with any firm with whom they can reach a satisfactory agreement. Firms also have freedom to hire who they please, subject to certain legal restraints on discriminatory behaviour to be discussed in Chapter 6. In isolated communities with low mobility, nepotism and direct personal relationships may dominate this matching of employers with workers, but in modern developed societies the bulk of the matching will be between parties who have no prior knowledge of each other. Workers will wish to discover the pecuniary and non-pecuniary rewards of each available wage offer, whereas employers will wish to learn the potential productivity of applicants in their workplace environment as well as the wage levels offered by other employers.

Economic theory belatedly acknowledged the presence of imperfect labour market information, and founded on work by Stigler in the early 1960s, the orthodox view is that wage rates are the crucial variable in this process of search. Workers search firms until they find an acceptable wage offer. Implicitly employers are conceived as taking a fairly passive role in this process; once they have fixed a wage level they hire those applicants of acceptable quality who are prepared to accept employment offers until they have no further vacancies. The competitive model also implies that workers and firms are always looking to make better 'deals' in the labour market. Workers are always hoping to find higher-paid jobs and firms hoping they can recruit at lower wages. This continual searching is also the consequence of certain labour market information only being obtained after a match is made. Workers only discover the social environment of the workplace and the realities of the supervisory and promotion structure after working in the firm. Similarly, employers only accurately discover many of the workers' personal characteristics after hiring. Thus search theory was initially developed to understand the anticipated high mobility in the labour market; search is not just to be found concentrated in entrants and re-entrants but by all existing participants in the labour market. The accuracy and appropriateness of this view have been recently challenged and we later survey this dispute.

The traditional economic arguments for a government employment agency have been in terms of improving the speed and quality of job-matchings. Although the first national employment exchanges in the UK opened in 1910, some municipal authorities had begun to collect registers of vacancies to help the search of unemployed workers in the closing decades of the nineteenth century. Improving labour mobility, the quality of the workforce and assisting manpower planning were also stressed in the early years of the employment service. The emergence of inflation as the major post-war macroeconomic constraint on economic growth and employment expansion led to a new emphasis upon the need to reduce 'frictional' unemployment, and the evolution of search theory provided a theoretical framework for the analysis of such unemployment. Search theory also provided a new rationale for a state placing agency: a centralised employment service could internalise some of the externalities of private search.

There are at present about 1000 Jobcentres and employment offices in the UK, and recent evidence suggests that they account for about a quarter of the 7 million annual 'starts' in the labour market. In 1986/87 2.6 million vacancies were notified and the service placed 1.9 million searchers. Most recent surveys, for example Smith (1988) suggest that about a third of vacancies are notified to the employment service, with the penetration rate rising in recessions and falling in booms. The penetration rate will also reflect structural changes in the labour market given the lower notification rate in the service sector, particularly in traditionally female jobs. The low penetration of the employment service was interpreted in the mid-1970s as reflecting employers' perception that applicants attracted from this recruitment channel were of low quality. It appeared that many employers at that time used unemployment as a proxy for unsuitability, associating employment offices with the least motivated unemployed job-searchers. One reason for the introduction of Jobcentres was to increase the perceived calibre of candidates they submitted, partly by attracting employed job-searchers, and so increase the penetration rate. Both of these changes appear to have occurred (MSC 1978; Ford *et al.* 1982), though employers are still more likely to notify vacancies than actually recruit Jobcentre applicants. It has been argued (OECD 1984) that the adoption of such a 'marketing' approach to employers is likely to heighten the conflict between the economic and social objectives of an employment service. The economic objective is to increase the penetration rate by always submitting applicants who best meet employers' perceived needs. This is likely to be inconsistent with the social objective of trying to combat the skewed distribution of unemployment by giving priority to groups who have special problems in competing for vacancies. We consider this conflict in this chapter together with recent concerns that government employment agencies may by their existence reduce the self-directed search of unemployed workers. First we must examine the actual search behaviour of workers.

5.1.2 Worker search

In most economies the data available on the aggregate search–hiring process are of poor quality. Few countries collect regular data on the amount and type of on-the-job search, that is search by workers already in employment. In the UK, the 1973 *General Household Survey* indicated that 11 per cent of heads of household were seriously considering a job change at that time. Recent surveys have indicated that about 10 per cent of males are dissatisfied with their present employment, a proportion which again has fallen during the recession. Slightly more is known about labour turnover; during the ten years after 1966 there was an annual average of 9.5 million cases of people leaving their employer, of which 1.5 million moved directly to another employer, equivalent to about 5 per cent of the labour force. Voluntary turnover is cyclically sensitive, with quits falling in a recession, and by 1985 job changes had fallen to about 7 million a year. Recent *Labour Force Surveys* indicate that about 10 per cent of those workers who remained in full-time and 7 per cent in part-time employment changed their jobs in the previous twelve months. The *General Household Survey* provides a similar picture with about 8 per cent of workers changing their employers annually, half the percentage of the early 1970s. This mobility is highly concentrated among the young, especially female entrants. The high concentration of job-changing is further illustrated by about a third of employees in the UK having tenure of at least ten years; as discovered in Chapter 3 the average length of completed job tenure for those currently employed was approximately twenty years in the early 1970s.

The form of this search in the British labour market is indicated in Table 5.1. About a third of those employees who started a job in the

Table 5.1   Search in the British labour market

| | Source from which employee heard about present job started in previous 12 months* | | Main method of unemployed seeking work† | |
| | Men | Women | Men | Women |
	(%)		(%)	
Jobcentre, careers offices	20‡	19‡	42	31
Private employment agency	2	3	1	2
Advertisements	20	22	29	42
Direct approach to employers	11	12	8	6
Friends and relatives	31	31	11	8
Other	5	3	3	3

Sources: 1986 Labour Force Survey, 1984 General Household Survey
* Direct approach by employers was the source for 10 per cent of men and women employees.
† Includes some unemployed who were not seeking work or did not state a main method.
‡ The *General Household Survey* is usually thought slightly to underestimate the importance of Jobcentres in securing employment.

previous year heard about the vacancy through friends or relatives. For males the next most important source of information was Jobcentres and advertisements, for females advertisements were the second most important source of information with Jobcentres third. Private employment agencies accounted for less than 3 per cent of these matches. For young workers and frequent job-changers a higher proportion heard about the vacancy they ultimately filled from Jobcentres and careers offices. Recent surveys confirm a decline in the importance of direct approaches to employers in successful job search for males and the growth of direct approaches by employers since the onset of recession. More data are available about search off the job, that is by the unemployed. Table 5.1 indicates that Jobcentres figure more significantly in such search; 70 per cent of the unemployed use them in their search. Jobcentres are especially important methods for the young and the long-term unemployed. The unemployed on average spend little time actually looking for work, less than five hours per week, and average only one application per month (Jackman 1985). In the USA the employment service is much less important with only a quarter of unemployed job-seekers using the service whereas direct approach to employers was being used by three-quarters of searchers. Personal contacts was listed as the major method of search by less than 10 per cent of these job-seekers.

5.1.3 Neoclassical search theory

The starting-point for modern theories of job search is the proposition that with imperfect information about labour market opportunities it is irrational for searchers to accept the first job offer. Given that wage variability exists, workers by prolonging search enhance the probability of discovering a better job offer. Thus search is a productive activity, an investment in accumulating knowledge which allows an optimal job acceptance policy to be formulated and implemented. The early emphasis in the literature was upon off-the-job search and hence unemployment was viewed as potentially a productive activity. The early popularity of the theory was due to the use made of the approach by both major schools of economic thought. Monetarists argued that misperceptions of the labour market conditions among searchers could explain short-run movements along the Phillips curve, while Keynesians used the approach to explain the weakness of price-adjusting models of the labour market.

Stigler (1962) originated the argument that in labour markets with imperfect information concerning existing market conditions and uncertainty concerning the future, instantaneous market clearing was impossible and search before contracting was efficient. Initially the theory was developed in an environment where an individual unemployed worker was confronted by a labour market where jobs were homogeneous in non-wage characteristics. Workers were assumed to know the overall distribution of wage offers they faced, but not know the wage offered, if any, by any specific firm. The traditional tools of capital and investment theory can now be applied to the problem of discovering an optimal search strategy. The solution can either be framed in terms of an optimal length of search or a sequential stopping rule, where search ceases when a wage offer exceeds or equals a pre-specified level, termed the reservation wage. Later theorists have concluded that Stigler's fixed sample rule is generally inferior to the reservation wage strategy and we concentrate on this approach. Prior to search the individual chooses a reservation wage which maximises the expected benefits from search. If the observed wage offer falls below the reservation wage the offer is rejected and search continues. The first offer of employment at or above the reservation wage is accepted.

For the traditional tools of equi-marginal analysis to be applied to the identification of the optimal strategy, the marginal benefits and costs of this search need to be identified. The benefits of search are higher expected lifetime earnings. As workers are searching a given distribution of wage offers, the higher their reservation wage the longer the expected duration of their search and the higher their expected post-search income. For a given normal distribution of wage offers, the increase in the expected wage from raising the reservation wage will decline as the reservation wage increases. The marginal benefit of choosing a higher reservation wage is therefore negatively sloped as illustrated in Fig. 5.1, because the chances of locating an offer above the reservation wage decline and because the expected longer search causes a depreciation of human capital and reduces the time period over which the higher wages are earned. A higher reservation wage implies a higher level of expected search costs, both the opportunity costs of lost income

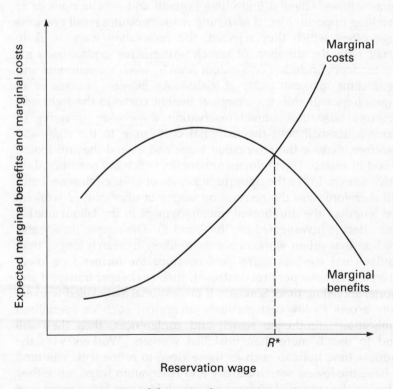

Fig. 5.1 Determination of the optimal reservation wage

and leisure and direct search costs. The marginal search costs may initially fall due to economies of scale in job search, reflecting geographical factors and indivisibilities such as suits and haircuts! However, as the most likely firms are searched first, together with other firms with low search costs such as those in the locality of the searcher, marginal costs will eventually rise. The optimal reservation wage will just equate the marginal benefits and costs consequential on any change in the minimum wage required to cease search, and therefore maximises the expected returns from search. At R^*, the optimal reservation wage, the marginal benefits from a small rise, higher expected income over the duration of the job, is equal to the marginal costs, largely forgone earnings for the anticipated extra period of search.

As the surveys by Pissarides (1985) and Mortensen (1986) indicate, much of the subsequent literature in this field has been concerned with uncovering the properties of this optimal reservation wage. The general conclusions about the nature of the underlying trade-off between discovering higher wage offers and enduring longer search are as follows. Given a finite time horizon and a finite number of searching opportunities, if searching workers cannot recall previous wage offers which they rejected, the reservation wage is likely to fall with the duration of search. Alternative explanations for this tendency include non-random search, wealth constraints and diminishing marginal utility of leisure. An increase in some or all wage offers will shift the marginal benefit curve to the right and therefore raise the optimal reservation wage. Any lowering of search costs will shift the marginal cost curve to the right and therefore increase the reservation wage and extend the anticipated period of search. Unemployment benefits which are conditional on active search, lower the opportunity costs of off-the-job search and will therefore raise the reservation wages of unemployed workers and lengthen the duration of unemployment in the labour market (this effect is investigated in Chs 7 and 8). The simple theory also predicts that urban workers are more likely to search longer than similar rural workers *ceteris paribus*, since the former face lower direct search costs per firm contacted, such as cheaper transport and shorter travelling time. Similarly if professional and skilled workers have access to low-cost methods of search, such as specialised publications, on-the-job search and conferences, then they will tend to search more than unskilled workers. Workers with the shortest time horizon such as those close to retirement, will tend to have the lowest search activity and reservation wage, since they calculate the stream of higher post-search incomes over fewer years and their marginal benefits curves are therefore below those of other workers.

The simple search model developed above has a major weakness in that it treats work and search as mutually exclusive alternatives. Rational behaviour requires all employees to conduct regular search in order to assess their current employment and prepare for wage negotiations. The problem to be solved by workers is to attain a maximising combination of income, leisure and search. Thus workers have to choose the intensity of search; they can combine work and search by adopting less intensive on-the-job search. The impact of changes in labour market conditions on search behaviour now becomes more complex. If the labour market tightens then more vacancies are available and reservation wages will rise, non-searchers may be encouraged to start on-the-job search while others react to the increase in the desired intensity of search by quitting and conducting off-the-job search. Unemployment benefits will distort the relative costs of on-the-job search compared to off-the-job search, raising the inflow to unemployment. In the early search models such as those in Phelps *et al*. (1970), job separations were always voluntary. Workers quit to take alternative employment or became unemployed in order to look for another job. Attempts were made to explain cyclical fluctuations in unemployment: workers misperceive real wage offers and are 'fooled' into extending or curtailing off-the-job search. However, such attempts have theoretical problems and are inconsistent with available data. Voluntary quits account for a minority of the inflow into unemployment and move pro-cyclically rather than contra-cyclically as predicted. Most voluntary quits occur because workers have received better employment offers from other firms. The availability of effective low-intensity and low-cost search methods, such as friends and newspapers, appear to explain the dominance of on-the-job search in the labour market.

More sophisticated search models address some of the above issues, and Hey and McKenna (1979) explain the reluctance of unemployed workers to accept temporary employment in terms of disturbance costs such as firm-specific training costs. Jovanovic (1987) generates pro-cyclical search and labour productivity and counter-cyclical unemployment movements by introducing shocks into the search model. The observed inverse relationship between tenure and the probability of quitting for male employees may reflect the need to experience the job before its full characteristics are discovered (McKenna 1985). Here workers accept an offer if the wage exceeds their reservation level; if on experience the job meets that reservation level they settle, otherwise on-the-job search or even voluntary quitting to unemployed search may occur. The almost infinite variations one can make to the assumptions of this approach, such as attitude to risk-taking, rate of time preference and knowledge about distribution of wage offers, have led to an explosion of literature in this area in the last twenty years.

5.1.4 Policy implications

As with any competitive-based theory, there is a presumption that market forces will generally lead to an efficient job-matching system, and workers and firms can be relied upon to design efficient search strategies. Within the confines of search theoretic models there appear two justifications for a government employment service. Firstly, governments can reduce the cost of search for workers by supplying information on outstanding vacancies, allowing workers to sample more firms per period of search and therefore raising their reservation wages. Such intervention may be justified on efficiency grounds if workers are myopic or if vacancy information has the characteristics of a public good, the collection costs being lower for governments than individuals or private companies. The national collection, collation and dissemination of vacancy information are comparable to a natural monopoly, and one where the government's role in data collection and unemployment benefits gives it a comparative advantage to fill. Salop (1973) and Barron and Gilley (1981) have developed models where indirect search via employment agencies leads to fewer contacts made with employers but a higher chance of locating an acceptable job offer per period of search. Here rather than the reservation wage being influenced it is the duration of unemployment which is reduced and their empirical results support this conclusion. Recently Pissarides (1984) and Lockwood (1986) have provided further arguments for intervention in the job-matching process. In this process one agent's trading costs can be reduced if agents on the other side of the market devote more resources to their search. Thus the more firms advertise their vacancies the easier it is for workers to target their search. Because of these externalities Pissarides shows that the steady state equilibrium unemployment rate generated by the search process is likely to be above the socially efficient level. Optimising agents ignore that their acceptance of a job offer saves the other party further search costs. These externalities are ignored when agents decide to enter a market, accept a match or search more intensely. Private employment agencies could internalise some of these externalities, but worker and job heterogeneity prevents such intermediation on any large scale. Lockwood argues that if we drop the assumption of firm and worker homogeneity then further kinds of inefficiency can be generated in the search process. High-skilled workers or high-productivity firms will cause low-skilled workers and low-productivity firms to have a low probability of acceptance in the matching process. For example, unemployed workers may receive no job offers even where they are the only applicant, and firms will make no offer to poorly matched or low-quality applicants anticipating that current output losses will be offset by the increased production of future, better-matched employees (Akerlof 1981). The market solution may represent a lower equilibrium acceptance probability for these disadvantaged agents than is socially desirable.

Although state employment agencies may limit the duplication of costly search and otherwise improve the efficiency of search, their role in reducing unemployment is ambiguous according to search theory. In both the UK and the USA governments have cut resources available to the placing service at a time of growing unemployment. The unemployed have been encouraged to search themselves back into work, the 'on your bike' strategy endorsed by a previous British Secretary of State for Employment. There is some theoretical support for such views in that search intensity of the unemployed may have fallen in recent years and this is considered later. Pissarides (1979) provided a different rationale; he assumed full registration of unemployed workers with employment offices and partial notification of vacancies, concluding that policies to encourage search outside of registered vacancies increased labour market efficiency. However, measures to increase the incentives for firms to register vacancies had an uncertain effect because it would dissuade the unemployed form undertaking self-directed search. Keeley and Robins (1985) also argued that the use of government employment services results in the reduction of total resources devoted to private search, probably producing an inefficient allocation of search resources by the unemployed. Both of these papers ignore any divergency of social costs and benefits from private ones in the job search process. Moreover given that all jobs and searchers are identical in Pissarides's model it is difficult to explain incomplete registration of vacancies where the public employment service makes no charge for its services. Partial registration requires that the internal costs of informing the agency exceed the total costs of private advertising and it is difficult to explain this difference unless the speed of filling vacancies differs significantly between recruitment methods.

Barron and Mellor (1982) provide a more convincing explanation of why employers do not automatically notify vacancies to the state employment agencies. Their reason is that firms do not view applicants arising from employment offices as perfect substitutes for applicants from alternative recruitment channels. Where payment of unemployment benefits are linked to evidence of active search, firms who register vacancies decrease the likelihood that applicants will actually accept any wage offer. Thus for some firms the increased likelihood of searchers contacting the firm is more than offset by the costs associated with the increase in the number of non-serious applicants. Such non-registering firms are likely to be those with high interview costs, typically those employing higher-skilled workers. Here we have the almost reverse of Pissarides's argument that any increase in employer contacts by unemployed workers was beneficial. A key difference is that Barron and Mellor's model includes heterogeneous workers with qualifications indicating productive potential. Employers derive a reservation index of qualifications, and workers are retained if monitoring confirms that their productivity exceeds wages. The higher the interviewing costs and the higher the reservation index of qualifications the more likely that the job will not be notified to the state employment agency. Their analysis highlights some of the fundamental problems with much of search theory, to which we now turn.

5.1.5 Limitations of job search theory

Search theorists acknowledge some weaknesses in existing analysis. In particular, how workers actually form expectations about the distribution of wage offers they face remains unclear, and their learning process needs to be modelled more rigorously. Above we noted that the early use of search theory to explain cyclical unemployment had been shown to be inappropriate. Gottschalk and Maloney (1985) using US data conclude that although the unemployed are more likely overall to make a successful transition to a better job than are on-the-job searchers, this is not true for the involuntarily terminated unemployed. In the UK unemployed searchers rarely reject job offers (Jackman 1985) and changes in the stock of unemployed workers are generally due to changes in outflow not inflow. To examine the experience of unemployed workers it is necessary to start from firms', not workers', search behaviour. Moreover search theory can tell us nothing about why firms directly adjust employment levels rather than reducing wage levels to encourage voluntary quits. Earlier work, we noted, assumed that while search is costly, job-changing is costless; it also ignored the presence of low-cost search methods and therefore failed to explain the dominance of on-the-job search. In short, conventional off-the-job search theory told us little about the majority of the inflow to unemployment and ignored the bulk of actual job-to-job changes of employment. Refining these areas, however, would ignore the fundamental weakness prevalent since the original Stigler paper. The very title, job search theory, reveals the problem. This emphasis upon the supply side of the job-matching process neglects the demand side and is inappropriate for the majority of labour markets. Only in the tightest of markets do a substantial proportion of workers pick and choose between job offers.

Barron, Bishop and Dunkelberg (1985) pointed out that the conventional search model which stressed searching workers receiving job offers and accepting or rejecting them via reference to a reservation wage, is an inaccurate description of actual labour market practices. Most vacancies are filled by a single job offer; it is the employer who chooses from a pool of searching workers, not the other way around. For Britain, McCormick (1988) shows that a chief explanatory variable for quits is the vacancy rate. Since only in the tightest labour market will a significant number of workers be able to choose between competing job offers, the reservation wage models of employee search need replacing by models which examine the determinants of employer search. When we refocus job-matching analysis in this manner it is the employer's perception of the characteristics of applicants which becomes crucial, not the applicants' search intensity or reservation wage which becomes central. No longer is there any reason to assert a relation between the duration and intensity of job search and the number of job offers received.

Little of search theory's treatment of the demand for labour has been concerned with these issues. Instead it has concentrated on establishing that differences in worker productivities generate inter-firm wage variability and therefore provide a justification for its supply-dominated approach. As individual job-searchers have different reservation wages then firms could raise the probability of applicants accepting the job offer by raising the wage offered. Firms can therefore substitute between length of search and wage levels offered for any given quality of applicant. When heterogeneous workers are introduced, firms have a choice of adjusting not only search and wage costs but also monitoring actual performance on the job. Different solutions to this choice will be a cause of wage variability within clearly defined labour markets. Since searchers would be aware of the search policy of firms, firms with fuller search strategies must compensate applicants for the reduced probability of a wage offer by raising the general level of wages offered.

The above discussion requires us to move away from traditional search theory to consider the determinants of firms' recruitment behaviour and its consequences for the efficiency of the job-matching process.

5.1.6 Employer search

Surveys by Rosewall and Robinson (1980) and Hedges (1983) suggest that about a third of British vacancies are notified to the employment service. Ignoring professional and executive labour markets, about a quarter of actual engagements are made through Jobcentres, with the highest shares being for manual workers especially in smaller plants. Firms are more likely to advertise through Jobcentres than actually recruit through them (Wood 1985). The survey by Hedges found that about half of manual vacancies are filled through informal methods and a third of non-manual vacancies. This largely takes the form of recruiting from friends and relatives of existing employees or internal promotions. Advertisements, especially in local papers, are as important as notifications to the employment service. It is important to note for later policy discussions the lack of symmetry between employer and unemployed workers' search. The latter rely much more on the employment service and much less on friends and relatives.

Employer search strategies will be modified by labour market conditions. Catt (1984) has explained how up until the late 1970s methods of recruitment were often passive, limited to interviewing 'cold callers', applicants who walked in off the street. Increasingly interviewing became more specialised, with personnel specialists taking over from line managers and some applicants being screened out prior to interview. With the massive increase in applications following the onset of recession at the start of the 1980s further modifications were made to hiring procedures. Manwaring and Wood (1984) agree with Catt that the recession was associated with a decline in casual callers, but suggest that their survey indicates that firms have not interviewed more applicants for each vacancy. Some firms screened out applicants with inferior qualifications; others, fearing workplace frictions and high turnover if they hired over-qualified applicants, have not raised required qualifications, relying even more heavily on informal information networks so as to restrict applications to manageable levels. Alternatively firms have erected low-cost screens to cope with the landslide of applications, either internal such as spot interviews, or relying upon Jobcentres to provide a short list. This conclusion of Manwaring and Wood (1984), that firms have reacted to the growth of applications by relying even more on informal recruitment channels, is especially difficult to square with traditional search theory.

5.1.7 Structuralist approaches

The evidence of widespread use of informal methods of recruitment and the earlier discovery of long tenure for the majority of employees is interpreted by the structuralist or segmented approach as reflecting the importance of internal labour markets in modern economies. The importance of firm-specific skills and worker morale encourages firms to adopt employment policies that limit turnover. Only in markets where technical skills are important, such as certain professional markets, and where turnover is not expensive, as in secondary labour markets and for young workers, will we experience high mobility and extensive job search. The long-term relationship which primary sector employers anticipate with recruits, leads them to adopt an extensive searching, screening and hiring process. Although existing employees should maintain job search to ensure that their employers are paying them their rent, some will subcontract this duty to trade unions and others will have confidence that their employers can be trusted to reflect changes in the external labour market. Hence on-the-job search is much less than anticipated by search theory.

A consequence of structured internal labour markets is that since firms will concentrate on retaining their best workers, partial success of this strategy implies that job-changers have a disproportionate number of less able workers. This produces adverse selection or the 'lemon' phenomenon in the labour market as initially analysed by Greenwald (1986). Employers are reluctant to hire job-changers and the consequential reduction of wages and opportunities for occupational advancement in the 'second-hand' market discourages mobility. This process strengthens the internal labour market and produces a very different world from that analysed by search theory above. Barriers to labour mobility created by adverse selection trap workers in unsuitable or disliked employment. Typically job changes and off-the-job search will be concentrated in the secondary labour market; established workers in the primary sector rarely change employer or become unemployed. In recessions, however, workers are displaced from good jobs and the characteristics and aspirations of unemployed workers become more diverse.

It is necessary to consider why informal methods of search are so common in modern economies. Reliance upon recruiting non-skilled manual workers through existing employees gives rise to an extended internal labour market (EILM). Recent surveys of employer recruitment strategies (Keil *et al.* 1984; Jenkins 1984; Way 1984) suggest that the common use of the EILM as a recruitment channel reflects both managerial and worker self-interest. For many managers the EILM represents a low-cost screening device, particularly conducive to recruiting a stable workforce. In structured internal labour markets reflecting highly firm-specific skills we earlier argued that a major task of personnel policies was to minimise costly turnover. Relying on present employees to act as recruiting agents is likely to ensure a supply of applicants with the required social skills to minimise workplace frictions. Such social skills are otherwise very difficult for firms to identify prior to employment. Jenkins reports that many managers often proxy the applicants' quality by that of the employee who introduces them, much like a private club. Others, again like a club, expect that the employee who recommends the applicant will act as an unpaid trainer and supervisor, reducing the firm's unit labour costs. For still other employers the EILM is favoured for the community it produces, the 'family firm' ethos, or for the industrial relations environment with which it is associated – though the built-in solidarity of the workforce can lead to bitter and lengthy industrial disputes when mutual confidence between employers and employees is lost.

The advantages for employees of recruitment via the EILM seem to be the improvement in social relationships at work (Manwaring 1984). Combining the social networks of family and friends with those of work improves the work environment, while securing the appointment of friends gives additional status in the community. For searchers an additional advantage which the EILM produces is the greater certainty about pecuniary returns, availability of overtime, operation of piece-rates and workplace environment. The EILM thus improves the quality and lowers the cost of information. It also reduces the costs of job-changing, because entrants already have contacts in the workplace who can ease their entry into the new social networks.

Where social stability is low, such as in new towns, or in periods or regions of low unemployment, then the EILM is unlikely to be the dominant recruitment channel. Similarly in higher-skilled employments where technical skills are more important than social skills, more formal methods of recruitment will be the main mechanism for obtaining new workers. In periods of high unemployment firms already using informal recruitment channels can rely on the EILM for all their manpower requirements. The low mobility of their workforce in such labour market conditions appears to induce firms to conclude that such practices are efficient. Other firms, who face severe product market and or financial constraints, try to reduce recruitment expenses by substituting informal channels of recruitment for more expensive formal ones. Surprisingly, Wood (1985) reports that there is little self-evaluation of hiring practices, even among large companies with professionalised personnel departments.

5.2 Search policy issues

The dominance of the EILM in many labour markets can explain the decline of 'cold-calling' or random search in recent years. Where many firms recruit through informal channels 'cold-calling' is inefficient. Thus any evidence which did suggest a decline in search intensity by unemployed workers in recent years would not necessarily indicate the decline of the work ethic. The substitution of informal search for the more traditional formal ones may be an efficient response to employer search strategies. This suggests that it is very difficult to define, and therefore measure, 'active' search or the intensity of search in the labour market, an issue to which we return in Chapter 7. The importance of the EILM also gives a new insight into the role of a state employment service. Earlier it was argued that the social and economic roles of the service may conflict. Maximising placements and penetration rate may lead to the service no longer giving special treatment to 'hard to place' unemployed job-searchers. In an economy where internal labour markets have developed, such 'disadvantaged' workers can neither price themselves nor search themselves into employment. Adverse selection and non-wage labour costs cause firms to screen out even unemployed applicants who offer to work for less than their existing employees. Their use of the EILM for recruitment may be a contributory factor in the concentration of unemployment experience among certain groups.

Those unemployed searchers without access to the social

networks of the employed workers will be disadvantaged in the job-matching process, and therefore over-represented in the stock of unemployment. Employers' use of the EILM makes 'who you know' rather than 'what you know' important for successful search. The inability of certain groups to gain the labour market information available through informal channels makes them particularly reliant upon Jobcentres in their search process. Hence the earlier observed contrast between the search strategies of those who found employment and those who remain unemployed. Predominant among those discriminated against by recruitment through the EILM will be entrants and re-entrants whose social circle will include fewer employed workers. Labour market discrimination will be cumulative since racial and religious minorities will again have fewer employed workers in their numbers. Holzer (1987) finds that up to 90 per cent of the difference in employment probabilities between white and black youths in the USA can be explained by differences in the use and effectiveness of informal search methods. A desire by employers to pursue discriminatory hiring practices while avoiding anti-discriminatory legislative constraints may be a further cause for the initial adoption of informal recruitment channels. In non-discriminating firms use of the EILM may lead to a high concentration of racial or religious minorities among their workforce. These groups' exclusion from large parts of the labour market contributes to their high unemployment rate, and to the declining probability of leaving unemployment as duration increases. These arguments are explored further in the discussion of discrimination in Chapter 6.

It is unlikely that the process outlined above represents a purely social problem. A priori there is no reason to believe that a strong relationship need exist between potential labour market productivity and access to the social networks of employment. The discrimination created by existing recruitment strategies of firms is accordingly unlikely to be efficient. There is some limited evidence that state employment agencies may presently help to offset some of this discrimination. Johnson, Dickinson and West (1985) in a study of searchers using the US employment service concluded that there were strong and widespread positive benefits obtained by women using the service, but not by men. The authors interpreted their results as reflecting the service's ability partially to offset women's lack of labour market experience and their inferior access to the informal networks of job-finding information. The widespread use of the EILM by employers in their hiring of new workers limits the ability of the employment service to increase their penetration rate under a voluntary notification system. Indeed early proponents of employment exchanges argued that for an effective service, compulsory vacancy notification was required. We return to this issue later in the chapter, but first we consider the recent operation of the employment service in the UK.

5.2.1 Jobcentres in a recession

In 1987 about 220 000 vacancies were notified to Jobcentres each month; this is close to pre-recession inflow levels, though the stock of unfilled vacancies remains below those levels and about 40 per cent of the stock are now temporary jobs. These figures indicate that the duration of vacancies has on average fallen during the recession. Of the labouring jobs notified to Jobcentres about two-thirds have been filled within a week and overall about three-quarters of the vacancies notified have been filled in recent years. Following a 1982 Rayner scrutiny less importance appears to have been attached to increasing the share of vacancies which are notified to Jobcentres. Instead more emphasis has been placed on reducing the average costs of placements and on attracting applicants for the various MSC employment and training schemes. The average cost of a placement fell from £92 in 1981/82 to £55 in 1986/87 in terms of 1986/87 prices, though minor accounting changes distort this comparison. Such figures tell us nothing about the quality of the placements made, though they have been used to proxy the efficiency of the service. The main reason for this fall in the average cost is that about two-thirds of placements are now made via the self-service system, and although the elimination of occupational guidance and centralisation of other specialist services also contributed to reduced costs, local Jobcentres have lost over 1000 staff in recent years. Expenditure on employment services accounted for less than 5 per cent of net MSC expenditure in 1986/87 and prior to the decision for their return to Department of Employment management was to decline in absolute and relative terms for the remainder of the planning period. One indication of this relative decline of the employment service in recent years is to compare expenditure to the number of unemployed registrants. Using 1985 prices, in 1976/77 expenditure on employment services per unemployed worker was £153; by 1984/85 that had fallen to just £40 (Adnett 1987). Similar cuts have occurred in the USA where federal support for the US employment service fell by 20 per cent in money terms between 1981 and 1983.

Earlier it was mentioned that governments had become concerned that state employment agencies may discourage self-directed search and this may be one reason for the above cutbacks. The previous discussion has indicated that it would be difficult to establish whether indeed the intensity of search has fallen. In labour markets where informal methods of recruitment dominate, self-directed search is inefficient. Nevertheless the expansion of social security provisions in 1966, the relaxing of qualifications for benefits during the 1970s and perhaps the changing attitudes to work and living off transfer payments which have been generated by mass unemployment, may all have reduced this search intensity. Since 1982 claimants have not been required to register at Jobcentres and a major reason for the reintroduction of Department of Employment management is to merge benefit payments and job search assistance. Recent papers by Layard and Nickell (1985a, b) have suggested that the search intensity of unemployed workers had fallen in the previous fifteen years. They present no direct evidence for this claim and proxy search intensity by increases in the ratio of notified vacancies to registered unemployment. Such a ratio will reflect the intensity of search of employers as well as workers and is distorted by structural changes in the economy and penetration of the employment service. As yet no study has provided any direct evidence on this issue and no study has claimed that changes in search behaviour were a significant cause of higher unemployment in the 1980s. The possible impact of unemployment and social security benefits on the intensity of worker search is considered in Chapters 7 and 8.

It was suggested above that although increases in the penetration rate of the employment service would enhance worker search, the reliance on recruitment through EILM made such increases unlikely within a system of voluntary registration. We now consider the practicalities of reintroducing compulsory vacancy notification. The 1920 Committee of Inquiry into the employment service supported such a proposal and other European countries have enacted legislation. In general compulsory policies have only operated in the UK in tight labour markets as a means of tackling labour shortages rather than unemployment. Adnett (1987) has suggested that the employment controls of the 1950s not only increased the relative importance of the employment service in the hiring process, they more importantly were associated with lower levels of unemployment for given levels of output.

The main arguments against compulsory vacancy notification which the present government has advanced are that it would distort vacancy data and prejudice employers' good relations with the employment service (OECD 1984). Given the widely acknowledged weakness of vacancy data as an indicator it is difficult to take the first argument seriously and the second mainly applies to firms not using the service. Although compulsory vacancy notification may promote efficient and equitable search in the labour market there is likely to be employer resistance to such policies. Any politically feasible new system must allow firms to recruit through their favoured channel. The danger persists that employers will continue to screen out Jobcentre applicants even if they had to register vacancies. One way to avoid this is to link the introduction of compulsory vacancy notification with a temporary job creation subsidy of the type discussed in Chapter 7. The subsidy could be administered by the local Jobcentres, payment of the subsidy being dependent upon employers recruiting additional employees from Jobcentre applicants. To minimise deadweight and displacement effects the subsidy could be targeted upon lower-skilled occupations in which both the unemployed and extended internal labour markets are concentrated. A fixed payment per additional employee would have the desired bias and be complementary to existing schemes. The long-term costs of such a scheme are unlikely to be large and the policy promises significant economic and social benefits.

5.3 Geographical mobility: theory and evidence

5.3.1 Introduction

Implicit in our previous discussion is that search and job-matchings are taking place within a local labour market. The recent recession increased disparities in unemployment between regions in the UK, generating renewed consideration of whether migration or regional policies could reduce these disparities. Efficiency losses can result if a potential match between an unemployed worker and unfilled vacancy is prevented by spatial factors or if these factors cause the quality of that match to differ between regions such that workers in some regions are consistently underemployed. The simplest forms of competitive models of the labour market expect regional unemployment differentials to be temporary, since resulting wage differentials should produce labour market adjustments. First, surplus workers compete down wages in high-unemployment regions which enables resident firms to gain a higher share of markets at the expense of firms in high-wage, low-unemployment regions. Second, high regional wage rates in low-unemployment regions induce an inflow of migrant or commuting workers seeking higher rewards for their labour and an outflow of 'footloose' firms seeking cheaper labour. To consider mobility within a regional, national or international context we have to recognise that substantial relocation or travel costs may distort this mechanism and cause persistent differentials in unemployment and wages. Standard neoclassical theory anticipates that the potential migrant, worker or firm, will compare the net present value of the higher returns from moving to another area with the costs of moving. In this section we initially examine the extent of mobility in the labour market and consider the persistence of regional differences. We then discuss the determinants of that mobility and try to discover the key constraints, particularly examining the role of housing. This leads to a consideration of existing UK policies to encourage greater locational mobility of workers and jobs.

5.3.2 Evidence on geographical mobility

The 1981 Census showed that just under 10 per cent of British households had changed their address during the previous year, slightly below the level of the previous census. Most of these moves are over short distances, with only 13 per cent being over 80 kilometres; the young and those employed in the higher occupational groups have higher incidences of mobility. If we define migration as moves between regions then its pattern has been a long-standing north–south movement towards the South-west, South-east (excluding the London area), East Anglia and the East Midlands. The majority of moves are not job-related; of respondents in a follow-up to the *National Dwelling and Household Survey* only 22 per cent cited job reasons (OPCS 1983). *Labour Force Survey* data indicate that of these job-related moves only a minority reflect changes of employer; mobility often therefore appears to reflect the strength of internal labour markets rather than the influence of external competitive forces.

Hughes and McCormick (1987) compare migration rates between the UK and the USA for heads of households who are in the labour force. Their figures indicate that both movement and migration rates are much lower in the UK by a factor of at least two to three times. One striking difference is in the migration rates for households whose head is a manual worker, the British rate being much lower than that for non-manual heads and both US rates. Such results have generated interest in the extent to which such low mobility of British manual workers is the result of council housing which provides for about 28 per cent of British households. Hughes and McCormick (1985) report that migration rates are about four times greater for owner-occupiers than for council tenants. There are only small regional differences in unemployment rates for non-manual workers and the migration pattern of manual workers does not appear to reflect regional differences in unemployment. Overall it appears that the majority of recent migration is irrelevant to the equalisation of wages and unemployment across regions; most moves are local, not job-related and few reflect a change of employer. However, Gordon (1986) does argue that until the 1979 recession net migration between regions was similar to differences in regional employment growth adjusted for the natural growth in the labour force. On this basis a responsive adjustment mechanism is claimed to be operating in the labour market.

The extent to which migration could increase efficiency depends partly on the significance of the regional mismatch contribution to total structural unemployment. The most commonly used method to proxy such mismatch is to compare ratios of unemployment and vacancies across regions. Indexes produced by such processes will be crude; we have already mentioned the problems of using vacancy data and unemployment data may also not be a consistent measure of active job-seekers across regions and time. In 1982 unemployment and vacancy data disaggregated by occupation and industry were no longer collected regularly in the UK, making any estimate of structural unemployment hazardous. Jackman and Roper (1987) discuss these problems but provide various indexes of regionally based structural unemployment. Regional indexes appear to move pro-cyclically, suggesting that regional imbalance is relatively unimportant in a recession. Overall it appears that since the mid-1970s regional mismatch has contributed much less to structural unemployment than occupational or industrial mismatch.

5.3.3 Migration decision-making

To analyse migration which reflects a change of employer within a neoclassical framework we need to utilise search theory developed earlier in this chapter. Workers continually search for better job offers or at least continually consider whether such search could be expected to yield net returns. This implies that workers accumulate knowledge of employment opportunities both within and outside their present local labour market. In comparing the net present value of offers outside with those within, workers should adjust for differences in commuting costs and the costs of having to move from the present market. Given that returns and costs vary between workers depending upon their personal and family characteristics, the neoclassical model predicts differences in migration rates dependent upon these characteristics. Thus for example, *ceteris paribus*, age should have a negative impact upon migration rate since the benefits of higher post-move earnings are discounted over fewer years. Other major determinants of the migration rate would be the costs of acquiring labour market information outside of the local labour market, availability of higher wage offers and the costs of moving, largely associated with housing and resettlement costs. For a discussion of policy we are particularly interested in any indications of market failure among these elements.

Information costs for many workers are likely to rise steeply outside of their local labour markets. Earlier the importance of informal informational networks in the labour market, especially for relatively unskilled and part-time employment, was established. These channels are unlikely to provide reliable information outside of the local labour market and searchers have to rely on more formal and costly search methods. The higher mobility of technical and professional workers may in part reflect the dominance of more formal methods in job-matching in these labour markets. Information of job opportunities in such markets is either acquired on the job or job advertising is structured nationally in trade journals rather than locally. Jobcentres have recently increased the availability of information on vacancies outside local regions by the provision of access by local offices to the National Vacancy Circulation System (NATVACS) data base, which contains details of on average about 3300 mainly hard-to-fill skilled vacancies.

The neoclassical theory of equalising net advantages suggests that regional differentials in labour market pressures and cost of living should generate an adjustment mechanism featuring changes in regional wage rates. Labour-scarce regions should bid away workers from high-unemployment regions by establishing a pay differential. However, regional wage rates for manual workers appear to be remarkably similar regardless of the large differences in unemployment rates. Pissarides and McMaster (1984b) find that relative wages react very slowly to differences in regional labour market conditions. Given the dominance of decentralised bargaining in the UK discovered in Chapter 3 this weakness of the wage adjustment mechanism is particularly surprising. The growth of multi-plant firms may have contributed to the uniformity of regional wage rates, though the importance of comparability and custom may be of more overall importance.

In order to consider a move workers need to acquire information not only on specific vacancies but on the general labour and housing market in other locations. Such search costs are generally fixed and may preclude inter-regional search by unemployed or low-wage workers. Although in net terms workers do tend to leave the high-unemployment regions the studies by Hughes and McCormick (1981, 1985) suggest that for manual workers being unemployed does not increase the intended migration rates. Given that the searcher has located and been offered a suitable job offer, acceptance requires that the expected net present value of additional earnings exceed the costs of relocation. The latter are usually interpreted as largely concerned with costs in the housing market, though some evidence also suggests that unsuccessful migration is often the result of psychic costs associated with an inability to adjust to changed social customs and norms.

Given segmentation in the housing market it is important to consider particular components of that housing market. Since the Second World War private rented accommodation has declined from 62 per cent to about 13 per cent of the total British housing stock with initially a growth of both council tenancies and owner-occupancy. The shortage of private rented accommodation together with a system of allocation of council housing via length of residency or period on waiting list, appears to have often prevented or penalised migration for those in rented accommodation. Hughes and McCormick (1987) suggest that although council tenants are as likely to seek to migrate as owner-occupiers for job-related reasons, they are much less likely actually to migrate. Hence the observed low inter-regional mobility of council tenants, even when adjusted for education, age and occupational differences. This is not true for private tenants who are the most likely segment of the housing market to move for job-related reasons. For owner-occupiers distortions are also likely to affect mobility; large regional differences in housing costs, stamp duties and tax-relief limits may raise transaction costs to prohibitive levels for all but the youngest workers. For those manual workers who are owner-occupiers, because manual wage rates vary little between regions whereas house prices vary significantly, real wages are often highest in areas of high unemployment. With the present system of benefits and property taxation even unemployment may not make migration financially attractive. Even in internal labour markets employers may face problems in adequately compensating workers for moves between high and low housing cost areas.

5.4 Mobility policy issues

5.4.1 Policies to encourage geographical mobility of workers

In the UK policies to subsidise migration originated in the inter-war years, though post-war regional policies concentrated upon the movement of jobs rather than workers. The most important schemes were the Employment Transfer Scheme (ETS) and more limited Free Forward Fare (FFF) which provided assistance with removal costs to enable unemployed workers with poor local job prospects to accept job offers in other local labour markets. Such policies are likely to create large displacement effects in a depressed national economy as unfilled vacancies disappear in even the prosperous regions. Reflecting this problem in recent years the schemes were reduced in scale and stringent regulations attempted to target the schemes on vacancies which were hard to fill. The numbers helped by these two schemes fell from 23 000 in 1979/80 to under 17 000 in 1984/85 at an average cost of just £240. Even at their height assisted migrants only accounted for about 5 per cent of net out-movements from depressed regions (Green et al. 1986). The impact of the MSC's geographical mobility schemes on migration was thus marginal and little is known about whether such intervention was justified. The ETS and FFF were withdrawn in 1986 on the grounds of both high administration costs and deadweight effects. An associated scheme, the Job Search Scheme, provided assistance towards search costs incurred by unemployed workers in extra-regional search, and was replaced in 1986 by a more closely targeted Travel to Interview Scheme, providing just £400 000 in expenses in 1986/87.

The Thatcher Government has shown much more concern with countering imperfections in the housing market than with subsidising directly relocation costs for workers. The National Mobility Scheme was introduced in 1981 to allow easier movement for council tenants between local housing authorities. Nearly 20 000 households moved in the first four years of operation, about a third of these for employment reasons, though of those who succeeded in gaining a nomination from their local authority two-thirds were rejected by their desired destination. Three-quarters of successful nominations were across regional boundaries. The scheme only requires participating local authorities to provide a quota of 1 per cent of lettings for incoming families which is unlikely to be optimal though the impact of privatising council housing stock makes any expansion difficult. Policies to decontrol private rented accommodation are to be implemented by the present government, though the favoured housing associations are not equipped to foster migration by manual workers.

5.4.2 Regional policy

The above discussion suggests that there are severe problems in generating sufficient migration to make a noticeable impact on regional mismatch. Any increase in migration would tend to widen other regional disparities and in particular raise congestion and social capital costs. In the post-war period such arguments led to a growth of regional policies aimed at moving employment opportunities into depressed regions. A wide range of policies were tried: tax incentives, employment subsidies, investment grants and location controls. Disillusionment with the impact of the constantly changing policy measures had led to total real UK Government spending on regional policies falling to less than a third of the mid-1970s level, with discretionary payments replacing automatic ones. At a time of increasing regional unemployment differentials government reduced the size of their regional policies.

The assessments presented to the House of Commons Public Accounts Committee (1984) indicate that over the period 1960–81 the overall net employment created or redirected by regional policy in assisted areas was between 250 000 and 445 000 jobs in manufacturing. If indirectly created jobs are included the range becomes 350 000–630 000. The various studies suggest that the real cost of a job created increased over this period due to loss of jobs created in earlier periods. At 1984/85 prices the cost per job created was around £38 000 even when inter-regional displacement effects are ignored. This figure largely reflected the high costs of job creation through the labour subsidy, the Regional Employment Premium, and the capital intensity of footloose manufacturing industry. This high cost and concern that in part this was due to continual policy changes encouraged a further revision of policies in 1979 and again in 1983. Despite evidence on their effectiveness location controls, Industrial Development Certificates, were suspended in 1981 and subsequently abolished. Tax breaks instead were given to firms locating in Enterprise Zones (1980) and Freeports (1984). In part these policy revisions reflected concern that assistance had been biased towards the declining manufacturing sector; certain service sector activities were made eligible for Regional Development Grants before their withdrawal in 1988. The movement towards discretionary rather than automatic payments also presents opportunities for targeting subsidies to minimise deadweight effects. However, the total expenditure on regional policy has been substantially reduced and more restrictive limits placed on individual payments and area eligibility. In a sense government regional policies have been displaced by the much cheaper Special Employment Measures to be discussed in Chapter 7. European Economic Community and local government initiatives have also eroded the importance of central government in this area.

5.4.3 Assessment of current policy

Regional mismatch in the labour market is inefficient and market forces do not appear effective in eliminating it. Greater labour cost differentials could be encouraged by a tax/subsidy system but employment appears to respond slowly to price signals in the regional labour market, hence the concentration on migration and regional policies. The discussion above suggests that any policy to encourage migration should target manual workers. This requires that the low-unemployment regions have to provide greater quantities of lower-cost housing. On labour market efficiency grounds a case can be made for a gradual move towards market-clearing levels of rents in private sector accommodation, though such reforms require co-ordination with reform of social insurance measures discussed in Chapter 8. Sales of council housing and restrictions on new council building make the desirable policy of increasing provision of such housing for in-migrants unrealistic. Housing shortages in prosperous regions may cause labour market inefficiencies, but to current owner-occupiers they represent windfall capital gains in the housing market and rents in the labour market. Resistance to any widespread building of low-cost housing in such regions should therefore be intense.

The failure of large inter-regional differences in the cost of living to generate compensating movements of jobs to cheaper regions in the UK indicates the problems which regional and migration policy face. Labour mobility cannot solve regional imbalance since it is the young, more skilled and more enterprising who move, generating a still more disadvantaged region. Yet regional policies have proved to be prohibitively expensive even in the relatively buoyant labour markets of the 1960s and 1970s. More recent government pronouncements argue that policy has concentrated upon the wrong spatial unit. The heavier incidence of unemployment in conurbations and general decline of the central core of these areas has redirected attention towards the inner city. Intra-regional mobility appears much more susceptible to labour market and planning policy than inter-regional mobility.

Further reading

The best introduction to search theory currently available is that of Pissarides (1985) which critically surveys its contribution to the understanding of labour market behaviour. Mortensen (1986) provides an alternative survey. The MSC's *Annual Report* and their corporate plan provided data and assessments of placing and mobility schemes, at least until the 'renationalisation' of the Jobcentres. The paper by Green *et al.* (1986) provides a widespread review of migration in a British policy context, while Armstrong and Taylor (1987) produce 1960s nostalgia with their critical review of what is left of British regional policy.

Chapter 6

DISCRIMINATION

Economists' concern with discrimination reflects their concern with both the efficiency and equity objectives of any economic system. Some economists have concentrated on whether resource misallocation due to discrimination causes substantial output losses. Others have approached the issue with a broader concern for equity, often reflected in the view that large persisting inequalities in opportunity represent a fundamental contradiction for any nation which believes in the economic and political virtues of a competitive economy. The burst of anti-discrimination legislation in Western economies in the decade following the enactment of the 1964 Civil Rights Act in the USA, was largely a reflection of this latter concern. Only recently have economists made systematic attempts to analyse the cause and effects of discrimination in the labour market and thereby made contributions to the assessment of such legislation. Largely these studies have been concerned with sex and racial discrimination, though age, health, sexual behaviour, size and national origin differences may also stimulate discriminatory behaviour. As early as the 1890s British economists investigated the causes of differences in the wages of women and men. Indeed the growth of female participation and retreat of sex segregation in the labour market under the pressures of wartime labour constraints led to the British Government establishing investigations of these wage differences. Both the 1919 and 1946 reports recommended that the government should eliminate the differences between the wages of men and women in the public sector, a policy not implemented at those times due to the cost. The demands of a war economy also stimulated early US Government action against racial inequalities in the labour market.

Phelps Brown's 1949 survey of these early British debates on sex inequalities made the still useful distinction between economists who stressed productivity differences and those who believed that institutional forces and social custom were the primary source of the earnings differentials. Only the latter group recognised the distinctiveness of discrimination, that women were treated fundamentally differently from men by employers and trade unions. This general problem of defining discrimination together with the latent divide between competitive and structuralist explanations became central elements of our review of economic theories of discrimination. These theories are then assessed in the light of empirical studies of the size and causes of sex and racial discrimination. This leads to a consideration of the appropriateness of existing anti-discrimination policy. First the extent of wage and employment differences between groups in the labour market needs to be established.

6.1 Evidence

Women constitute about 40 per cent of Western economies' labour forces but in all of these economies women receive lower wages than men. Mincer's survey (1985) indicates that for full-time workers, women's hourly wage is about two-thirds to three-quarters of that for males. Such wage variations give no indication of discrimination since the source of the difference may be in the group's different labour market characteristics, such as education or experience, or in the household's division of labour. As can be seen from Table 6.1, ratios for the earnings of full-time female workers range from just over half male rates in Japan to almost equality among manufacturing workers in Sweden. In all countries apart from the USA, the female rate rose relative to males over the twenty years from 1960. Mincer estimates that about one-quarter of the total unadjusted wage gap closed in this period. The apparent stability of the earnings ratio in the USA has aroused much interest especially because it was one of the first countries to introduce equal pay and equal employment legislation. We return to this problem later. This widespread narrowing of the differential has occurred during a period of rapidly rising female participation rates, especially among married women. Growth rates in participation differ between countries and have been associated with declines in fertility and increases in real wages and divorce. In the UK the relative earnings of females rose rapidly in the early 1970s; since 1976 there has been no discernible trend. The cause of the rise has been disputed and we consider this debate when the impact of equal pay legislation is examined.

Table 6.1   Comparisons of relative wages by sex 1960–80

	Ratio of women's to men's wages*		
	1960	1970	1980
Australia	0.59	0.59	0.75
UK	0.61	0.61	0.79
France	0.64	0.67	0.71
West Germany	0.65	0.69	0.72
Italy	0.73	0.74	0.83
Japan	0.46	0.54	0.54
Sweden	0.72	0.84	0.90
USA	0.66	0.65	0.66

Source: Mincer (1985) Table 3
* Hourly wages, aggregate, except: Australia: weekly, full-time workers; UK: hourly, manual workers; France: annual full-time workers; Italy and Sweden: hourly, manufacturing workers.

Sex discrimination in the labour market may also be indicated by the flatter age–earnings profile of female workers discovered in Chapter 3 and by differences in the distribution of employment between industries and occupations. Jonung (1984) describes the extent of sex segregation in the British, Swedish, US and West German labour markets. The pattern of segregation is similar in these countries with women over-represented in service, clerical and social work and under-represented in administrative and manu-facturing occupations. Sex segregation or occupational crowding appears particularly strong in the USA where about 80 per cent of female employees work in occupations where 70 per cent or more of employees are female. The 1981 Census found that in England and Wales about 46 per cent of females worked in occupations which were at least 70 per cent female. Table 6.2 indicates the form of sex segregation in the UK, with nursing and teaching contributing to over-representation in the lower professional group. Clerical work has increasingly become female-dominated and the growth of female employment has been biased towards part-time unskilled manual work in which group 10 per cent of employed women now work. A more detailed examination of the nature and causes of sex segregation appears later; we note that although the median occupational status of women is only just below that of males, they have a significantly lower average status (Greenhalgh and Stewart 1985). This result stems from the concentration of women in lower-level non-manual jobs and although women have begun to enter some higher-level male-dominated occupations quite rapidly,

Table 6.2   Occupational distribution of female workers in the UK 1951 and 1981

Occupational group	Female workers as a % of total workers in group		Distribution of female workers by group	
	1951	1981	1951	1981
Professional				
Higher	8.3	11.1	0.5	1.4
Lower	53.5	56.4	8.2	14.5
Employers and proprietors	19.9	21.5	3.2	3.2
Managers and administrators	15.2	18.7	2.7	5.0
Clerical workers	58.8	71.0	20.4	28.9
Foremen, inspectors and supervisors	13.4	20.4	1.1	2.0
Skilled manual	15.8	14.5	12.8	6.1
Semi-skilled manual	40.7	44.8	43.1	30.0
Unskilled manual	20.3	42.0	8.0	9.0
All occupations	30.8	39.9	100.0	100.0

Source: Mallier and Rosser (1987), compiled from Tables 3.6 and 3.8

these women represent a small proportion of the total female labour force who are still concentrated in 'female' occupations.

Greenhalgh and Stewart (1987) found that British women received significantly less full-time training than males. Although sex differences in employment between industries appears to be less for younger workers in the UK, young females are still less likely to receive training, especially of long duration (MSC 1987b). Discrimination may also be reflected in the higher levels of under- or unemployment among female workers. Distortions caused by differences in measurement and unemployment compensation schemes make international comparisons of unemployment by gender difficult. There is some evidence that the higher mobility of women in and out of paid employment leads to higher unemployment in many developed countries (Björklund 1984).

Differences in wages between majority and minority racial groups have no common international dimensions. In the USA the mean earnings of year-round full-time adult black males is about 70 per cent of that for white males. For females the difference is much smaller, about 5 per cent. In both cases there was a rapid reduction in the earnings differential in the late 1960s and early 1970s. In the UK the male earnings differential appears smaller, though there are significant differences between the various racial minorities. Once again no direct indication of discrimination is to be drawn from these figures as racial groups will differ in productivity characteristics and tastes. It is not just current labour market earnings which may indicate discrimination; minorities may suffer from occupational crowding, irregular employment or from more expensive search or commuting. In the USA Blacks are crowded into 'bad' jobs, though again their relative occupational attainment improved more rapidly after 1964 (Freeman 1981). Typically unemployment among black American youths is at least twice the rate for whites and recent *Labour Force Surveys* in the UK indicate that for all age-groups the unemployment rates for those of West Indian and Asian origin were about twice that for whites. Once again such differences do not prove discrimination since characteristics differ between racial groups. However, the 1985 survey indicated that for West Indians the scale of the unemployment rate difference increases with educational qualifications.

6.2 Defining labour market discrimination

We have seen that a comparison of the average gross hourly earnings of full-time adult workers in the UK indicates that women receive about three-quarters of male earnings. Orthodox theory would therefore suggest that females face a lower demand curve than males, have a lower supply curve or that both of these differences underlie the earnings differential. These possibilities are illustrated in Fig. 6.1 which concentrates solely upon differences in wage rates. Wage rates for females, w_f, may lie below that for males, w_m, if women face a lower demand curve due to perceived or actual productivity differences or have a lower supply curve due to differences in investments in human capital or tastes.

Discrimination only occurs when some superficial personal characteristic is used in an attempt to restrict an individual's opportunity for economic or social advancement. To assume that the above earnings difference, $w_m - w_f$, is solely attributable to discrimination would require that male and female workers are alike in every respect apart from sex. Differences in earnings, which reflect differences in tastes or education and training, may not be discriminatory if such tastes reflect unconstrained choice and if equal opportunity for educational investments exist. Earnings

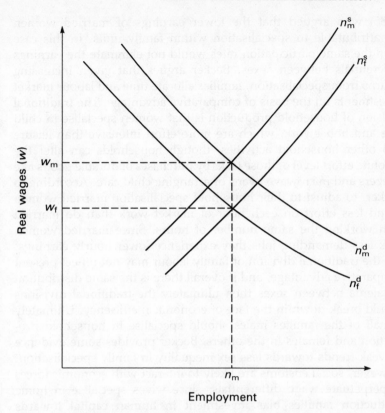

Fig. 6.1   Possible causes of gender wage differentials

differentials may be broken down into a wage gap and productivity gap, with typically only the former being taken as an indicator of the size of labour market discrimination. Thus if women anticipate less attachment to the workforce then it may be optimal, given the arguments developed in Chapter 4, for them to invest less in education and specific training than males. An earnings gap would be observable even for those with ex-post equivalent tenure and experience, since women anticipated lower participation. Similarly from our analysis of search theory developed in Chapter 5, less attachment to the workforce may lower the reservation wage of women searchers relative to that of males since they anticipate wage gains from further search to be discounted over a shorter period. Human capital and search interpretations therefore view sex wage differentials as potentially economically efficient.

The human capital approach has been augmented by Becker

(1985) who argued that the lower earnings of married women are attributable to specialisation within family units. In this case even the same participation rates would not eliminate the earnings differentials between sexes. Becker argues that given increasing returns from specialisation, families allocate time and labour market investments on the basis of comparative advantage. The traditional division of household production is that women specialise in child care and housework, which are more effort intensive than leisure and other household activities, though households can alter the absolute effort level of those tasks by purchases of durable goods like freezers and microwave ovens or arranging child care. According to Becker, to adjust to their household specialisation married women spend less effort on each hour of market work than do married men working the same number of hours. Since married women seek less demanding jobs they experience lower hourly earnings. But the traditional division of family labour may not reflect present comparative advantage, and if overall there is the same distribution of talents between sexes then ultimately the traditional divisions should break down in the face of economic inefficiency. Ultimately in half of the families males should specialise in household production and females in the others. Becker provides some evidence of weak trends towards less sex inequality in family specialisation. However, social customs are likely to interact with economic forces to perpetuate wage differentials; since wives specialise in home production families bias investment in human capital towards husbands and sons. Hence the comparative advantage of husbands in labour market production is transmitted to the next generation. Both the human capital and family specialisation approaches suggest that women are paid less because they are worth less. Their lack of human capital and desire for less demanding jobs makes their supply curve lower than that for males, and because they are less valuable to employers they receive lower wages.

It may be helpful to relate the above arguments to our diagrammatic representation of human capital theory developed in Chapter 4. If women had the same tastes, family roles and faced the same labour market opportunities as males then the supply and demand functions for investment in human capital would be identical and optimal investments would be identical. However, if role specialisation causes women to have less attachment to the labour market then they face lower rates of return on their investments as the benefits accrue over a shorter period, depreciation of capital is faster off the job and they will search less. Hence D_f, the demand for human capital of females, lies above D_m, the curve for males.

On the supply side this difference may make lending institutions less likely to lend to female investors and induce firms to ask female trainees for a larger share of the training costs. This raises the rate of interest which females have to pay for a given investment in human capital: the supply curve for females S_f, lies above that for males, S_m. This situation is shown in Fig. 6.2, and the optimal investment for female workers is accordingly at I^*_f which is a lower level than the optimum investment for males, I^*_m. Alternatively, labour market discrimination may cause women to receive lower returns on their investments. In this case D_f again lies below D_m, women accordingly invest less and this causes relative female earnings to be even lower as a consequence. Here human capital effects reinforce labour market discrimination.

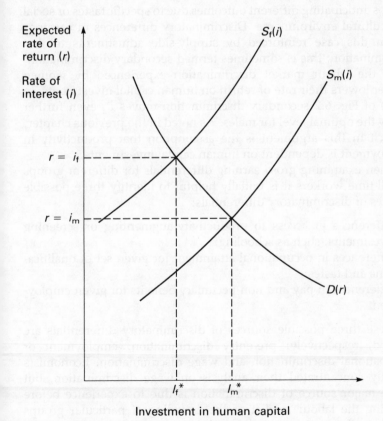

Fig. 6.2 Sex differences in optimal investments in human capital

Differences in characteristics, motivations and tastes between different groups make defining labour market discrimination extremely problematic. A conventional definition is unequal treatment in terms and conditions of employment for groups of equal productivity (Sloane 1985); such a definition requires discrimination to reflect forces on the demand side of the market. Employers must exhibit a preference for one group of workers over another group with identical supply characteristics. Such employer preference may reflect their own prejudice or that of their workers, consumers or even government. Whether such prejudice results from a subjective dislike of a group or from ignorance, which leads employers to underestimate one group's productivity, has important policy implications, improving information being much easier to achieve. This demand-side approach can be combined with human capital theory which explains differential investments due to different groups anticipating different outcomes due to specific tastes or social and cultural environments. Discriminatory differences in earnings are in this case reinforced by supply-side adjustments to that discrimination: this is sometimes termed secondary discrimination. Thus the labour market discrimination experienced by women further lowers their rate of return on human capital investments: in terms of Fig. 6.2 secondary discrimination moves I^*_f even further below the optimal level for males. As noted in the previous chapter, implicit in this argument is the assumption that productivity in employment is dependent on human capital investments.

When examining gross earning differentials for different groups of full-time workers it is initially helpful to identify three possible sources of discriminatory differentials:

1. Differences in access to productivity-augmenting or screening investments, such as schooling;
2. Differences in occupational attainment for given set of qualifications and tastes;
3. Differences in pay and non-pecuniary benefits for given employment.

These three possible sources of discriminatory differentials are termed, respectively: pre-entry discrimination; employment or occupational discrimination and wage discrimination. Economists initially concentrated their analysis on wage discrimination, but if the major source of discrimination is due to experience before entering the labour market or the crowding of particular groups into a small range of occupations, then such analysis may have little policy relevance. Accordingly we discuss theories and evidence of each type of discrimination before proceeding to a consideration of policy.

6.3 Pre-entry discrimination

Unequal schooling investments between groups may reflect supply- or demand-side factors. Unequal provision of public funds may cause differences in the quality and quantity of schooling available to different groups, while different expected returns to investments, attitude to risk-taking or access to capital markets may cause differences in the demand. The extension of voting rights to women eventually ensured similar access to education, though non-market skills were often emphasised rather than vocational ones (needlework instead of technical drawing). In the mid-1980s female school-leavers in the UK were three times as likely to have an A level pass in English or French as males but only one-third as likely to have a pass in mathematics and physics. Such striking differences are likely to reflect predominantly sex-role socialisation rather than educational provisions, though evidence is lacking on their relative importance. In the USA there is some evidence that the quality of schooling has differed by race (Welch 1973). Thus although the median educational attainment of black males was only 0.4 years less than that of white males in 1980, differences in quality appear to explain part of the racial earnings differential.

It was earlier suggested that women may demand a smaller quantity of, or less vocational, schooling because of differences in life-cycle labour force participation. Thus role specialisation, both institutionally and biologically determined, may discourage investments due to accelerated depreciation of capital. Women who expect to be absent from the labour force for long or frequent periods will choose occupations in which the costs of intermittent partici- pation are lowest, typically those occupations with little on-the-job training. This human capital approach suggests that women will be under-represented in professional jobs partly as a consequence of optimal investment strategy. Both this human capital approach and Becker's allocation of time model suggest that there will be marked differences in occupational attainment between married and single women. Such differences would reflect different investments in education and training and also different family care commitments, rather than discrimination in the labour market. However, different expected returns for different groups from the same investments may reflect anticipated occupational and wage discrimination and thus any attempt to estimate the relative importance of pre-entry discrimination is problematic.

6.4 Post-entry discrimination

6.4.1 Competitive theories

The catalyst to modern economic studies of discrimination was Becker's study (1957) which utilised traditional neoclassical tools. He assumed that employers have a 'taste' or preference for discrimination and are prepared to sacrifice profits to exercise this taste. Here profit maximisation is no longer synonymous with employer utility maximisation. Employers, or more precisely managers, may therefore refuse to hire black or female workers in competitive markets, even where their marginal product exceeds the marginal costs of hiring. Thus white males and other favoured groups of workers receive higher wages than in a non-discriminatory market, since labour supply has been restricted. Black or female workers receive lower wages because they are viewed as inferior substitutes for white male workers of the same quality, and wage differences are required to induce their employment. If there is a dispersion of discrimination tastes between employers and identical production functions, employers who discriminate less will have lower labour costs and therefore under competitive conditions should be able to eliminate more discriminatory firms from the market. Ultimately only non-discriminatory employers should survive; persisting discrimination is therefore indicative of non-competitive markets or severe transaction costs, reflecting the influence of government, trade unions or monopolists.

In principle Becker's model yields testable propositions. There should exist a negative relation between the size of wage discrimination and the proportion of favoured workers in the industry workforce. Medoff and Dick (1978) found weak evidence for this relation in their study of racial discrimination in American labour markets. An alternative, but less direct, test is that wage discrimination should be positively related to product market concentration; Heywood (1987) reviews previous US studies and provides his own analysis which supports this proposition. In general the same conclusions follow if it is employees or consumers, not employers, who exhibit a taste for discrimination.

In this case if different groups are perfect substitutes for each other then competition should eliminate wage discrimination, but the end result would be segregated workplaces. Once again the Becker approach assumes that the taste for discrimination is independent of any benefits obtained from discrimination. Women or blacks are excluded because of the supposed deterioration in the work environment their presence creates, not because of any financial benefits from the restriction on the supply of labour. The source of this taste remains problematic.

A major problem for neoclassical analysis is that discrimination is a social not an individual phenomenon, it is a dominant group which discriminates against a minority group. For discrimination to persist in competitive markets there needs to be some kind of group pressure which restricts the behaviour of employers. Explanations for such group pressures are generally inconsistent with a neoclassical framework, with its emphasis on an individualist choice theoretic approach. Akerlof (1976) assumes that individual utility depends upon prestige as well as consumption levels, and that prestige depends in part upon compliance with social customs. Believing that others are racialists and male chauvinists can make it rational for an individual worker or firm without such tastes to comply with such behaviour in the labour market. Alternatively since discrimination is always practised against minorities, the taste for discrimination may in fact be a taste for dominance and power which directly yields utility. We consider these approaches later.

An alternative approach to the analysis of discrimination still within the framework of neoclassical analysis is to consider the consequences of employers having imperfect information about applicants' potential productivity. Arrow (1972) and Phelps (1972) consider cases where it is costly to acquire such information; in these markets employers will wish to find a proxy to predict the employability of particular applicants. Race and sex being easily observable characteristics, applicants may be considered to have the mean productivities of previous workers hired with these characteristics. If firms, for example, have in the past observed that on average white males had the highest productivity or have subjective beliefs to that effect, statistical discrimination can occur against some female or black applicants, though within-group discrimination occurs against the higher-productivity members of all groups. Figure 6.3 illustrates this situation: employers believe that the mean, realised productivity of male applicants, P_m, lies above that of female applicants, P_f. Since the employer prefers male applicants where possible the shaded area represents low-productivity male workers

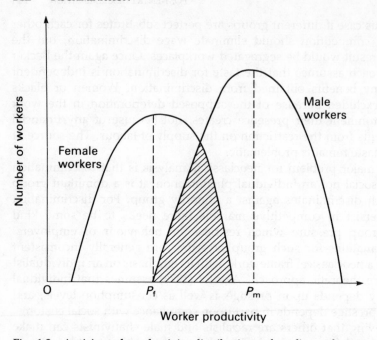

Fig. 6.3 Anticipated productivity distributions of applicants by sex.
Shaded area illustrates individuals experiencing positive or negative
discrimination

who may experience positive discrimination and female workers
who suffer negative discrimination.

Employers react to the anticipated lower productivity of women
or blacks by offering employment only at a lower wage. Where
there are restrictions on the payment of lower wages then such
applicants may be screened out completely. Blacks or women will
only be hired on equal terms in industries and occupations where
their 'inferior' characteristics are unimportant to productivity. This
leads to occupational crowding, and to a further depressing of wages
in those occupations.

If the stereotype is accurate, such as a belief that women
live longer, then there need be no inter-group discrimination in
aggregate. The probability of a job offer depends on the average
productivity of the group. Initially economists believed that this
form of statistical discrimination was efficient, since employers were
making use of a low-cost proxy to aid decision-making in a world
of imperfect and costly information. If such behaviour is efficient
then any attempt to eliminate statistical discrimination by legisla-

tion would reduce national output. However, when supply-side responses, both in participation and human capital investments, to this form of screening are considered (Lundberg and Startz 1983; Schwab 1986) it is no longer clear that the use of the screen is welfare improving. Since disadvantaged workers' skills are less accurately estimated by employers they have less incentive to invest in human capital and search or substitute market work.

Stereotypes to be accurate need to be continually updated, but the information necessary for this process is expensive to acquire. Where labour markets are experiencing rapid changes stereotypes may rapidly become outdated and erroneous discrimination can occur. Hiring decisions reflect outdated information and therefore are biased. For example, employers may not distinguish between immigrant black workers and those born locally. If the observed low productivity of immigrants was due to the limitations of their native countries' educational or training system, then race is no longer an appropriate stereotype when black workers are predominantly locally educated and trained. Such prejudice or erroneous discrimination should not persist in the long run in competitive markets; firms with accurate stereotypes will displace those with obsolete stereotypes. Tight labour markets which force employers to experiment with groups not normally hired for particular occupations would therefore increase the speed of adjustment of stereotypes.

Moreover 'true' stereotypes while reflecting employers' previous experience are also likely to reflect self-fulfilling expectations. If employers only hire females or blacks for dead-end jobs, the behaviour induced by such tasks will conform to that anticipated by employers. Thus where productivity is job based, stereotypes may be self-perpetuating. Alternatively because potential employers find it difficult to ascertain the quality of disadvantaged workers, current employers may be reluctant to promote them since to do so provides a signal to competitors. Milgrom and Oster (1987) argue that talented women and blacks may therefore get hidden by their employers, receiving lower pay and status than other workers of similar ability. In this case competition fails to eliminate discrimination, but unlike the Becker model the process is costly to society as job-matching is inefficient for these 'invisibles'.

So far wage and employment discrimination has been considered within a neoclassical framework, and it has been argued that the presence of elements of monopoly in product markets can sustain wage discrimination. Monopolists are not threatened by lower-cost non-discriminatory firms penetrating their markets. It is also likely that women are more likely to suffer from monopsony than males.

In families where husbands possess a greater stock of human capital or have a comparative disadvantage in house and family care, family income maximisation implies that wives bear disproportionally the costs of family care. Married women will therefore tend to be less geographically mobile and to search and commute smaller distances. Particularly in less urban areas, married women will face a small number of potential employers who can therefore exercise their monopsony powers to reduce wage offers to this group. Where blacks are heavily concentrated in specific locations then monopsony may also reduce their relative earnings. As discussed in the previous chapter, women and racial minorities may also face higher search costs since they have poorer contacts with the informal networks of information in the labour market. This increases the costs of quitting and of on-the-job search, resulting in a greater immobility and making their labour supply more inelastic to the firm. The profit-maximising monopsonistic firm will therefore offer them lower wage rates than that offered to white male workers.

6.4.2 Structured labour markets

The above approaches suggest that competition in the labour market should in the long run eliminate inter-group wage discrimination. The persistence of discrimination is therefore attributed to the weakness of competitive forces. Trade unions, monopoly and monopsony are the ultimate cause and therefore the appropriate target for policy. Approaches to discrimination within segmented labour markets start from a presumption that firms' employment policies are largely independent of market conditions: 'insiders' can resist competition for good jobs by 'outsiders'. Wage discrimination will therefore be a feature of firms with structured internal labour markets since competitive forces are unable to undermine discriminatory labour market practices in primary labour markets (Shorey 1984). Discrimination in the primary labour market will reflect managers' own social attitudes and an awareness that their present employees would resent and resist any changes in the customary divisions of jobs. Thus childhood socialisation, sex-specific schooling or biological and anthropological differences give rise to a socially dominant division of market/non-market work between the sexes. Employers in allocating applicants between and within primary and secondary labour markets merely reflect such social customs. The radical version of this approach attributes this segmentation of the labour market to employers' desire to fragment their workforce and so reduce their bargaining power. Employers' tastes for discrimination are therefore induced by the expectations that such tastes are profitable.

In segmented labour market models, employers with established internal labour markets hire workers on the basis of future productivity. Employers reflecting social custom may assume that girl entrants to the labour market have no long-term commitment to the labour force or that blacks have higher turnover rates and therefore exclude both groups from the structured internal labour market. The 'employability' of applicants may also be proxied by educational qualifications, in which case minority applicants may fail to gain access to the 'good' jobs. Here it is pre-entry discrimination which is crucial in explaining earnings differentials. Alternatively firms may hire on the basis of performance in tests; such tests may be sex or culturally biased, leading to black or female applicants being screened out. Statistical discrimination or subjective judgements by personnel staff also prevent entrance to primary sector jobs by such applicants. Because of vertically structured internal labour markets in this sector, there is low mobility between the primary and secondary sectors of the economy. Thus black entrants unable initially to gain a 'good' job enter the secondary sector where they experience high job turnover, frequent unemployment and little on-the-job training. Their work record accumulated in the secondary sector will prevent their transfer to 'good' jobs, the stereotype is confirmed and discrimination is perpetuated. Given that firms rarely hire large quantities of new workers and are usually making marginal adjustments to their workforce, the preferences of their existing employees will influence hiring decisions. Where employees are unwilling to work with blacks or women, employers wishing to reduce turnover or X-inefficiency may acquiesce and the workplace remains segregated. Segregation in the primary labour market may also result from the use by employers of their current workforce for recruitment. Hiring from among the friends and relatives of existing workers sustains the existing racial, and perhaps sexual composition of the workforce.

The radical version of the structuralist approach emphasises employers' desire to reduce workers' bargaining power. Here managers may wish to integrate the workplace, while segregating by occupation. The tension between majority and minority employees will reduce their cohesiveness and therefore their bargaining power. This 'divide and rule' strategy will tend to lower wages of both groups, benefiting profitability. White or male workers interpret the low wage as reflecting the competition from black or female employees and the divisions grow. Unions may become the agents of the majority workers and in alliance with employers strengthen employment and wage discrimination against minority workers. This political–economic approach views discrimination as just one feature of the inherent conflict between capital and labour. Elimination of discrimination for this approach requires fundamental reforms or replacement of the capitalist system.

6.5 Empirical studies

The earlier discussion of neoclassical theory suggests that discrimination arising from employees' tastes will lead to segregated workplaces, whereas employer-based discrimination will lead to earnings differentials, which will persist in non-competitive markets. The imperfect information theories and the existence of segmented labour markets can explain occupational crowding and hence resulting earnings differentials. It is not easy empirically to distinguish between the alternative theories or to separate discriminatory elements from non-discriminatory differences in tastes and motivations. This has led to most researchers estimating discrimination as a residual, rather than directly to test specific models. Most attempts to measure the extent of discrimination start from the Mincer earnings function introduced in Chapter 4. Earlier studies inserted a race or sex dummy variable into the function, the significance and size of the coefficient on the dummy variable being taken as a measure of discrimination. However, such an approach is likely to produce a biased coefficient on the dummy due to measurement errors in the regressors and omitted productivity-related characteristics. By only allowing the intercept term in the equation to vary it also assumes that the returns to education and other characteristics do not vary between groups, an assumption rejected by most empirical studies.

More recently it has become standard to estimate separate regressions for each group, so allowing discrimination both to affect the intercept of the earnings equation and also influence the coefficients on personal characteristics. It is possible to break down earnings differentials between groups into three sources: differentials resulting from different personal characteristics, different coefficients on those characteristics and different intercept terms. The latter two terms are often taken as the appropriate measure of discrimination. Indeed wage regressions have increasingly been used as evidence by groups claiming discrimination in US courts. An example of the standard approach is given by Goldin and Polachek (1987), following Oaxaca (1973). Let

$$y_m = g_m (x_m) \qquad [6.1]$$

and

$$y_f = g_f (x_f) \qquad [6.2]$$

where y_m and y_f = mean male and female earnings;
g_m and g_f = the male and female earnings functions of the type introduced in Chapter 4.

Then the mean earnings of females if they had male characteristics are:

$$y_{fm} = g_f (x_m) \qquad [6.3]$$

It follows that $(y_{fm} - y_f)$ is the difference in mean earnings explained by differences in measured productivity-related characteristics. Thus the portion of the wage gap explained by differences in characteristics is:

$$c = \frac{y_{fm} - y_f}{y_m - y_f} \qquad [6.4]$$

Hence one measure of discrimination is

$$d = 1 - c \qquad [6.5]$$

Such an approach ignores pre-entry discrimination and assumes that different returns to attributes are not reflecting autonomous tastes. If we take the view that attributes such as innate talents, tastes and motivation are randomly distributed, then all three components can reflect discrimination. A review of many of the problems which such estimation methods present can be found in Sloane (1985). There is a lack of studies at the company level which look behind these earning functions and consider the source of discriminatory differences. Economists have also generally avoided the issue of the efficiency losses resulting from discrimination, implicitly assuming that their estimates of the private costs of discrimination proxy social costs.

6.5.1 Empirical studies of sex discrimination

The bulk of existing empirical studies are of the US labour market; Cain's survey (1986) shows that the conventional measure of labour market discrimination, the mean unexplained portion of the gross differential, the d from above, varies from 0.51 to 0.87 for women depending upon specification. The estimate for discrimination is much lower when labour market experience is included and adjustments made for occupational structure. It thus appears that at least half of the actual earnings gap in the USA cannot be attributed to differences in human capital factors. As repeatedly emphasised, this in part represents discrimination but also non-discriminatory differences in tastes and characteristics not measured in the explanatory variables. Madden (1987) provides an example of a more direct attempt to test the importance of human capital and discrimination elements in gender differences. Human capital theory explains sex differences predominantly in terms of female workers having less job-specific human capital, hence displaced male workers should suffer a greater wage loss than displaced female workers. Her study found that in the early 1980s US female workers actually experienced a greater short-term wage loss, a result more supportive of the discrimination interpretation of earnings differentials. The apparent stability in the gross earnings differential in the USA in recent decades is interpreted by O'Neill (1985) as initially reflecting the decline in the relative skill of female workers as the participation rate increased. Entrants represented a higher proportion of the female labour supply and this tended to lower the relative skill in terms of education and job tenure. More recently high unemployment and large total inflows have put downwards pressure on wage rates for inexperienced labour in the USA and therefore again depressed gross female relative earnings.

British estimates of sex discrimination from earnings functions have usually produced a d of around 0.5, therefore indicating that female wages could be about 10 per cent higher if discrimination was eliminated (Sloane 1985). The range of estimates provided by British studies is still fairly large; Dolton and Makepeace (1986) surprisingly found a large d for female graduates at an early stage of their careers. Miller (1987) reports results broadly typical: the 1980 *General Household Survey* shows that there was a 39 per cent difference in hourly earnings between married men and women. Of this one-fifth can be explained by differences in wage-related characteristics and another two-fifths by the impact of non-participation. This leaves a 14 per cent wage differential which cannot be explained and is usually attributed to discrimination.

If single and married females have different tastes and lifestyle then the separate estimation of an earnings function for both groups may produce different estimates of discrimination. Since it is common to assume that single women are more likely to approach male attitudes to work and have uninterrupted work experience, any earnings differential between single males and single females may be a better measure of discrimination. Differences between married and single men and between married and single women can be attributed either to family role differences or discrimination specifically on the basis of marriage. Greenhalgh (1980) was the first to apply this approach to British data. Her results were broadly comparable to US studies in that educational qualifications had a similar influence for both sexes, but female age–earning functions were flatter because of the smaller impact of experience on their earnings. Greenhalgh estimated discrimination by comparing the actual earnings ratio with a hypothetical ratio based upon the assumption that the groups differed only in measured productivity characteristics. Ratios of 1.1 : 1 between single men and single women were obtained and similar ratios were generated between married men and single men, and single women and married women. The latter two differentials apparently reflected marital status discrimination, though the lower adjusted earnings of married women may also reflect locational immobility and different work history patterns. Less qualified single women appear to suffer from above-average discrimination in Greenhalgh's study. These estimates do not distinguish the impact of child-rearing separately from marriage and a general problem with this sort of approach is that women who participate in the labour market may be atypical, and the participation decision needs to be treated endogenously.

The asymmetric effects of marriage on male and female earnings is well established empirically. Whether the boost to male earnings which marriage appears to provide is a reflection of specialisation or discrimination against single men remains to be resolved. For females more recent work suggests that the source of adverse effect of marriage on earnings appears to be linked to the presence of children; Dolton and Makepeace (1987) find that although participation falls with marriage earnings are not separately influenced in the absence of children. Their study of the graduate labour market finds a range of estimates for residual earnings differential of between 4 and 25 per cent between the sexes. Such a wide range suggests another reason why it is unwise to select a single estimate of discrimination; such estimates are not only highly sensitive to specification but also by sample selection.

The usefulness of the wage equation approach to the measurement of discrimination appears to be challenged by the results of a stimulating US/Canadian study by Kuhn (1987). He finds that the extent of wage discrimination against a woman as measured above, is not positively related to the probability that she will report discrimination in a confidential survey. The elimination of all wage discrimination would only reduce the percentage who report discrimination by a third in his study. Indeed his study suggests that in particular young well-educated women behave as if they experience considerably more discrimination than earnings functions indicate.

Even if earnings functions do give insights into the size of discrimination they tell us little about the nature of that discrimination. The relative importance of occupational segregation in labour market discrimination is in dispute. Sloane and Siebert (1980) concluded that females were not unduly concentrated in low-paying occupations and that earnings differentials were predominantly due to differences in pay within occupations. Miller (1987) using very broad occupational groups finds that the presence of occupational segregation contributes little to the size of the gender wage gap in the UK. More disaggregated British studies of the distribution of occupations by sex have rejected such conclusions, and there is now much agreement that much of women's inferior position is due to occupational crowding (Dex and Shaw 1986). Hakim (1981) produced strong evidence of segmentation by occupation and industry, concluding that the broad sex structure of occupations had not changed significantly between 1901 and 1979. Whether such segmentation reflects employment discrimination or taste differences cannot be considered by aggregative studies. Aldrich and Buchele (1986) conclude that American studies suggest that occupational segregation is a significant, but not dominant, source of earnings differentials. Once again more disaggregated studies suggest a greater weighting should be given to occupational segregation. Bielby and Baron (1986) find a very high degree of sex segregation within occupations in their study of Californian firms. Such segregation did not reflect human capital differences but statistical discrimination by employers. This in turn resulted from inflexible organisational policies which were rarely adjusted unless subject to outside intervention.

For occupational crowding to be a significant cause of earnings differentials, predominantly female jobs must either be undervalued by the labour market or female workers are underemployed in those jobs. Norwood (1985) concludes that within occupations in the USA men and women are generally paid the same wages for specific jobs, but there are a smaller number of women in senior jobs. Less than a third of the women employees surveyed in a 1980 British study thought they had promotion prospects, while over a half desired promotion. Greenhalgh and Stewart (1987) provide limited evidence that the returns from recent full-time training are larger for both single and married women than for men. If employers artificially restrict the supply of training opportunities for women then human capital theory interpretations of earnings differentials are invalidated. Craig, Garnsey and Rubery (1984) studied smaller British companies and concluded that women's jobs were predominantly low paid whatever the characteristics of the job or worker. Ferber, Green and Spaeth find similar results for the USA, concluding that 'It is not mainly what women do, but what is done to them that keeps them in an inferior position' (1986: 56). Such conclusions are particularly important for our policy discussion below.

Non-participation appears to account for the major part of the gender differences in wage levels and employment structure. Female attachment to the labour force is less peripheral than is often implied by human capital interpretations of earnings differentials. Although female participation tends to rise with labour market expansion, the process is not fully reversible and Owen and Joshi (1987) find relatively few 'discouraged' female workers in their study of the last recession. Stewart and Greenhalgh's (1984) longitudinal study finds that two-thirds of female employees in the survey have had only one interruption of labour force participation, though women with more frequent interruptions are less likely to be in employment with career ladders, a finding consistent with all models of earnings differentials. Again it is married women who experience much less upward mobility and have tended to move into the low-status, and often part-time, occupations left by upwardly mobile groups (Greenhalgh and Stewart 1985). Only about half of women returning to the labour force after child-rearing retained their previous occupational status, such downwards mobility being more common in the UK than in the USA. This pattern of occupational mobility across childbirth reflects the structural changes of the British labour market with the growth of the service sector and increased part-time working (Dex 1987).

The stability of traditional roles in the family suggests that socialisation may be an important element in sex inequalities in the labour market. There have recently been attempts to include sex-role socialisation as an explanatory factor in models of discrimination.

Corcoran and Courant (1987) test a model of educational attainment using US data and find that young non-black women with brothers acquire significantly less education than those without brothers, the effect diminishing with income. This suggests that families treat boys and girls differently in the quantity as well as the quality of schooling. Psychologists have established the gender differences in tastes and personality traits which socialisation induces, and their importance to labour market inequality is likely to become a fertile area in future research.

There have been few disaggregated studies of sex discrimination in the UK though the limited study of Siebert and Sloane (1981) suggests that sex discrimination occurs only in certain plants and industries. There is still much disagreement on the sources and extent of sex discrimination in the labour market. At this time majority opinion appears to believe that significant discrimination does occur and that when occupations are disaggregated, employment discrimination is probably more important than wage discrimination. There is also general agreement that discrimination against single women is smaller than that against married women, with the former decreasing over time and the latter reflecting the consequences of child-rearing interruptions. If the disfavoured treatment of married women reflects productivity losses due to depreciation effects of labour market withdrawal, then it may be, as Fuchs concludes, that: 'In order for women to earn as much as men in competitive markets they will probably have to behave like men with respect to subjects studied in school, choice of jobs, postschool investment, and commitment to career. This could result in extremely low fertility or in large numbers of children receiving inadequate care' (Fuchs 1986: S268). However, this rather begs the extent to which markets are actually competitive and even more fundamentally whether social norms concerning the family division of labour are sensitive to policy changes. One could as easily argue that if men behaved more like women then earnings differentials would be eliminated, without the supposed social side-effects. We return to these issues later.

6.5.2. Empirical studies on racial discrimination

American studies indicate that once productivity characteristics have been adjusted, the residual discrimination against black males is of the same dimensions as that for females, Cain's (1986) review showing a d of between 0.39 and 0.66. Dickens and Lang (1987) find that a substantial proportion of this differential is explained by the concentration of black workers in secondary sector employment, the differential disappearing in the primary sector. Racial discrimination appears to have also reduced the hours worked by blacks as they face higher levels of unemployment and involuntary part-time employment. For well-educated and younger blacks, Hoffman and Link (1984) suggest that labour market discrimination has largely been eliminated. This reduction in discriminatory differences made family background a much more important cause of income inequality in the USA. Smith and Welch (1987) estimate that proportionally there are three times as many poor black families as white; the major reasons for this disparity are the greater instability of black families, 40 per cent female-headed, and the lower activity rates of black adults. Income inequality among male blacks has increased and poverty has become more spatially concentrated: the 'underclass' cannot escape the ghetto (Danziger and Gottschalk 1987). The consensus that discrimination against middle-class blacks in the USA disappeared in the 1960s and that occupational mobility is now class, rather than race determined, has been challenged. Datcher-Loury (1986) suggests that blacks have more unstable middle-class status than whites, reflecting family instability, and that the income gains of younger blacks may not be sustained over their total labour market experience. In recent years the proportion of black high-school graduates going on to college has dropped significantly, suggesting further uncertainty about the permanence of reduced inequality.

Earnings data for the UK indicate substantial differentials between white and minority racial workers, and earning functions for males suggest that d is higher than in the USA, indicating that the lower earnings of minority workers are not primarily due to differences in characteristics. Mayhew and Rosewell (1978) showed that immigrants were more occupationally crowded than the population as a whole, but that the type and extent of crowding differ significantly between immigrant groups. Disaggregated studies by location and race have recently suggested large differences in the extent of earnings differentials (McCormick 1986b) and that discrimination also takes the form of greater commuting and search costs as well as lower pay (McCormick 1986a). Because racial minorities account for only about 3.5 per cent of the economically active population in the UK, aggregation of different nationalities into a non-white group is usual with existing data sources. Most studies have used data in which first-generation immigrant West Indian and Asian workers dominate and education and training dissimilarities between their country of birth and the UK may distort the earnings functions. All these factors urge caution in the interpretation of British studies which attempt to compare earnings functions of whites with those of non-whites.

McNabb and Psacharopoulos (1981b) found the earnings function for black workers was much less responsive to personal characteristics than that of white workers. Black workers appeared to receive a lower return on education and experience and these lower rates of returns were the major cause of the earnings differentials. Stewart (1983a), using *National Training Survey* data, also discovered a flat age–earnings profile for black immigrant workers and lower returns to education. However, in his study the data allowed examination of the cause of this difference in earnings functions and the lack of occupational progression among black immigrants appeared crucial: it was occupational rather than pay discrimination that was the predominant cause of the differential. Estimates of discriminatory earnings differentials of around 10 per cent have been common in British studies of racial discrimination, though some of this may reflect inferior quality or inappropriate education received in the country of birth. Although young blacks suffer higher unemployment than similar whites, Blackaby (1986) and Dex (1984) provide some support to the suggestion that young blacks in employment are no longer significantly discriminated against, though they may still experience later labour market discrimination through a dearth of on-the-job training or promotion opportunities.

6.6 Policy implications of theory

The conventional case for specific anti-discriminatory as opposed to anti-poverty policies in the labour market rests upon the belief that earnings differentials between groups in society do not exclusively reflect differences in productivity-influencing characteristics or tastes. It presupposes that different groups within the labour market experience different treatment purely because of their membership of that group. Whether such discrimination is inefficient remains problematic to competitive theorists. The disfavoured group are underemployed and the favoured group overemployed as a consequence, and potential output is therefore reduced. However, neoclassical economics takes tastes as given, hence if tastes are a fundamental cause of discrimination then inefficiency cannot be assumed. Since economics does not distinguish between the ethical merits of different tastes then neoclassical economics provides no support for anti-discriminatory policy (Cain 1985). Non-competitive theorists who are less willing to attribute both discrimination to tastes and productivity to the workers' characteristics are more prepared to support intervention on economic grounds.

The previous discussion indicates that there are several possible causes and forms of discriminatory behaviour, and if it is desired to reduce such practices the appropriate policy response will be determined by the relative importance of specific causes and the particular market environment. A particular policy measure which is an appropriate response to one type of discrimination may only reinforce discrimination when different causal factors are in operation. For example, if measures are introduced to eliminate pay discrimination this will tend to cause additional employment discrimination as more employers introduce discriminatory hiring practices. What is required here is a 'policy mix', where complementary policies are combined to reflect the importance of the various discriminatory causes. In this section the frequently recommended policy responses are discussed and related to the causes of discrimination. There are four main types of policies advocated: increased competition; compensatory public finance; intervention into wage-fixing and intervention into hiring decisions.

6.6.1 Increased competition

Neoclassical approaches suggest that inter-group discrimination should be undermined in the long run by competitive forces in the labour market. According to this general approach anti-discriminatory policies require the strengthening of competitive forces in the product, labour and capital markets. Market forces should force discriminating employers out of the market or lead to their take-over by non-discriminatory ones. Thus monopoly and restrictive practices legislation and the deregulation of capital markets have potential importance as anti-discriminatory devices. Measures to increase labour market competitiveness are also likely to be beneficial according to this approach. Any policy which increases labour mobility should reduce the extent of occupational crowding and monopsony in the market and therefore reduce the potential for discrimination. Measures to reduce restrictive practices of employers and trade unions, to reform housing markets and reduce commuting costs may therefore assist the undermining of discriminatory labour market practices. While increased competition should increase the costs of acting on prejudice, that is on incorrect information, it is not clear than even within the neoclassical approach this tackles the underlying cause. If there exists a preference for discrimination which results from a lack of contact between groups, increased competition may not reduce segregation significantly and therefore fails to attack the fundamental cause of discrimination. Increased competition is also unlikely to break down discrimination resulting from social custom. Any attempt to increase competition is likely to have an impact on discrimination only in the long run. The structuralist approaches suggest that given the ability of internal labour markets to isolate themselves from external market forces, even in the long run the effects are likely to be small.

6.6.2 Compensatory public finance

The government can directly finance and produce goods and services that the market fails to provide. Where poverty or false discounting of expected returns have caused certain groups to under-invest in human capital accumulation the government could provide training opportunities. Where social customs dictate a sexual division of labour where women are largely responsible for child care, one response could be for governments to provide day-care facilities (Schmid 1984), or as in the USA provide tax concessions for child-care expenses when both parents are working. The greater gaps in employment and subsequent greater downwards occupational mobility of British mothers compared to those in the USA which Dex and Shaw (1986) discovered appear linked to these differences in child-care provision. Legislation requiring employers to provide for paid maternity leave can also prevent downwards occupational mobility for mothers. The benefit system may also sustain social customs, since mothers, especially the poor and unmarried, may face high marginal tax rates on labour market incomes.

The tax and benefit system could be amended to compensate directly groups discriminated against, a system which made it financially advantageous to divide home and market work more equally could help offset prevailing social customs. Empirical evidence suggests that the substitution effect of a rise in married women's wages dominates the income effect, accordingly any alteration in their marginal tax rates is likely to have a large impact on their supply of labour. Alternatively, reflecting the popularity of Becker's taste model of discrimination, a tax–grant policy to influence wage-fixing and hiring decisions could be implemented. A tax on employing members of favoured groups could provide revenue to subsidise employment of discriminated workers. In Chapter 4 we saw how such policies have been implemented to attempt to improve the allocation of training resources, but no such policies have been implemented to improve the allocation of employment. The danger that such a system is likely to benefit most those employers who previously discriminated most can be avoided if the grant is paid for employing above some norm ratio of minority workers and the levy imposed for those below that norm. The administrative costs of deciding upon and implementing appropriate norms appear to be the major economic obstacles to such a policy, though these were surmounted in the case of training norms.

The government is a major purchaser of goods and services in all developed economies. As such it has the power to reduce discrimination through its own behaviour as a purchaser. American experience discussed later suggests that making public contracts dependent upon non-discriminatory behaviour or even affirmative action can have a major impact on eliminating such practices in the labour market.

6.6.3 Wage-fixing legislation

One of the most frequently advocated anti-discriminatory measures is intervention directly into wage determination. Wage equalisation policies attempt to ban wage discrimination directly. The mildest form of intervention into wage-fixing is a minimum wage law which seeks to reduce wage discrimination against low-wage groups. The impact of such policies again depends upon the actual cause of discrimination. Neoclassical theorists believing in the underlying efficiency of competitive wage-fixing view such interference with market forces as harmful and counter-productive. If black and white workers, or female and male workers are in fact close substitutes for each other, then any attempt to enforce higher wages for the dis-criminated group must reduce their employment opportunities. If it is employers' tastes which underlie discrimination then employment discrimination will replace wage discrimination, wage differences between groups are replaced by differences in unemployment, and the disadvantaged group could even suffer a net loss of income due to such equal wage legislation. Where equal wages laws only apply to certain labour markets then occupational crowding is likely to occur in those markets not covered by the law, putting further downward pressure on wages in these markets. With both statistical and erroneous discrimination equal wage legislation again leads to differences in unemployment rates replacing wage discrimination. The adjustment mechanism is weakened as fewer members of the disfavoured group are hired, and this results in a slower dissemination of information regarding correct productivity distributions between groups. However, where discrimination arises from monopsony, wage equalisation can eliminate wage differences and, depending on relative elasticities, actually increase employment opportunities for the discriminated group. Additionally wage equalisation legislation can be beneficial where social customs are preventing economic forces from eliminating discrimination.

Where the major cause of discrimination is occupational crowding of certain minority employment groups into secondary labour market jobs, equal pay legislation is largely irrelevant. Segmentation means that there is little impact on either earnings differentials or on employment opportunities for discriminated groups. As different groups are segregated they are not doing the same jobs and are not close substitutes for each other. This leads to a discussion of how in practice to define equal pay. If firms can define equal pay narrowly then segregation by specific work task will occur to avoid the consequences of the legislation for its wage bill. Hence proponents of intervening into wage-fixing argue for a change from 'equal pay for equal work' to 'equal pay for work of equal value'. Proponents of comparable worth argue that jobs within a firm can be valued in terms of inputs of effort, skill and responsibility. Equality of remuneration should hold when comparable characteristics generate jobs of comparable worth to a firm. This equality requires an upwards adjustment of wages in traditional female occupations; comparable worth policies have been attempted in Canada, certain US states and Australia, and they are assessed later in this chapter.

6.6.4 Positive discrimination and affirmative action

Where the major cause of earnings differentials between groups is believed to be occupational crowding which does not reflect qualifications and taste differences, then the policies discussed above are generally ineffective. In this situation the advocated policy is either positive discrimination, the establishment of job quotas for certain groups, or the affirmative action policies which give encouragement to the employment and promotion of minority groups. Positive discrimination can take various forms from specifying quotas for schooling, training, occupations or individual employers. Quotas are effective in eliminating discrimination due to employer or employee prejudice or social custom, since better information produced by greater contacts creates more accurate stereotypes of the discriminated group. Where labour markets are segmented then this elimination of discrimination based on prejudice will also result in a reduction of both earnings and unemployment differences between groups. Quotas may also be effective in combating discrimination occurring prior to entry into the labour market or in offsetting the consequences of discrimination against previous generations. In the latter case 'inferior' applicants from discriminated groups may be favoured over applicants from advantaged groups in the short term. This is based upon a belief that qualifications or performances in hiring tests may be biased indicators of ability and employability for members of groups who have suffered historically from discrimination. This may reflect the influence of environment on human capital decisions, imperfections in the capital market which constrain the investment decisions of those with low family incomes and wealth, or the result of tests which are culturally or socially biased. Such policies are advocated by those who believe that competitive forces are unable by themselves to eliminate discrimination. The break-up of segregated workplaces and the reduction of occupational crowding are assumed advocates to produce efficiency gains greater than any losses resulting from interference with firms' hiring decisions.

The belief that positive discrimination may conflict with other objectives in society such as freedom of contract and individual justice has led many only to advocate such policies in extreme situations. For some reason positive discrimination is typically tolerated more commonly in the elimination of employment discrimination against disabled workers than in the case of racial or sexual discrimination. Affirmative action programmes for minorities have sometimes become substitutes for mandatory quotas. Linking government contracts to the implementation of internal policies to eliminate discriminatory behaviour and targeting government training and other manpower policies have been widely adopted in the USA.

In some of the theories of discrimination previously considered, majority groups may benefit directly from the practice by receiving higher wages and better non-pecuniary returns from work such as status and power. The elimination of discrimination may therefore reduce the returns from work for members of the majority group.

There is likely to be resistance to the implementation of effective anti-discriminatory policy and widespread evasion would pose a threat to its effectiveness. Governments have therefore stressed the moral, social and political dimensions of anti-discriminatory legislation and minimised the impact of their policies on the long-term economic well-being of the majority group. Compliance with legislation will reflect the costs of conforming relative to the expected costs of violating the law (Beller 1978). The former will reflect how successfully the measure has defined and targeted discrimination. Where minority groups are a small proportion of the total workforce resistance is likely to be small. High prevailing levels of aggregate demand are also likely to facilitate the introduction, implementation and acceptance of legislation by lowering the costs of conforming. Affirmative action policies are therefore much easier to conduct where employment opportunities for white males are plentiful. Compliance will also reflect the penalties imposed for violating the law, adjusted for the probability of the violation being detected and the penalty enforced. In slack labour markets targeting special employment programmes at the discriminated groups presents an alternative policy approach to those outlined above. However, where discrimination is the result of incorrect or imperfect information, or crowding, it is unlikely that such programmes will be effective without any expansion of employment opportunities. Having established the importance of linking policy to cause we now turn to a consideration of policies actually implemented in developed Western economies.

6.7 The impact of current policies

6.7.1 Policies to reduce sex discrimination

In France and West Germany discrimination by sex is forbidden by their constitution, in Sweden employers and trade unions have almost negotiated discrimination away, elsewhere legislative changes have been used to reduce discriminatory earnings differentials. The USA was the innovator in the introduction of equal pay, anti-discrimination and affirmative action legislation, and initially we consider the development and impact of these measures. The Second World War had a lasting effect on the structure of the labour force in many countries, the range of 'female' jobs rapidly expanded and impetus was given to legislators to introduce equal pay measures. Although many individual states had introduced some form of equal pay law in the immediate post-war years it was not until 1963 that the Federal Equal Pay Act was finally passed. The measure required the introduction of equal pay 'for equal jobs the performance of which requires equal skill, effort and responsibility', a much narrower measure than many previous bills which would have enforced equal pay for jobs of comparable value or skill. In the next year Congress prohibited employment discrimination by race and sex in Title VII of the Civil Rights Act. For the next twenty years there was, however, no upward movement in the gross female earnings ratio. Detailed research suggests that inequalities within firms were reduced and occupational segregation may also have been weakened by the measures, especially from the 1970s.

Although the 1970s saw an improvement in American women's occupational opportunities (Zalokar 1986) a large proportion still work in traditional female jobs in clerical and the caring professions and are largely unaffected by equal pay legislation. This supposed failure has led to proposals to raise wages in women's jobs by the introduction of equal pay for jobs of comparable worth. This attempt to move policy forward from a concern with pay discrimination towards attacking employment discrimination has generated much debate, recently reviewed by Aldrich and Buchele (1986). Figart (1987) concludes that evidence from individual states with comparable worth legislation suggests that by itself such measures are not sufficient. Comparable worth raises entry level and average wage rates for women, but does not produce the same job ladders as are available in 'male' occupations. Equal pay legislation together with the 1972 removal of sex discrimination in higher education appear to have reversed the role of college education in reinforcing sex inequality (Nord 1987). Also significant has been the experience of positive discrimination in the USA. Executive Order 11375 issued in 1968 required federal contractors not to discriminate on the basis of sex, adding to existing requirements on race and religious discrimination. It sanctioned the ending of federal funding if a violation is discovered and forced contractors to have an affirmative action programme that actively hired and promoted women and minorities. Comparisons of the growth of minority and female employment in firms covered by the executive order with similar non-contractor establishments suggest that affirmative action has been generally successful in reducing employment discrimination (Leonard 1986). However, for white women, unlike other targeted groups, there is no evidence of any occupational advancement resulting from affirmative action. Affirmative action especially raises the demand of black females as they fill two quotas and this may explain why black female relative earnings have risen. However, in periods of recession and weak enforcement the impact of this measure appears small.

British anti-discriminatory legislation borrowed significantly from American experience. The Equal Pay Act was passed in 1970 and fully implemented in 1975. It required that men and women be paid the same wage if they were employed in the same or broadly similar work. In 1984 to comply with a European Court ruling the basis for claims became equal pay for work of equal value, though only within the same employing agency and when a job evaluation scheme has not been applied. In 1975 the Sex Discrimination Act was also enacted, making it illegal to discriminate on the grounds of sex in certain areas of employment, education, housing and other services. Individuals can take their case to Industrial Tribunals, though financial compensation for victims has been minimal. The Act applies equally for men and women and therefore makes reverse discrimination in favour of women generally illegal. The Sex Discrimination Act established the Equal Opportunities Commission to monitor the two Acts and enforce compliance. However, the commission has found it difficult to utilise its enforcement powers in practice and has usually worked through persuasion and education rather than compulsion.

The impact of the two Acts on earnings differentials, discrimination and employment has been the subject of several recent studies. Snell, Glucklich and Povall (1981) report employers often minimised their obligation under the Act by moving workers and changing job content, during the transition period of the Equal Pay Act. The impact of the Equal Pay Act may therefore have been to worsen occupational segregation. The requirement that women covered by collective agreements, employers' pay structures or Wages Council's orders be paid at or above the lowest male rate did appear to eliminate much pay discrimination in non-segregated firms and occupations, even among the smaller companies. Their survey of employers also concluded that although the Sex Discrimination Act had eliminated overtly discriminatory hiring and promotion practices, it had not significantly altered firms' actual labour market behaviour, while the continuation of the use of incremental pay scales and promotion based on length of service continued to operate against reduced earnings differentials. The failure to confront the consequences of segregated workplaces and the concentration of women in low-paid employment had therefore undermined the effectiveness of the legislation. Rather than adopt

Table 6.3   Women's earnings relative to men's: UK 1970–87

Average gross weekly earnings*: women's as % of men's†

April	1970	63.1	1981	74.8
	1975	72.1	1982	73.9
	1976	75.1	1983	74.2
	1977	75.5	1984	73.5
	1978	73.9	1985	74.1
	1979	73.0	1986	74.3
	1980	73.5	1987	73.6

Source: Employment Gazette Nov. 1987, based on results of the new earnings survey
* Full-time workers aged 18 and over, excluding overtime and workers whose pay
was affected by absence.
† Since delays in particular settlements may affect the earnings of one sex more than
another in a given year.

this workplace study of the impact of the measures, most other investigations have adopted an aggregate econometric approach, and these are now considered.

As Table 6.3 indicates, relative female earnings rose rapidly in the UK between 1970 and 1980. It is difficult to resist the temptation to link this rise in female relative earnings shown in Table 6.3 directly with the introduction of anti-discriminatory legislation in the UK. However, there are alternative interpretations of this trend. The occupational crowding of female workers means that structural changes in the economy can cause changes in relative pay. The general level of economic activity may also have an impact as women are concentrated in jobs with low training which may increase in relative pay during a tight labour market. Exogenous male or female labour supply changes, increasing female unionisation or the impact of income policies are additional candidates to explain the increase. Whether the rise in female relative earnings reflects reduced discrimination remains an empirical issue. Chiplin, Curran and Parsley (1980) attribute most of the increase in female pay during the Equal Pay Act transition period to the operation of flat-rate income policies, though they make no attempt to estimate the impact of cyclical and structural change on relative earnings. Tzannatos and Zabalza (1984) and Zabalza and Tzannatos (1985a) attempt a more sophisticated investigation of the problem. They found that the change in the distribution of female workers and changes in the industrial wage differentials had little impact on the overall movement of female relative wages. The improvement in relative female earnings was due largely to a reduction in wage differentials within industrial sectors. On inspection they conclude that anti-discriminatory legislation appeared to have a large positive effect on relative female earnings and relative employment. The impact had been to shift the demand curve for female labour, and depending upon whether one views the depressed earning capacity of non-participants as discriminatory, Zabalza and Arrufat (1985) estimate that the Acts have reduced discrimination by between 30 and 50 per cent. Whether this reflects an impact effect or a permanent change in the labour market remains an important issue. The conflict in findings between studies conducted at the firm level which are pessimistic about the impact of the Acts and studies at the aggregate level which have suggested large effects remains puzzling.

Given the fear that reduction of female earnings differentials would reduce employment prospects for female workers it is important to consider the impact of legislation on female job opportunities. If male and female workers are close substitutes for each other then the employment consequences should be large. If, alternatively, there is strong segmentation in the labour market then male and female workers may not be close substitutes for employers and the employment response is weak. Joshi, Layard and Owen (1985) report that the 15 per cent rise in relative earnings of female workers in the mid-1970s did not appear to cause any decline in the relative demand for female workers. Pike (1985) concludes that although female full-time and part-time workers are close substitutes for each other as are part-time women and youths, full-time females are not close substitutes for males and may even be complementary to youths. Thus just as segmentation may have diluted the impact of equal pay legislation on earnings differentials it has also limited the employment consequences of reduced income inequality. However, it is likely that there was a decline in job opportunities for female part-time workers following the enactment of legislation.

In 1972 the Australian Conciliation and Arbitration Commission decided to switch from the principle of 'equal pay for equal work' to 'equal pay for work of equal value'. Australian experience with the introduction of comparable worth appears to confirm the small employment consequences of anti-discriminatory legislation. The 1972 decision appeared to have a major impact on relative female earnings; female average hourly earnings rose from 76 per cent of males to 86 per cent, at little cost to female employment growth (Gregory and Duncan 1981). Though problems remain concerning the evaluation of traditionally female jobs (Short 1986), any job evaluation requires value judgements to be made concerning the measuring and weighting of specific characteristics.

The conclusion that women's inferior labour market position was largely due to occupational segregation together with the reduction in pay discrimination following legislation suggests that more concern should be given to the impact of policies on occupational status. American women appear to achieve greater upwards occupational mobility than British women. Dex and Shaw (1986) show that British mothers spend more time out of the labour force after childbirth than American mothers and are more likely to return to part-time work and experience downward mobility on return. These three factors are obviously interrelated, and maternity leave and tax provisions for child-care expenses appear to influence the speed of return to the labour force after childbirth. In the UK it also appears that mothers who wish part-time employment find such jobs are heavily concentrated in low-grade jobs. Improving the status of part-time jobs and reforming tax systems may therefore have an important role in reducing female wage inequality.

6.7.2 Policies to reduce racial discrimination

In the period since the passage of the 1964 Civil Rights Act in the USA blacks have experienced large gains in education, occupational attainment and earnings relative to whites. However, there remain large differences in unemployment and poverty rates between racial groups. Median annual earnings of black males remain at about two-thirds of those for white males and have not risen significantly since the mid-1970s. The increase in relative earnings have been greatest for young, well-educated and female blacks, and the extent to which these changes reflect successful anti-discriminatory policies has been widely debated as Brown's (1982) survey indicates. The increase in the relative earnings and occupational status of blacks could be due, *ceteris paribus*, either to shifts in the labour supply curve of blacks relative to whites or an increased demand for black labour relative to that of whites. On the supply side some economists have emphasised increased human capital investments by blacks, while others point to qualitative improvements in schooling. In addition expanded social programmes may have reduced black participation rates, especially of those with low labour market earnings, hence both reducing the relative supply of black labour and directly raising relative black earnings. On the demand side the principal force raising the relative demand for black labour is likely to be the impact of affirmative action initiatives and equal employment opportunity legislation on corporate recruitment and promotion policies. The incidence and the timing of the gains seem to suggest that it is the demand shift which has been the strongest influence, a conclusion largely confirmed by empirical studies (Freeman 1981). Affirmative action has especially benefited black females as they fill two quotas, and while middle-class black males also benefited it appears to have had little long-term impact upon male racial differentials (Smith and Welch 1987). The contract compliance programme has apparently raised the demand for blacks in highly skilled white-collar and craft jobs more than that for unskilled and semi-skilled workers. Thus the affirmative action initiative appears to have been complemented by government training programmes which have increased the supply of educated and trained minority employees. The Equal Employment Opportunity Commission, established to police the Civil Rights Act, has limited powers and relies heavily upon conciliation to settle disputes. Thus the courts have become a visible and important source for change.

In the UK, the 1968 Race Relations Act made unlawful discrimination on the basis of race, colour, ethnic or national origin in the areas of employment, housing and the provision of goods and services. The 1976 Act set up the Commission for Racial Equality to police the legislation, though individuals complaining of discrimination had direct access to courts. Overt racial discriminatory behaviour has been virtually eliminated, but the extent to which it has been replaced by hidden discrimination remains uncertain. Surveys have suggested that up to a half of firms discriminate against racial minority applicants in recruitment; largely it appears on statistical grounds or reflecting prejudice of existing employees. It is just in these areas that positive discrimination appears to have been effective in the USA. The indications that young black applicants may face less discrimination than their parents is one sign that attitudes may be changing and erroneous stereotypes are being eroded.

6.8 Conclusions

It has been established that modern economies still have significant areas of discrimination in their labour markets. In competitive markets orthodox theory implies that if women and blacks behaved as white males, earnings levels would converge. Existing studies suggest that such analysis is too simplistic; social norms are an important part of the operation of labour markets and competitive forces are often weak. This implies that if society wishes to reduce earnings inequality between groups then government intervention is required. Equal pay policies are an effective way of reducing wage discrimination, but inadequate as occupational segregation is common and non-participation a major cause of earnings differentials. Affirmative action policies have been effective for certain groups, especially black females in the USA. Comparable worth appears to have further improved the position of female workers where implemented, but again is inadequate to combat fully the lack of upwards occupational mobility among certain groups. Surprisingly compensatory public finance policies have rarely been tried in this area, though tax concessions for child-care costs may be an effective way of maintaining female occupational status during motherhood. No single policy is sufficient to tackle discrimination and the need is to co-ordinate a collection of effective policies which foster comparable worth and comparable work.

Successful anti-discriminatory programmes can only be pursued in sympathetic environments. Economic growth is a major requirement for effective policy action. Increasing the numbers of new 'good' jobs and reducing available supply of labour help to produce an atmosphere conducive to behavioural change and changes in social norms. American experience has also shown that the operation of the courts can help to achieve changes in the climate of opinion. The acceptance of the 1987 legal decisions that the Rotary Club, by excluding women from membership, was perpetuating male dominance in managerial and professional decision-making, was indicative that previous decisions on sex and racial discrimination had indeed reformed US public attitudes. It is therefore significant that a majority of boards in the UK did not discuss the consequences for their companies of the Race Relations Act and almost 40 per cent failed even to discuss equal pay legislation (Marsh 1982).

Further reading

Mayhew in Bain (1983) provides a comprehensive introduction to the study of discrimination in the UK. Mallier and Rosser (1987) compare women's labour market experience in the UK and the USA to which Dex and Shaw (1986) provide a necessary supplement. A good place to start a more rigorous investigation of the topic is D'Amico's (1987) recent, short and critical overview of the economic approach to discrimination. The most comprehensive recent surveys of theory and empirical studies are those by Sloane (1985), Cain (1986) and Dex and Sloane (1988). Both are fairly advanced and the former more sympathetic to competitive approaches, and Fischer (1987) provides an easier theoretical survey with a structuralist bias. Zabalza and Tzannatos (1985b) provide a detailed examination of the impact of legislation on the employment and wages of women in the UK.

Chapter 7

UNEMPLOYMENT

In 1986, fifty years after the publication of Keynes's *General Theory of Employment, Interest and Money*, the official male unemployment rate in the UK was at 14 per cent, compared to a mean rate of 1.5 per cent between 1941 and 1970. While recently the British rate has been relatively high by international standards, all major economies have suffered levels of unemployment unknown since the 1930s. Over the last fifty years economists of all persuasions had told generations of their students that the Keynesian revolution had permanently eliminated the problem of mass unemployment. The reappearance of mass unemployment at the end of the 1970s has caused extensive debates about its origins and the appropriate policy responses. Ironically, these debates have followed much of the pattern of those which were generated by the publication of the *General Theory* itself. Rejuvenated neoclassical economists explain the rise in unemployment in terms of institutional restrictions on the operation of labour markets, the operation of trade unions and of unemployment insurance schemes having distorted both demand and supply sides in the labour market, causing the natural (equilibrium) rate of unemployment to rise. Unemployment since it reflects the weakness of competitive forces in the labour markets, is a microeconomic problem requiring microeconomic policies. As in the 1930s, even the increase in central government's budget deficit during periods of economic recession is viewed with alarm by certain economists. In contrast Keynes argued that unemployment was compatible with competitive markets, concluding that governments had to use macroeconomic policies to adjust levels of aggregate demand if acceptable levels of employment were to be sustained.

The 1980s replay of this theoretical and policy debate is the central concern of this chapter. First it is necessary to define our terms carefully, to gain some ideas of the costs of unemployment, and to acquire some overview of its present extent and composition. This is followed by a review of current explanations of unemployment, particularly concentrating upon their ability to explain the pattern of recent British unemployment. Existing policies are then reviewed and analysed, and the chapter concludes with a consideration of alternatives to current British policy.

7.1 Unemployment: methodology and evidence

7.1.1 Defining unemployment

Many disputes concerning unemployment could be clarified or resolved if it was recognised that the term is used to describe several different concepts in the literature. To some people unemployment measures the underutilisation of the potential workforce, including those who in certain situations would enter the labour market. Here the extent of underemployment of workers is as significant as the number without any employment. For many economists, it is a measure of immediately available, non-employed workers willing to accept market-clearing wages. In this latter case it is active job-seekers who are the appropriate criterion for measurement. For many policy-makers, unemployment is the currently adopted measure of registrants for, or claimants of, unemployment and social security benefit. As such the total can be adjusted by altering incentives to register or benefit eligibility regulations; since only about a third of the unemployed receive unemployment benefits in the UK and the USA such changes can produce large changes in the unemployment counts. Thus debates about the 'true' level of unemployment are often futile, since the number of unemployed will depend upon which definition is adopted. As illustration, official British unemployment figures fell by 150 000 in the year to March 1987; Charter for Jobs (1987) claims that two-thirds of this reduction was the result of administrative and statistical changes and the remainder to the expansion of the Special Employment Measures. Overall the latter policies are thought to have reduced measured unemployment in the UK by about half a million in the mid-1980s.

The convention adopted in the UK in 1982 for counting unemployed was based upon the number claiming benefit (unemployment benefit, supplementary benefit and National Insurance credits) on

the day of the monthly count, and willing to do any suitable work. It
has since been amended to exclude certain groups of school-leavers,
students and occupational pensioners; the many recent changes
have been documented by Southworth (1987). Such a measure
will overestimate unemployment to the extent that some claimants
are non-active searchers, are only prepared to work at unattainable
wages, have already found employment or are fraudulently making
claims. It will be sensitive to the level of benefits, as well as to the eligibility requirements. On the other hand it excludes certain groups
which other measures would include, such as discouraged searchers
not entitled to benefits, predominantly re-entrants into the labour
market. Those in part-time, who wish full-time employment are also
excluded, as are some early retirees. A movement towards a US-style
survey-based count of the unemployed would produce yet another
measurement of unemployment, again dependent upon definitions
of active job-seeking and on levels of remuneration available.

Which is the most appropriate definition of unemployment
will depend upon one's belief about how labour markets operate.
For example, neoclassical analysis views labour markets as price
adjusting, and unemployment should measure the difference
between the supply and demand for labour, the emphasis being on
active searchers and unfilled vacancies. However, supply of labour
is dependent on the real wage rate, non-labour market earnings
and non-market work and leisure opportunities. Accordingly the
level of unemployment will change as any of these variables
change or when the demand curve shifts due to changes in
the firm's environment. Once it is recognised that the appropriate
definition of unemployment will depend upon the theoretical
framework adopted and upon the particular issue of concern, then
consistency of measurement becomes the real issue. Care should be
taken in any historical or international comparison to ensure that
the data are consistently defined. In the following pages figures
for unemployment refer to current official series unless otherwise
stated. This convention is certainly not meant to indicate that these
figures reflect the most useful definition of unemployment, since
governments may have an interest in adopting definitions which
minimise the numbers unemployed.

7.1.2 Costs of unemployment

Given the problems of actually defining what the term 'unemployment' means, it is necessary to establish the importance and unique-

ness of the concept. Unemployment is important because it is costly, both to individuals and to society as a whole. Firstly, unemployment imposes costs upon society; labour is perishable and labour not utilised for production causes a permanent loss of output and therefore consumption. Secondly, unemployment imposes suffering upon individuals, not just in terms of forgone consumption, but the associated low self-esteem often results in behavioural and physical health problems and family/marital instability. We now consider the composition and interaction of these components.

In an average recession in a developed Western economy GNP will fall below potential by about 5 per cent for two years. In crude terms this is equivalent to around £2000 per family. On average, disposable income will only change by about half this level, as the tax and benefit system initially absorbs some of this change. Concentrating on the output losses of increased unemployment since 1979, Matthews and Minford (1987) estimate annual losses of only about £5bn. or just over 1 per cent of British GDP in 1986. Such a low figure is produced by unemployment being concentrated among low-productivity workers and offsetting gains in the form of increased leisure and non-market production. The main way in which society shares the cost of unemployment is through the changes in government spending and tax receipts. In 1981 the British Government estimated that every additional 100 000 unemployed cost the exchequer £340m. in lost taxes and increased benefit spending. In fiscal year 1981/82 the full cost of unemployment to the budget, including loss of indirect taxes, may have been as high as £13bn., that was equivalent to over 6 per cent of GDP (Knight 1987).

For individuals the pecuniary costs of unemployment will be dependent upon the income lost, offset by the receipt of unemployment benefits and increases in leisure and search time. These costs will rise with the duration of unemployment, since long-term unemployed receive lower benefits, diminishing marginal utility of leisure, and a falling reservation wage, explained in Chapter 5, promises lower lifetime earnings when hired. Estimates of income loss of unemployed workers for 1980 in the UK suggest that single workers lost about a third, while married persons with a large family lost less than a fifth of expected income in work (Dilnot and Morris 1983). In addition, adverse selection and firm-specific human capital investments will cause many unemployed workers to suffer downwards occupational mobility on re-employment.

The above calculations of the exchequer and individual costs of unemployment are poor proxies for the total costs to society of unemployment. The earlier estimates ignore the external costs of unemployment upon employed workers' productivity: high unemployment reduces on-the-job search (Adnett 1986) and depresses reservation wages, both causing workers to tolerate jobs which underutilise their abilities. In addition, crime levels, sickness and social disruptions all appear to be positively related to the level of unemployment, though the magnitude and direction of causation have been difficult to establish. In Allen *et al.* (1986) there are several studies of the impact of unemployment and Smith (1987) reports survey evidence which suggests that unemployed men are twice as likely to commit suicide and suggests overall that unemployment at the level of the mid-1980s was responsible for killing 3000 persons per annum in the UK. Such claims need to be assessed with caution since careful studies of the relationship between unemployment and physical sickness find no association once the influence of skill levels was removed (Narendranathan, Nickell and Stern 1982). Finally, as was argued above, labour cannot be stored; an unemployed worker can never regain his lost output, and preventing a worker from working may also reduce his future productivity. Human capital will depreciate with unemployment, and among the long-term unemployed cognitive and even social skills will be lost when not exercised.

The importance of unemployment is dependent upon the costs which it imposes on society. The arguments above suggest that these costs are often large, and will tend to increase with the level and duration of unemployment in the economy. Evidence in the next section suggests that unemployment is highly concentrated among certain groups, accordingly the bulk of these costs are borne by a relatively small proportion of the total population. In a democracy because unemployment costs are borne by a minority the political tolerance of unemployment may be high. However, efficiency and equity objectives may require governments to pursue policies which aim to alter the distribution, as well as the level, of unemployment.

7.1.3 The behaviour and composition of unemployment

There have been dramatic movements in the level of unemployment this century. In the UK, unemployment rates averaged 4.4 per cent between 1851 and 1920; 14 per cent 1921–40; 1.5 per cent 1941–70; 4 per cent 1971–80 and 11.2 per cent in the first half of this decade. Unemployment trends are strongly correlated internationally; this is illustrated in Table 7.1 where unemployment definitions have been standardised by the OECD. Even given the international differences in labour market adjustments identified in Chapter 3 recent movements have been similar. Since 1979 the UK has moved from a low- to a high-unemployment economy.

Table 7.1   Standardised unemployment rates in major OECD countries (per cent of total labour force)

	1970	1975	1980	1985	1986	1987*
USA	4.8	8.3	7.0	7.1	6.9	5.9
Japan	1.1	1.9	2.0	2.6	2.8	2.8
West Germany	0.8	3.6	3.0	7.2	7.0	7.0
France	2.4	4.0	6.3	10.2	10.4	10.8
UK	3.0	4.3	6.4	11.2	11.1	9.8
Italy	5.3	5.8	7.5	10.5	10.5†	—
Canada	5.6	6.9	7.4	10.4	9.5	8.8
Major seven OECD countries	3.2	5.4	5.6	7.6	7.1‡	—
EEC average	2.6	4.4	6.5	12.0	11.0‡	—

Source: QECD Quarterly Labour Force Statistics, 1987 Number 4
* Figures are for third quarter.
† Figures are for July 1986.
‡ Figures are for October 1986.

The increase in unemployment has been especially marked in the EEC, with Scandinavia and Japan having lower rates and smaller increases. Comparison with growth in the size of the labour force suggests that there is no strong international or historical relationship between the two series. Of particular interest for the UK is the cause of the dramatic increase in registered unemployment at the end of the 1970s. Unemployment trebled in three years and remained on that much higher plateau till 1986.

Some initial understanding of the underlying causes can be gauged if we move away from stock measures of unemployment. The identity which links the stock of unemployment to the underlying flows is:

$$\text{Change in the stock of unemployment} \equiv \text{inflow} - \text{outflow}$$

The unemployed are not an unchanging group of individuals; in the mid-1980s each month about 400 000 became unemployed and roughly the same number left the stock of unemployed, not all to employment. Changes in the number of unemployed can therefore be caused by changes in the number becoming unemployed or changes in the numbers leaving unemployment. Alternatively for an assumed constant level of unemployment:

$$\text{Stock of unemployment} = \text{inflow} \times \text{average duration} \\ \text{of unemployment}$$

Thus in February 1988 the UK stock of unemployment was 2 665 500 and the inflow over the previous quarter was 1 018 200 thus:

$$\text{Average duration} = \frac{2\,665\,500}{1\,018\,200} = 2.6 \text{ quarters} = 34 \text{ weeks}$$

Thus if the stock of unemployment had been constant and if all the unemployed had the same completed spell of unemployment, that spell would have been about thirty-four weeks.

If we concentrate upon the rise in unemployment in 1979/80 then surprisingly there was only a modest rise in the inflow to unemployment, of the order of 70 000 per month, largely through increased redundancies (Pissarides 1986). However, outflow did not rise and as a consequence the average duration of unemployment increased, particularly it appears because the shorter spells of unemployment lengthened. This behaviour of unemployment in recent years appears to have been experienced in other developed economies; Gregory (1986) reports a similar increase in duration of unemployment for Australia. It therefore appears that to understand the movement of unemployment in recent years we have to explain why the unemployed did not leave unemployment at the previous rate. Was it because there were insufficient jobs available or did the unemployed become less active in their search activity and more at ease with the state of unemployment? One insight into the failure of outflow to respond to the rise inflow is gained when we note that newly notified vacancies to Jobcentres fell by almost a half at this time. Seven years later the inflow of vacancies had still not reached its 1979 level. This suggests that our later discussion should concentrate on reasons why firms have not hired workers rather than why the unemployed have not sought work or why firms created redundancies.

In September 1987 the median spell of unemployment of those currently unemployed was about forty weeks, over five times the US figure. However, the median figure fails to indicate the very skewed distribution of unemployment in a modern economy; in July 1987 about 1.25 million, that is two-fifths of the total, had been unemployed for over a year. Other Western European countries had similar proportions, though two-thirds of Belgium's unemployed have been jobless for over a year; in contrast this proportion is around a tenth in North America, Scandinavia and Japan. The Department of Employment (1986) provided a detailed analysis of the duration of British unemployment in the mid-1980s. It showed that of those becoming unemployed about a quarter left unemployment within four weeks, yet a fifth were still unemployed a year later. Prospects of leaving unemployment worsen with duration; those unemployed for two years had less than a 40 per cent chance of leaving unemployment in the next year. These long-term unemployed represent a particularly important group. This is because, as suggested above, duration is probably a better measure of the social costs of unemployment, and because the chance of leaving unemployment diminishes with the duration of unemployment. This may reflect both a morale-discouraged worker effect which leads to reduced job search, or alternatively statistical, or erroneous discrimination against the long-term jobless by employers. The rapid increase in the numbers of this group is thus important, as is the suggestion that nearly half of this group who do find employment return speedily to the stock of unemployed.

Considering the composition of the unemployed, we find very different experience among different groups, examined in some detail in Sinclair (1987: Ch. 1). The high concentration of unemployment among the young reflects a chronic tendency to become unemployed, but generally for short spells, while the unemployment among the elderly reflects a low probability of becoming unemployed but a long duration for those that do. The skewed distribution of unemployment experience also reflects the powerful positive effects which the experience of unemployment, and especially the length of that initial spell, has on the probability of future unemployment. The unskilled experience much higher unemployment than skilled workers, largely due to longer duration. Hughes and Hutchinson (1986) report that unskilled males accounted for 6 per cent of the active labour force between 1975 and 1981 but 15 per cent of the typical unemployment cohort and 66 per cent of the long-term unemployed. If we divide the UK from the Wash to the Bristol Channel then the 'south' contains half of the employed but only a third of the unemployed. The traditionally buoyant, but heavily manufacturing, West Midlands by the mid-1980s became the region with the longest median spells of unemployment. We have already discussed the large racial differences in unemployment incidence in Chapter 6.

Unemployment is at present heavily concentrated among certain high-risk groups in the labour market. Increased labour market flexibility of the sort discussed in Chapter 3 suggest that under-employment and intermittent employment are likely to become an increasingly common labour market experience. We now turn to explanations for the level and pattern of unemployment in developed economies.

7.2 An introduction to the development of modern theories of unemployment

A simple division of theories of unemployment will assist our review. Consider Fig. 7.1 which illustrates a labour market initially in equilibrium at a real wage of w^* and employment level of n^*. Let us subject this market to a contractionary shock so that the demand for labour contracts to n^d_1; at every real wage employers wish to hire less labour. If neoclassical economics is right and labour markets

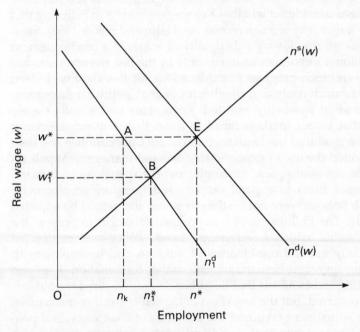

Fig. 7.1 Theories of unemployment

are best described as auction markets, wages rapidly adjust to clear the market and a new equilibrium occurs at B where real wages and employment are lower at w^*_1 and n^*_1. At B, demand matches the supply of labour so the lower employment level need cause no expansion of unemployment; that level still depends on market imperfections which prevent actual employment levels from achieving the equilibrium, n^* or n^*_1. Alternatively, Keynesians start from a presumption that prices are 'sticky' at least in the short run, thus initially quantity has to adjust, hence the market moves to A. Here assuming that quantity is fixed at the short end of the market, employment has contracted to n_k and therefore unemployment has risen by $n^* - n_k$. We now investigate the present form of these alternative views concerning labour market behaviour.

7.2.1 Keynesian theories

Keynes's argument is nowadays usually interpreted as being that wages cannot be relied upon to fall in the face of unemployed workers, and that any movement towards lower wages may not be effective anyway in clearing the labour market. Keynesians have tended to emphasise the 'stickiness' of wages and only recently have economists considered whether Keynes was correct in believing that flexible wages may worsen recessions (Hahn and Solow 1986). Similarly, though the downwards rigidity of wages is a crucial element in traditional Keynesian analysis, only in the last twenty years has there been much progress in explanations for this rigidity. Indeed there was much confusion whether it was the rigidity of real or money wages that was being asserted. Keynesians traditionally merely stated that labour markets failed to clear, that demand deficiency therefore produced inadequate employment opportunities and then championed the use of expansionary demand-management policies to tackle any widespread unemployment. Expansions of demand encouraged firms to expand output, and therefore employment, but such policies were not costless as prices also would be adjusted upwards. The Phillips curve was originally thought to present the policy 'menu' which governments faced. Policy-makers decided the socially optimal combination of inflation and unemployment, adjusting aggregate demand to achieve that combination. Lags and forecasting errors meant that disturbances from desired output levels still occurred, but the weakness of the self-correcting mechanism of price adjustment favoured the adoption of counter-cyclical policies. The recognition that a trade-off existed between the inflation rate and unemployment rate caused the term 'full employment' gradually to disappear from the literature, just as in the neoclassical model there was a range of possible employment levels rather than a unique level which corresponds to the optimal level.

Some economists have queried whether the above emphasis on wage rigidity is appropriate and instead concentrated on another element of Keynes's analysis of unemployment, communication failure (Leijonhufvud 1968). Modern developments of this argument have concentrated upon the idea that trading is more costly in a thin market. The lower the level of activity on one side of the market the higher the search costs on the other side of the market, an argument first developed in Chapter 5. Expectations can be self-fulfilling; expectations of low economic activity discourage people from trading and therefore generate low activity. Howitt and McAfee (1987) provide an example of such a model; their model displays multiple equilibria at different unemployment rates. Both high and low unemployment can result at the same real wage rate, due to these externalities in the search process.

7.2.2 Monetarist critique

Beginning in the late 1950s the neoclassical counter-revolution gradually undermined Keynesian arguments for counter-cyclical fiscal policies. New theories of aggregate consumption expenditure, of crowding out, of the demand for money, the adoption of floating exchange rates, and above all the reinterpretation of the simple Phillips curve, weakened the case for policies aimed at stabilising employment levels. Keynesian economics had become focused upon the manipulation of aggregate demand to the exclusion of other issues, and the failure of these models to explain the emergence of stagflation gave added impetus to the emerging monetarist critique. According to the Phelps–Friedman expectations-augmented Phillips curve, governments could no longer manipulate employment by macroeconomic policies. The tendency of the labour market to clear was now reasserted, but equilibrium was now consistent with a positive, 'natural' level of unemployment. In much of the literature the term 'natural rate' is used interchangeably with the non-accelerating inflation rate of unemployment, or the NAIRU. Although some prefer to use natural rate only in competitive markets, we will make no distinction between the terms. The size of this natural rate was dependent upon the extent of imperfections in the labour market, what previously had been termed frictional and structural unemployment. Thus occupational and locational immobilities, imperfect information, union and government interference could all give rise to unemployed workers and unfilled vacancies, although there was overall balance between the demand and supply of labour in the market.

A diagram of the natural rate of unemployment is illustrated in Fig. 7.2. The demand side of the labour market is now defined to exclude vacancies and we distinguish between the total supply of labour, n^t, and the amount of workers willing to accept offered jobs, n^e. At w^* the number of workers willing to accept offered jobs equals existing employment and the number of existing vacancies does not induce any change in the real wage to alter the flow of applications. The difference between n_1 and n^* measures the difference between the total supply of labour and the amount of employment offered and accepted and hence represents the natural rate of unemployment. Factors which cause the total labour supply to diverge from the number of workers willing to accept offered jobs causes the natural rate of unemployment to increase. Thus increased mismatch

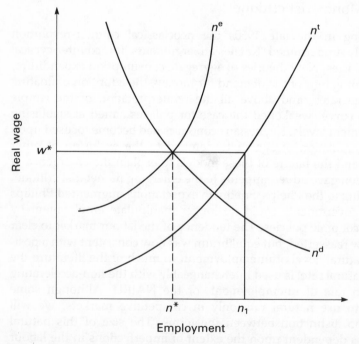

Fig. 7.2 The natural rate of unemployment

shifts the n^e curve to the left and increases the natural rate since vacancies and searching workers are becoming less compatible.

An alternative approach which we concentrate upon later has been to view this NAIRU as that level of unemployment necessary to make the target real wage rate of workers and target mark-up of firms consistent with the production capabilities of the economy. If there is insufficient unemployment target wages will exceed feasible levels and inflation will result.

The term 'natural rate of unemployment' does not imply an optimal level of unemployment in the economy, since in part it reflects avoidable inefficiencies. However, attempts by government to reduce unemployment below this natural rate by expansionary macro policies would cause excess demand. If we assume that decision-makers form expectations adaptively, that is current forecasts are based upon previous forecasts revised by a fraction of the forecasting error, then excess demand will lead to unexpected increases in wage and price inflation. In the short run workers are 'fooled' into supplying more labour and less search and leisure, hence unemployment falls. As the expectations of decision-makers would eventually be revised in the light of current inflationary experience, persistence with expansionary policies would cause a continual rise in the rate of inflation. The 'accelerationist' hypothesis thus suggests that only in the short run, while expectations are unadjusted, is there a trade-off between unemployment and the rate of inflation. In the case of expansionary policies, workers and employers are 'fooled' into a temporary increase in employment above the desired level by misperceptions of the real wage. However, this deviation is only a short-run experience, and as no government could contemplate a continuous acceleration in the rate of inflation, unemployment could not be permanently reduced below the natural rate. In cases of deflationary policies or shocks, employed and unemployed workers are fooled into rejecting employers' wage offers and the inflow to, and duration of, unemployment temporarily increase. According to this approach, to reduce unemployment permanently the labour market had to be made more competitive and hence, microeconomic policies were required to lower the natural rate.

7.2.3 New classical theory

A major weakness of the above approach is that decision-makers can be repeatedly fooled in the short run, reflecting the way expectations are formed in the model. The new classical approach is to maintain the market-clearing assumptions of the Friedman–Phelps approach and to assume that expectations are formed rationally; Lucas (1981) and Lucas and Sargent (1981) contain many of the major contributions of this school. In such a model anticipated changes in fiscal and monetary policy can have no impact on real variables since decision-makers merely revise their expectations of the future price level. Systematic macroeconomic policy is now impotent with respect to the level of unemployment; no trade-off between unemployment and inflation exists even in the short run. In the long run, and when expectations are correct in the short run, unemployment will be at the natural rate. If the natural rate does not change much through time, the actual rate of unemployment in the economy will tend to move randomly around it, reflecting unexpected shocks which cause expectational errors and hence deviations from the natural rate. New classical economics thus produces the final eclipse of Keynesian policy prescriptions, and attempts to reduce unemployment by expanding aggregate demand merely cause rapid upwards adjustments of prices. The reasons for this conclusion lie not in the adoption of rational expectations *per se*, but in combining rational expectations with flexible wages and prices. The key issue thus remains the same as in the debates of fifty years ago: are labour markets best described as price or quantity adjusting in the short run?

Before we discuss the current state of that debate we need briefly to consider some of the developing critique of new classical theories of unemployment. Unemployment does not appear to move randomly over time as predicted by the simple model above. Some new classicists have argued that the natural rate moves cyclically, explaining the cyclical movement of the actual rate of unemployment as reflecting lagged adjustment to surprises. Problems remain with the causes of these persistent, yet unpredictable, shocks and whether the expectational errors are sufficient to cause the large observed movements around the natural rate of unemployment. Once again it is the microeconomics of price- and wage-fixing which remains unclear in this approach.

7.2.4 The present state of theories of unemployment

Since the mid-1970s both Keynesians and neoclassical economists have belatedly turned their attention to the issue of how markets adjust to demand fluctuations. The essential divide is still between neoclassical economists who largely see high unemployment as reflecting a high natural rate, and Keynesians who see it as reflecting the consequence of a contraction in aggregate demand, causing a long-term deviation from the natural rate. Traditionally the division has also been interpreted as reflecting Keynesian stress on involuntary unemployment and neoclassical on voluntary unemployment, Keynesians believing that workers are supply constrained in the labour market, while in some versions of the neoclassical approach unemployment is either efficient off-the-job search (discussed in Ch. 5) or a rational response to low labour market productivity and relatively high unemployment insurance benefits (discussed in Ch. 8). Thus Lucas writes, 'To explain why people allocate time to ... unemployment we need to know why they prefer it to all other activities' (1986: 38). The distinction between voluntary and involuntary unemployment has always been problematic since definitions differ. Redundant teachers could deliver newspapers, if they choose not to when such jobs are available are they voluntarily or involuntarily unemployed? In more recent models any distinction breaks down as, say, workers in aggregate may prefer unemployment as a response to demand reductions, but the specific individuals who actually lose their jobs do so unwillingly. Wage rigidity may directly influence the natural rate of unemployment if it is the unemployed, rather than firms and employed workers, who exhibit a reluctance to adjust their reservation wage levels when market conditions weaken. Initially we consider recent evidence of wage rigidity, and discuss explanations for that rigidity which emphasise firm and employee behaviour.

7.2.5 Evidence of wage rigidity

The debate about the degree of flexibility of wages in the economy is not directly about the variability of wages, but about how responsive wages are to disequilibrium pressures in the labour market. In other words, the key question concerns how effective wages are in clearing the labour market rather than how stable they are. To illustrate, a country with a high inflation rate will tend to have a greater variability of money wages than a low inflation country, but this tells us nothing about the comparative labour market adjustment processes in the two countries. Flexibility is a much more elusive concept than variability, as it formally requires disequilibrium labour market forces to be modelled, and such work is in its infancy (see for example, Beckerman and Jenkinson 1986). As mentioned in

Chapter 3, the UK does appear to require relatively large changes in employment to absorb shocks; Coe (1985) measured short- and long-run real wage rigidities from estimated wage equations. For the UK a total rise in the unemployment rate of about 6 per cent was required to offset a real shock which would otherwise cause a 1 per cent rise in inflation. Estimates for other major Western economies were lower, down to less than a 0.3 per cent rise in Japan. An alternative approach is to examine how real wages behaved in the middle of the 1980s when one in seven of the British workforce were unemployed. As revealed below, most recent British studies indicate a low elasticity of real wages with respect to unemployment and at the aggregate level real earnings grew throughout the period of the recent growth of unemployment, though real wages fell slightly till 1982. Oswald (1986a), using disaggregated data for relatively unskilled and poorly paid jobs, supposedly the most competitive markets, found relatively little real wage flexibility, even in the secondary labour market. Robinson (1987) in his disaggregated study found greater evidence of flexibility, a third of the surveyed occupational groups having lower real wages in 1984 than in 1979. This general failure of British real wages to decline in the early 1980s was reproduced in West Germany and France, though in the USA as indicated in Chapter 3 it is nominal, not real wages which appear to be rigid.

7.3 Deviations from the natural rate of unemployment: theories of wage rigidity

In traditional analyses of competitive labour markets any change in market conditions produces a speedy adjustment of wage levels ensuring that labour demand and supply are balanced, and unemployment is only a temporary disequilibrium phenomenon. Currently explanations of why firms and/or workers prefer to adjust to contractions of demand for output by reducing employment rather than wages is something of a growth industry. This growth of theoretical work on wage rigidity in the 1970s can be attributed to several convergent forces. The development of the structuralist approach and observations that contemporary employment spells were much longer than previously assumed, stimulated interest in how strongly attached workers and firms would adjust to temporary changes in demand. The disappearance of a strong negative relationship between inflation and unemployment, and the development of expectations-based models of inflation also aroused interest in the origins of long-term contracts between workers and firms, and the influence of unions in the form of those contracts. Above all, as discussed above, the reluctance of inflation to fall in many Western economies at the end of the 1970s at a time of historically high levels of unemployment, required investigation. Either the natural rate of unemployment was increasing over time, or the labour market was not adjusting to that natural rate. Several excellent surveys of theories of wage rigidity exist (Lindbeck and Snower 1985; Stiglitz 1986; Mitchell 1986) to which readers are referred for more details; we have already discussed many of the arguments briefly in Chapter 2. The different approaches are not mutually exclusive, and the allocation of particular arguments among the following headings is to an extent arbitrary.

7.3.1 Staggered contracts

One way of producing wage stickiness if not rigidity is to assume that the wage contracts are for a finite period of time and renewal dates of these contracts are staggered. Even with rational expectations, when aggregate demand contracts wage adjustments must also be staggered, since contracts prevent adjustment until renewal. Indeed when contracts do come up for renewal it will be in the interests of parties to make only partial adjustment since they can take advantage of groups whose renewal dates are later and who are trapped into higher wages. Non-synchronisation of contracts can therefore lead to a long drawn out adjustment of wages to lower levels of aggregate demand; such a model was developed by Taylor (1979).

7.3.2 Implicit contract theories

Surprisingly one of the first attempts to explain wage rigidity originated within the market-clearing tradition; implicit contract theory was developed originally to explain the high incidence of temporary lay-offs in the American economy. The implicit contract literature has been surveyed by Rosen (1985), the basic hypothesis being that workers are more risk averse than firms. Given that workers also have less access to capital and information markets and that long-term job tenure is desired by both sides of the market, firms are encouraged to provide some form of wage and employment insurance for their employees. Profit-maximising firms will have no incentive to reduce real wages when demand for their output falls, as to do so would cause too much income fluctuation for their workers. The problem with this approach is that lay-offs may also cause income fluctuations, and hence implicit contracts need not specify lay-offs as the agreed response to product market contractions. To generate temporary lay-offs as efficient practices for firms we need to postulate a system of unemployment compensation which supports the income of laid-off workers, or high search costs for laid-off workers which prevent their seeking alternative employments. Differences in attitudes to risk-taking between workers and firms do not appear sufficient by themselves to explain wage rigidity.

7.3.3 Efficiency wage arguments

An alternative approach to wage inflexibility is to build upon models of internal labour markets which emphasise the employers' need to ensure that workers supply acceptable levels of effort for agreed wages. Such models reject the neoclassical theory which views production as determined by a purely technical relationship between inputs and outputs. Akerlof and Yellen (1986) bring together a collection of recent papers developing this approach. Employers' pay and employment policies must generate incentive effects and penalise employee 'shirking'; the actual productivity of workers becomes a function of the wage paid. Firms may now be reluctant to lower wages in the face of excess supply of labour because productivity may fall even faster, raising labour costs per unit of output. A feature of such models is that they can explain why high unemployment, inflation and productivity growth can coexist and may thus be particularly relevant to recent Western experience.

The earliest versions of this positive relation between productivity and wages can be found in Marx, where because the industrial reserve army (the unemployed) acted as a discipline device, firms had an incentive to fix wages at a level which produces an excess supply of labour. Later economists emphasised improved nutrition as the cause of this positive relationship; more recently costly turnover and a negative relation between wage levels and voluntary separations have been advanced (Stiglitz 1987). Alternatively, where firms cannot easily distinguish the employability of applicants, or where they cannot for legal or sociological reasons differentiate wages between individual employees, they may adopt a high-wage strategy. The presumption is that the quality of applicants depends upon the wage offered, a higher wage produces a higher-quality workforce. Still another version develops Marx's argument by stressing the high costs of monitoring workers. Discipline in the firm requires that workers are rewarded for 'good behaviour', and penalised for shirking. By paying workers above alternative employments, firms encourage workers to protect their 'rents' by adopting acceptable patterns of behaviour. It is not clear that these theories always produce wage rigidity rather than payment by seniority; linking relative nominal wages to tenure would be equally efficient in many of these models. Akerlof (1982) argued that actual productivity depends upon workers being convinced that employers are treating them fairly; money wage cuts represent unfair behaviour and are therefore avoided. This efficiency wage approach is very close to the next group discussed, insider–outsider models of wage rigidity; the two approaches are evaluated in Lindbeck and Snower (1987).

7.3.4 Insider–outsider models

Both the efficiency wage and insider–outsider approaches argue that wage reductions need not lower total unit labour costs. While efficiency wage theories are built upon the assumption of firms' imperfect information of employees' productivity, a competing theory starts from existing employees having market power due to costly turnover. These insider–outsider models can also explain the persistence of unemployment; unemployed workers cannot in reality price themselves into jobs by undercutting present employees. Such models are in essence models of structured internal labour markets, though their origins lie in Okun's work (1981) in which turnover costs are a source of wage rigidity in internal or career labour markets. Given search, screening, negotiation and training costs, firms have an incentive to make a long-term relationship attractive to employees. Thus insider wages paid to current employees exceed the level of competitive or outsider wage rates. The workers in the external labour market cannot undercut the 'monopoly wages' of insiders, because of these productivity differences and non-wage costs. Hence the unemployed cannot price themselves into jobs as lower wages do not lower unit labour costs and unemployment persists. Neither firms nor currently employed workers need have any incentive to change their behaviour. Existing employees prefer higher wages to providing job opportunities for outsiders, the employment of which may in the long run reduce their rents. The presence of unions will tend to lead to a greater exploitation of employees' bargaining power and may further increase the stock of unemployment (Lindbeck and Snower 1986).

7.3.5 Union behaviour

The analysis discussed so far cannot explain why explicit contracts between firms and unions traditionally specify wage rigidity and allow employers to choose employment levels unilaterally. The mutual interest in, and acceptance of, redundancy or lay-offs by reverse seniority (last in first out, hence LIFO), means that senior workers need not fear displacement, except in the case of complete plant or firm closure. While flexible wages may help the job security of junior employees, they represent unwanted income fluctuations for senior ones. Where union decision-making reflects the interests and votes of senior or median members, they will favour downwards wage rigidity. Alternatively if laid-off workers leave unions, or members are risk neutral and the low probability of unemployment is offset by the higher rewards from work, downwards wage rigidity will still be specified in collectively bargained contracts. Given that unions and employers anticipate a long-term bargaining relationship, and that strikes are expensive for both sides, optimal bargaining strategies may favour wage rigidity. In summary this approach suggests that flexible wages are absent from collectively bargained agreements because unions do not wish them.

7.3.6 Summary

Models exist which combine the various causes discussed above. In McDonald and Solow's version (1985) a secondary labour market is added to a unionised primary sector. Now unemployment consists in part of workers laid off from the quantity-adjusting primary sector, who are unwilling to consider a 'bad' job in the secondary labour market in the interval before rehire. In addition the slow adjustment of wages in the secondary sector causes frictional unemployment; in equilibrium there will also be a group of workers queueing for 'good' jobs to become available in the primary sector. Bulow and Summers (1986) develop a similar model though with an efficiency wage bias. Such models are consistent with US evidence that the wage differentials between primary and secondary sectors widens in weak markets and that aggregate employment is more flexible in the primary sector. Oswald (1986a) cites psychological studies to support his propositions that workers gain utility dependent upon the gap between aspired and achieved wage, where the latter adjusts to past achievements and experiences. Since utility losses from achieving below aspiration also appear to exceed utility gains from a similar excess over aspiration, workers may be very resistant to wage reductions. If workers therefore have kinked utility functions with respect to wage offers a wide range of theories of wage determination can produce downwards wage rigidity. The above modern theories of wage rigidity can explain many of the previously puzzling features of unemployment in Western economies: unemployed workers cannot price themselves into internal labour markets; existing employees will not in aggregate accept lower wages in preference to lay-offs; work-sharing is not a viable alternative given that once again this would imply senior workers subsidising junior ones.

Most of the above models suggest that downturns in aggregate demand will produce increases in unemployment above the natural rate, as firms initially adjust employment rather than wages. However, the policy implications of unemployment deviating from the natural rate for considerable periods of time remain unclear. The response of wages to fluctuations in demand is asymmetrical. While wages are slow to fall as demand contracts, the above models generally suggest that firms, employees and unions all favour price adjustments to expansions of demand. Any expansionary policies implemented by governments to reduce unemployment will thus risk stimulating inflation, which will be compounded by adjustment of expectations. Hence the interest of many economists who have developed the above models in combining expansionary policies with anti-inflationary policies, or designing expansionary packages which minimise inflationary consequences. We return to a consideration of these policy implications after we have examined the modern neoclassical explanation of unemployment.

7.4 Determinants of the natural rate of unemployment

For those economists who reject wage rigidity as all but a very temporary phenomenon in the labour market, unemployment is always adjusting speedily to the natural rate. Hence any increase in unemployment sustained over time must indicate an increase in the natural rate of unemployment. In principle in an imperfectly competitive world the NAIRU can increase either because the feasible real wage which the economy can sustain has fallen or wage-fixers' target wage has risen relative to that feasible wage. The actual level of the equilibrium rate of unemployment thus depends partly on frictions in the operation of competitive markets. Imperfect information, as we discussed in Chapter 5, leads to rational unemployed workers and labour-constrained firms searching the labour market. Unemployment and unfilled vacancies in part reflect productive search by decision-makers. Heterogeneity of workers and jobs add to informational imperfections and also reduce the mobility of labour between occupational and industrial sub-markets. Thus mismatches between the characteristics of unemployed workers and requirements of unfilled vacancies will lead to persisting unemployment. Technical progress which alters the required characteristics of workers, changes in the pattern of national and international demand, and the imperfections and lags in the educational and training markets discussed in Chapter 4, can all generate increases in the natural rate of unemployment. Locational immobility of both workers and jobs discussed in Chapter 5 will also lead to unmatched workers and firms even where there is overall balance in the labour market. Here the geographical distribution of social capital, non-economic dimensions to locational decision-making and other relocation costs generate equilibrium unemployment.

Few economists have argued that recent changes in the natural rate have been predominantly generated by reductions in the economy's feasible wage. In principle there are several factors which could have produced such changes. The two oil shocks in the 1970s reduced Western economies' feasible real wages as purchasing power was reallocated to the oil-exporting countries. The partly associated widespread slow-down in productivity growth in the 1970s also reduced the feasible growth of real wages in Western societies. However, both of these factors are more relevant to explaining unemployment in the 1970s than to more recent experience. Economists accepting this view of the labour market have therefore concentrated on factors which could have raised the target real wage in society. Three major sources of such changes in the natural rate of unemployment have been emphasised: trade unions; income taxes and social insurance; and government wage and job security legislation.

7.4.1 Trade unions

Trade unions, by interfering in the operation of market forces, will distort market outcomes, directly they increase the natural rate of unemployment by reducing inter-firm and inter-occupational labour mobility. Closed shops and union-sustained skill demarcations not only cause inefficiency, but by increasing the segmentation of the labour market they increase the extent of mismatch. Inter-union disputes may further limit mobility and also contribute to an increase in the unemployment rate. Indirectly unions may also contribute to a higher natural rate by the upwards pressure they place on wage rates. Possible reasons for unions preferring wage increases to employment increases have already been discussed above and models of union behaviour are developed further in Chapter 8. Given a downward-sloping demand curve for unionised labour, any increase in wages which unions obtain for their members above the competitive level must reduce employment opportunities. In a fully unionised economy the size of the union mark-up, the excess over competitive wage rates, must have a negative relation to the employment levels. However, no Western economy is fully unionised, and to sustain this argument it is necessary to explain why unionised firms with higher wages are not priced out of markets by non-unionised firms. Imperfectly competitive product markets may be one cause, but some economists such as Minford *et al.* (1983) combine the impact of unions with that of the operation of unemployment insurance schemes. Workers displaced from unionised markets as the mark-up increases, do not put downwards pressure on wages in non-organised sectors because unemployment and social security benefit levels dissuade unemployed workers from pricing themselves back into jobs. This is to argue that while unions have shifted the demand curve for labour to the left, the development of unemployment insurance and social security systems have also shifted the supply curve of labour upwards. This latter possibility is now examined.

7.4.2 The replacement ratio and voluntary unemployment

To analyse the possible disincentive effects of income taxes, social insurance and transfer payments we have to return to the concept of the reservation wage, developed in Chapter 5, and relate it to the replacement ratio of an individual worker. The total benefit entitlement of a worker (or family) out of work, compared to total net income in work, is termed the replacement ratio. The replacement ratio may be high for a particular worker because the social security payments are high in comparison to available labour market earnings or because tax and National Insurance contributions are high at low wage levels. A high replacement ratio may produce a moral hazard, by inducing workers to reduce search intensity and raise their reservation wage so that low wage offers are rejected. The consequences of such widespread behaviour, which reduces effective labour supply, must be to increase wages and reduce employment at the bottom end of the market. Redundancy payments may also contribute to higher unemployment by extending the duration and reducing the intensity of search of recipients. As individual workers face replacement ratios dependent upon their potential net labour market earnings and entitlement to benefits, it follows that if jobs are rationed in the labour market the replacement ratio will affect the distribution of unemployment, rather than the level. The stock of unemployed workers will in this case contain a disproportionate number of workers with high replacement ratios.

Where wage offers are high and the tax and insurance system progressive, replacement ratios will tend to be low and have little impact upon unemployment. Thus given conventional assumptions of worker motivation of utility maximisation, it is the level of benefits relative to labour market wages together with the marginal utility of increased leisure and non-market work which are critical to supply decisions, not the absolute level of those benefits. Hence a recession that lowers the relative wage of unskilled workers also raises their replacement ratios. 'Poverty traps' can occur when loss of means-tested benefits create marginal implicit tax rates on labour market income of over 100 per cent, hence eliminating short-run financial incentives to supply more labour. Similarly, an 'unemployment trap' causes an unemployed, unskilled worker to face a marginal implicit tax of over 100 per cent on supplying any labour. Where the payment of some benefits is linked to active search for employment, then the extent to which disqualification from benefits is likely will also influence the natural rate of unemployment. As we shall see, it is difficult to find a single appropriate measure of the replacement ratio and given that the size of the ratio will also influence the proportion of the unemployed who claim benefits, we again face problems concerning the definition and measurement of unemployment. The contributions which employers make to the national system of insurance will also influence employment levels. Such contributions represent a tax on employment and therefore alter desired factor ratios and levels of output. In the USA unlike the UK the possibility that employers may also face a moral hazard is recognised and insurance contributions are experience weighted: the more frequently workers are laid off the higher the firm's contributions.

7.4.3 Wage controls and employment protection legislation

It may not be just the benefit/income ratio which has set too high a floor to wage levels. Governments who set, directly or indirectly, minimum wage levels may be preventing wages from clearing the market and hence contributing to the NAIRU. In the UK such policies took the form of the Fair Wages Resolution, which required government contractors to pay minimum prevailing wages to employees; extended to all employers in 1975, it was repealed in 1980. In addition, in the mid-1980s there were twenty-six Wages Councils which laid down minimum rates of pay and conditions of work for about 2.75 million employees. Of these about 80 per cent were female, two-thirds were part-time and the Councils covered 20 per cent of all employees under eighteen years of age. Wages Councils effectively set minimum wages for a large group of lowly paid workers, though in recent years up to half of these workers have been covered by a union collective agreement. There is some dispute concerning how widespread has been non-compliance (Mayhew 1985) and whether the Wages Councils have actually raised wage rates above competitive levels. Unless reform of the tax and benefit system is combined with policies to abolish government wage-fixing, the effect of any lowering of wages will be to raise the replacement ratio for workers in these sectors of the economy.

In many Western countries the biggest influence that the government has upon wage levels is as an employer in its own right. If public sector wage levels influence levels in the private sector, then government constraints on its employees' wages may lower the NAIRU. However, there will also be microeconomic consequences of such policies; if the relative pay of public sector workers falls then the quality of public sector employees and hence of output may diminish.

The natural rate of unemployment may also be increased by employment protection and health and safety legislation which imposes higher fixed labour costs on employers. The former may alter the desired division of labour input between number of workers and hours per worker. If firms are reluctant to hire new workers because of higher firing costs then although their total labour input may not change, an increase in hours worked per worker may cause measured unemployment to rise. Firms will also be less willing to fire workers as they may be required to make redundancy payments. The net effect on measured unemployment is therefore not clear; the regulations will tend to reduce inflow into unemployment while also reducing the outflow back into jobs. The impact of the measures on labour market efficiency is equally unclear. Redundant workers incur losses due to depreciation of firm-specific human capital, their resulting search represents another private and social cost. If the labour market does not internalise these private and social costs of making workers redundant then targeted redundancy payments schemes may be efficient (Hamermesh 1987). The significance of the 1972 Act, which gave workers a right to claim unfair dismissal after tenure qualification, remains a debated issue to which we return below.

7.5 Towards an assessment: accounting for the rise in British unemployment

We have now discussed the major determinants of the natural rate of unemployment and it is time to review all current theories of unemployment. At the extremes we get some striking differences in explanation. Thus according to some versions of the efficiency wage arguments since employers proxy quality by the reservation wage of applicants, workers can remain unemployed because their reservation wages are too low. In practice Keynesian and neoclassical approaches to the determination of unemployment are not mutually exclusive. A period of persisting high unemployment may reflect both unemployment above the natural rate and an increase in that rate over time. While some Keynesians are uncomfortable with the concept of a unique equilibrium level of unemployment, most are prepared to accept that competitive forces work in the long run. Similarly many neoclassical economists acknowledge that deviations from the natural rate can persist for significant periods of time. The key question is therefore to identify the quantitative importance of the various influences at any moment of time. The latter qualification is important as the relative importance will be likely to change over time and over the cycle. This empirical debate is very intense at present, and any survey of contemporary opinion is hazardous. Initially we concentrate upon British experience, particularly on the causes of the rapid expansion of unemployment in 1979–81 and the persistence of a high level in the 1980s.

7.5.1 The competing stories

The rise in British unemployment beginning in 1979 is usually attributed to a combination of disinflationary macroeconomic policies, adverse shocks and increasingly inefficient labour and product markets. Economists differ over the relative importance to be attached to each of these factors, though there is general agreement that some explanations popular with non-specialists are unimportant. The belief that the electronic technical revolution has displaced significant numbers of workers ignores the job-creating influence of new techniques and products which historically always dominate in the long run. The slow-down of labour productivity growth discussed earlier makes the technological unemployment argument untenable, if output per person has been growing less rapidly then employment cannot be falling in relation to output. Similarly to explain higher unemployment in terms of labour force growth is to ignore the historical fact that employment and labour force grow together. The growth of foreign competition in manu-factured goods has also been suggested as a major culprit. While increased import penetration may affect the composition of the labour force it has no obvious impact on the level of unemployment, especially when the British trade balance was in surplus for most of this period. Increased occupational and geographical mismatch in the labour market is a further factor which has been suggested to explain increasing unemployment. Jackman and Roper (1987) find that although the above factors caused an increase in structural imbalance in 1979–81, there was no evidence that mismatch was growing in the UK in the 1970s and early 1980s, indicating that reduced mobility and structural change were not significant contri-butions to rising unemployment. Finally, the argument that capital shortages prevent sufficient employment opportunities ignores the importance of the service sector in employment growth and the sensitivity of capital formation to demand pressures. We are left with two competing approaches, broadly representing the Keynesian and neoclassical perspectives.

A broadly Keynesian interpretation would be as follows.

Monetary policy in the late 1970s and early 1980s was much tighter than the behaviour of the monetary aggregates indicated. Fiscal policy was also restrictive, with public capital formation significantly lower and some resulting job losses in the public sector (Hadjimatheou 1986). After adjusting for the impact of inflation on debt charges and for cyclical influences, the structural or full employment budget moved into substantial surplus (Miller 1985). The combined effects of these policies together with the impact of the international recession was to restrict consumption expenditure and raise real interest rates. This depressed the capital goods sector of the economy. The higher real interest rates together with the continuing impact of North Sea Oil exploitation caused sterling to appreciate against other currencies. This intensified the recession in the export and import-substitutes industries, and given the rigidity of wages the impact was largely upon employment levels. Hence the 17 per cent fall in manufacturing production and the halving of the profit rate in 1980. Indeed the fall in manufacturing employment of 2.4 million between 1974 and 1983 almost exactly mirrors the rise in unemployment over this period. According to this story unemployment rose more rapidly in the UK than elsewhere because tighter demand-management policies, greater shocks, and the greater rigidity of real wages all increased the need for employment adjustment. The last cause particularly reflects the nature of wage bargaining in the UK which is biased towards wage push, an argument fully developed in Chapter 8.

The above Keynesian interpretation can explain the rise in unemployment, but its weakness is in explaining the persistence of unemployment at the higher levels till 1987. An alternative and broadly neoclassical interpretation would be to stress the factors causing the NAIRU to increase during this period. All the recent attempts to estimate the NAIRU for the UK suggest an upward trend over the last twenty years. Layard and Nickell's (1985a) paper suggested that the NAIRU for male workers was around 2 per cent between 1955 and 1966, and then doubled by 1967–74 and doubled again between 1975 and 1979. From that level of around 7.8 per cent the NAIRU again rose to 10.7 by 1980–83. Davies's (1985) summary of three recent studies suggests a rise of around 2–4 per cent between the late 1970s and the mid-1980s, that is about half the actual rise in unemployment. Some neoclassical economists would argue that the slow downwards adjustment of wage settlements during this period indicates that unemployment must have been close to the NAIRU level and hence these studies underestimate its rise in recent years. Greater mismatch between workers and jobs may have been the cause of this rise, perhaps due to changes in the relative price of energy or growth of the service sector. Additionally the unemployed may have become less available for work, due to higher replacement ratios, reduced pressure from benefit offices on recipients to find work, or a general reduction in the work ethic. The Thatcher Government's tight monetary and fiscal policy together with external shocks did reduce inflation after 1980 by raising unemployment above the rising NAIRU. As the Thatcher Government changed target and introduced tighter controls on unions, deregulated markets and reduced implicit tax rates, the NAIRU began to fall; according to Matthews and Minford (1987) it fell from 3.7 million in 1981 to 1.6 million in 1985.

The problem with this interpretation is that many forces appeared to be reducing the NAIRU before 1982 and the movement of inflation appears difficult to reconcile with that of unemployment. Since 1979 earnings-related unemployment benefits have been abolished, employers' National Insurance contributions have fallen and trade union power has fallen. Some economists, trying to interpret the same experience, question whether viewing the NAIRU as independent of the level of demand, or composition of the unemployed, is appropriate. Solow (1986) quotes studies of the natural rate in the early 1980s which suggested that the NAIRU was 2.4 per cent in Austria and 8.0 per cent in West Germany, with it having risen from 1.6 per cent over the last ten years in the latter country. Solow queries such large differences over time and between apparently similar countries. Additional concern with the monetarist interpretation stems from the rapid growth of British wages in the 1980s despite high unemployment apparently in excess of the estimated NAIRU. Given that the fundamental prediction of NAIRU models is that unemployment in excess of this level reduces the rate of wage inflation, doubts have grown over whether a unique well-defined NAIRU exists for the UK. Matthews and Minford (1987) respond to these doubts by arguing that real wages respond only slowly to unemployment in excess of the NAIRU, an argument which Keynesian economists had previously championed.

The striking coincidence that estimates of the natural rate have moved up with the actual rate of unemployment, suggests some form of 'hysteresis' and Cross (1983) provides a good introduction to this important topic. Pure hysteresis means that the current value of a variable depends upon history, the variable having no tendency to move towards any particular level. The behaviour of the NAIRU may reflect a causal influence from current and past levels of unemployment to the current NAIRU, perhaps because insiders not outsiders determine wage levels. Jenkinson (1987) investigates several possibilities for this influence and particularly important in this context appears to be the behaviour of the long-term unemployed. The long-term unemployed become discouraged, causing a reduced intensity of search, their loss of skills make them less attractive to employers and they therefore have little downward impact on wage pressure. The NAIRU will increase as the proportion of long-term unemployed rises; support for this proposition has come from a wide range of models (Layard and Nickell 1986; Budd, Levine and Smith 1987; Hall and Henry 1987). Higher unemployment may also reduce labour market efficiency as on-the-job search is reduced and this results in lower labour market mobility among employed workers and increases mismatch. Whether there is a unique NAIRU is a much debated issue with both Pissarides (1986) and Carruth and Oswald (1986) rejecting the proposition of multiple equilibria.

7.5.2 The Layard and Nickell model

Any empirical investigation of the post-1979 unemployment experience must allow both Keynesian and neoclassical mechanisms to operate. A good example is Layard and Nickell (1986, 1987) where the economy is characterised by imperfect competition, firms' mark-up on costs reflects demand conditions and workers strive to raise their real wage. In this sort of model the NAIRU is where the 'feasible' real wage implied by the pricing behaviour of firms equates the 'target' real wage implied by the behaviour of wage-bargainers. As firms' mark-up on wages rises with output and employment is positively related to output, it follows that the real wage falls as employment rises; this is the price-setting curve shown in Fig. 7.3. The positively sloped wage-setting curve derives from the argument that wages are a mark-up on expected prices and that this mark-up increases with employment.

In this type of model any increase in wage-push pressure shifts the wage-setting curve leftwards and real demand has to be reduced to stabilise inflation, the new equilibrium position has higher real wages and lower employment and hence greater NAIRU. Demand has to be low compared to potential output and unemployment high in order to induce bargainers to settle at the feasible real wage. In the short term unemployment can diverge from the NAIRU due to demand shifts but in the medium term the economy returns to the NAIRU. Unemployment is hence determined by supply factors in the medium term and demand factors in the short term. In these

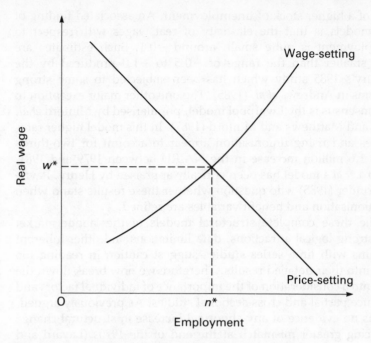

Fig. 7.3 Interaction of target and feasible real wages

types of models a key element is the extent of wage push for any given level of demand. Wage push will be determined by the extent of imperfections in the labour market, union militancy, import prices, replacement ratios and employers' labour taxes.

Results from this model suggest that demand factors played significantly little role in the growth of male unemployment in the 1960s and 1970s, where union militancy and in the 1970s the rise in real import prices appear to be the dominant causes of that growth. The picture dramatically changes when we consider the rise in male unemployment in the late 1970s where demand factors alone explain around 85 per cent of the rapid rise in male unemployment. Layard and Nickell conclude that although the influence of unions and replacement ratios may have caused an increase in unemployment in the 1960s and early 1970s, demand factors dominate recent increases. McCallum (1986) reaches similar conclusions about the importance of restrictive fiscal and monetary policy, and additionally rejects the suggestion that Europe has greater wage rigidity than other developed economies. Pissarides (1986) adopting a flow analysis, again finds a fall in the demand for labour, largely reflecting lower aggregate demand, as the dominant cause of a higher stock of unemployment. An associated finding of such models is that the elasticity of real wages with respect to unemployment is quite small, around -0.1. Such estimates are much smaller than the range of -0.5 to -1.0 produced by the Treasury's 1985 study which has been subjected to some strong criticisms in Andrews *et al.* (1985). The one other major exception to this consensus is the Liverpool model, popularised by Minford *et al.* (1983) and Matthews and Minford (1987). In this model higher rates of taxes and rising unionisation appear to account for two-thirds of the 1.6 million increase in the NAIRU between 1979 and 1981. Minford *et al*'s model has been critically appraised by Henry, Payne and Trinder (1985) who question whether these results stand when the unionisation and benefit variables are refined.

While these complete structural models of the labour market have strong logical attractions, data limitations and other inherent problems with time series studies suggest caution in reading too much into their detailed results. Therefore we now break down the issue into a consideration of the importance of individual factors and introduce partial and cross-sectional studies. As previously argued, there is no evidence of any abnormal increase in structural change producing greater mismatch at the end of the 1970s (Layard and Nickell 1986), accordingly we concentrate on the three main sources of an increase in NAIRU introduced above.

7.5.3 The impact of trade unions' and employers' bargaining behaviour

In Chapter 3 we noted that about 80 per cent of manual and 50 per cent of non-manual workers are covered by collective agreements, agreements which in the UK typically determine wages and leave employment to employers' decisions. The extent to which unions' and employers' behaviour produces unemployment depends upon how collectively bargained outcomes differ from individually bargained ones. What bargains would exist in a world without unions is impossible to determine and the only crude estimate of the impact of unions is to try to measure the union wage differential. Such a differential purports to measure the difference in pay between workers of equal characteristics in collectively and individually bargained employment. In both the Layard and Nickell and Minford models it is increases in union militancy which express themselves in attempts to increase the union differential, thereby increasing wage push and raising NAIRU.

In order to test this proposition it is necessary to define and proxy union militancy, a problem which has plagued researchers in this and allied areas. In most cases researchers use union militancy to mean a measure of the union's relative bargaining power and their willingness to use that power in negotiations. Minford adopts the proportion of workers organised, the unionisation rate, as the best proxy though there is no obvious causal link from changes in membership to militancy. His empirical work suggests a strong union impact upon unemployment; between 1964 and 1979 a 1 per cent increase in the unionisation rate was associated with a 0.25 per cent increase in the unemployment rate. On disaggregating by industry Minford's results suggests union differentials in excess of 50 per cent, three or four times the normal estimated differential. Such a large differential for otherwise homogeneous workers appears unlikely given even weakly competitive product markets. When labour quality differences are included in the analysis the union differential is much smaller; Stewart's (1983b) analysis using individual data suggests a differential in single figures. Moreover when Minford's unionisation rate measure is refined and the analysis extended to cover the post-1979 period the influence of unions on unemployment seems to disappear (Henry, Payne and Trinder 1985). Layard and Nickell proxy union militancy by directly using a measure of the union differential, once again an imperfect measure as its movement will reflect labour quality and market forces changes. While they find that unions have a direct impact on current unemployment of about 2 per cent, we have seen that their model indicates that unions have not been an important cause of high unemployment in the 1980s. Nickell and Andrews (1983) similarly find a significant union effect, but no indication that this effect has risen in recent years. Pissarides (1986), again using the union differential as a proxy, notes that the differential changed little in the 1970s, but rose sharply in 1980–81 as unions resisted real wage reductions even in the face of employment contractions, suggesting that they may have been significant causes of unemployment since 1979. However, in his empirical results unions accounted for less than a tenth of the 1979–83 rise in unemployment. Given the inherent weakness of empirical work in this area it would be wrong to make any strong conclusions.

7.5.4 The impact of the replacement ratio

The impact of the tax and benefit system on the incentives to work has been a heavily researched area in recent years, partly reflecting governments' fear that moral hazard was widespread. In comparison with other OECD countries the UK does not appear to have an especially high replacement ratio for unemployed workers (Chan-Lee, Coe and Prywes 1987). However, the abolition of the earnings related supplement in 1982, and the Social Security Act of 1986 together with various other taxation and benefit changes were motivated by a concern about disincentive effects on labour supply and the perceived need to reduce voluntary unemployment. The measurement of the extent and impact of disincentives and voluntary unemployment is extremely problematic, data and modelling problems abounding. This topic is considered in detail in Chapter 8; broadly our findings are that there appears a consensus (Beenstock 1987b) in micro studies that variations in individuals' replacement rates are not associated with any large differences in unemployment duration. Macroeconomic investigations produce no such agreement.

7.5.5 Wage controls and employment protection legislation

The importance of wage controls in the rise of British unemployment since 1979 appears to be small. Wages Councils were ineffective in even maintaining the relative pay of workers under their jurisdiction. Between 1974 and 1984 the average earnings of full-time workers covered by Wages Councils fell from 73 per cent of average pay to 65 per cent; it seems unlikely therefore that the councils made a major contribution to unemployment. Deregulation in the 1960s and 1970s appears to have produced some slow-down in the contraction of those industries, though the experience of the clothing industry suggests that demand responses to wage cuts are small (Marshall and McCormick 1985). Similarly the Councils appear to have made little contribution to wage push; Nickell (1985) has pointed out that the wage pressure has been highest among high-income groups, with the bottom 10 per cent of male workers taking a real wage cut, pre-tax, between 1980 and 1984.

The impact of employment protection legislation on unemployment and wage pressure remains unclear. Many studies of the period since 1970 interpret the positive time trend on unemployment in their models as the impact of such legislation but few direct tests of the proposition are available. As discussed above, the measures will tend to reduce both inflow to and outflow from the stock of unemployment, and Nickell (1982) finds evidence of such changes.

His results suggest a net favourable impact upon unemployment, but the result remains tentative. Surveys of employers suggest little overall disincentive effect, though small firms may have been significantly dissuaded from hiring new workers. The reintroduction of freedom for firms to fire workers in their first two years of employment thus appears unlikely to have any major impact on hiring behaviour. The possibility that employment protection legislation has caused the substitution of part-time for full-time, especially young, employees has not been directly tested. National Insurance contributions are equivalent to about 7 per cent of labour costs and changes from the 1960s onwards have made part-time employees cheaper (Hart and Trinder 1986). International comparisons suggest that non-wage labour costs are relatively low in the UK (Chan-Lee, Coe and Prywes 1987) and the study by McKee, Visser and Saunders (1986) indicates that the total marginal tax rates on labour use in the UK are also below the OECD average.

7.6 Policy implications

It seems clear from our survey above that there is general, but not universal, agreement that deficient demand was the biggest factor in causing the rapid rise in unemployment at the end of the 1970s. However, we need also to examine the persistence of unemployment close to that high level. Whether we wish to use the term NAIRU or not, the long-term level of unemployment will depend upon the degree of money wage pressure at any given level of demand. Any increase in wage pressure must in the long term tend to increase the level of unemployment consistent with constant inflation. Any attempt to offset increases in unemployment by expanding the level of aggregate demand must tend to raise the inflation rate over time. On the other hand, policies which seek to reduce the NAIRU without raising demand will slowly lower the inflation rate and only in the long run stimulate employment. We appear to have a crucial asymmetry in the labour market: contractions of demand work disproportionately through employment while expansions of demand favour wage not employment increases. It follows that to reduce unemployment it is necessary to reduce wage pressure by supply-side policies while at the same time raising the level of real aggregate demand. If the stimulus to aggregate demand can be targeted at high-unemployment groups then the inflation costs of raising employment can be reduced.

This conclusion will serve to structure our discussion of policy. Initially we consider recent British Government attempts to reduce wage pressure. This is followed by a consideration of even more radical proposals for changes in the operation of the tax and benefit system to influence wage pressure. We then assess the alphabet of job subsidy and job creation schemes encompassed in the Special Employment Measures. The lessons being learnt from these schemes are used to investigate the desirability of innovative manpower policies in combination with Keynesian-type policies, general reflation combined with some form of incomes policy. Before commencing this discussion it is important to state the dimensions of the current British problem: economic growth averaging 4 per cent over about four to five years if unemployment is to be brought down to around 2 million (Layard 1986). This may well be an underestimate of the additional jobs required as the new jobs created in recent years have been filled by a higher proportion of unregistered unemployed workers than previously anticipated. While demographic factors become favourable to reduction of unemployment by the middle of the 1990s, to make an impression before that requires the sort of performance only previously sustained in the UK in the mid-1930s. The task facing any British Government is therefore immense, requiring a co-ordinated policy response.

7.7 Current British Government policies

In March 1985 the British Government published a White Paper, *Employment: The Challenge for the Nation* (Cmnd 9474), which summarised their interpretation of the causes of, and cure of, high unemployment. It rejected deficient aggregate demand as a contributory factor and argued that any significant increase in public sector investment expenditure would merely crowd out private sector spending. Instead the document concentrated upon failures in the operation of the labour market. One major concern was the inflexibility of the labour market; policy actions in the areas of education, training and mobility were discussed as means of reducing the natural rate. The main emphasis was upon the problem of achieving a 'sensible' growth of income in a free society. As the government rejects any centralisation of bargaining through incomes policy, it follows that policy has to influence bargaining behaviour. Reducing wage pressure therefore requires either strenthening employer power or weakening that of unions and individual workers. While some of the more doctrinaire reasonings were abandoned before the 1987 General Election, the 1985 White Paper provided a framework for a variety of policies which are now examined.

7.7.1 Weakening worker bargaining power

The Thatcher Government has passed three Acts and is currently enacting a fourth aimed directly at weakening trade union bargaining strength. By making it more difficult for unions to organise, retain members and strike effectively, the legislation hopes to weaken union bargaining power. The detailed nature and impact of these measures are considered in Chapter 8. The recession has obviously reduced union power and the true test of the policy awaits a return to higher levels of economic activity. The policy is not directed at unofficial strikes and presupposes that closed shops are a direct contribution to wage pressure and to inflexibility in the labour market. There is little evidence that employers take this view, and outside of the public sector the new legislation has not as yet been widely used. The history of industrial relations legislation in the UK suggests that it can have little impact upon union–employer relations without the co-operation of both sides. It is the climate of industrial relations, rather than the legal environment, which appears to lead to a reduction of conflict and extension of co-operation. Thus while there is likely to be some reduction in wage pressure or alternatively higher productivity growth resulting from these initiatives, few economists expect any major impact on unemployment in the short or medium term.

At the individual worker level, the White Paper claimed that the fear of unfair dismissal actions has had a major impact upon firms' hiring policy. Accordingly the qualifying period has been quadrupled to two years, reverting to the conditions in the original 1971 Industrial Relations Act. Again we have seen above that there is an absence of any hard evidence to support this assertion. The government has repealed the Fair Wages Resolution and the Schedule of the 1971 Act extending its cover, at the same time reforming or abolishing many of the Wages Councils. The 1986 Wages Act removed workers under twenty-one years of age from the scope of the Wages Council system. The objective of these measures is to create greater flexibility in wage levels in these industries, allowing workers to price themselves into jobs. These measures are likely to reduce wage pressure at the lower end of the labour market, though as explained above it is not this segment which has been generating the greatest pressure. Marshall and McCormick (1985) conclude that abolition of some Wages Councils does not appear to have had any major impact upon employment in those sectors. Among higher-paid groups government action has been more limited, reducing some monopoly rights in the money market and of professional workers, such as solicitors and opticians, and also encouraging more competition, especially by advertising. The overall impact of these measures is likely to be small.

As an employer the government has directly reduced wage push by applying explicit guidelines for public sector pay. On average since 1980 pay has been rising significantly more slowly in the public than in the private sector. Zabalza and Kong (1984) suggest that private sector pay does not respond to public sector levels, which implies that the macroeconomic impact of public sector restraint is small. However, the impact on the quality of labour applying to the private sector may be significant, if one assumes that such a change would generate faster economic growth.

7.7.2 Labour cost changes

Changes in taxation can influence wage pressure by changing the relationship between disposable income and real labour costs. In the early 1980s non-wage costs were about 30 per cent of total labour costs, compared with about 20 per cent a decade earlier (Hart 1984). In real terms employers' National Insurance contributions including the surcharge doubled between 1967 and 1982, and reached almost 10 per cent of labour costs in 1981. As a wage tax operating between upper and lower income limits for each employee, National Insurance contributions are essentially a payroll tax. These limits encouraged the employment of part-time workers to escape that lower limit and also subsidised the employment of higher-paid employees. The restructuring of contributions in the 1985 Budget attempted to end this bias and stimulate the demand for low-paid labour. In sum the abolition of the surcharge has reduced the inflationary consequences of any wage push, while the removal of the upper limit reduced labour market distortions.

Wage pressure will also reflect employees' taxes and National Insurance contributions. If employee direct tax rates are cut then workers should require less increases in their pre-tax earnings to achieve their target net wage. Although direct taxes have been cut since 1979, increases in National Insurance contributions and expenditure taxes have meant that the married man on average manual earnings experienced no reduction in his tax burden between 1979 and the end of 1986. International comparisons of taxing employment incomes, using purchasing-power parities, suggest that tax rates and progressivity were not particularly high in the UK in the mid-1980s (Board of Inland Revenue 1988). Whether earlier concentration on reducing employers' National Insurance contributions, rather than employees' tax and insurance burden, had a net beneficial impact on employment remains unclear. The consequences for the supply of labour of these changes are discussed in Chapter 8.

Minford *et al.* (1983) have argued that what is required is a more radical revision of labour market intervention. In their model benefit levels provide a floor for unskilled wage rates and therefore prevent price adjustment in the labour market. Given that they estimate a high elasticity of unemployment with respect to benefit levels, they recommend the 'capping' of benefits for unemployed workers at 70 per cent of previous net earned income; such policies already operate in several Western European countries. Minford *et al.* would combine 'capping' with the introduction of tougher eligibility for benefits including 'workfare': requiring the unemployed after a period of search to accept any job offer made at the going rate. In order to increase incentives and close the 'poverty trap', Minford *et al.* argue for a major rise in tax thresholds and a large increase in child benefit. The abolition of means-tested benefits in kind and replacement with more generous family income supplement are also advocated. The 1986 Social Security Act moved somewhat in this direction and this issue is discussed more fully in Chapter 8.

7.7.3 Fiscal and monetary policies

One area not stressed in the 1985 White Paper was monetary and fiscal policy; up to that period the Thatcher Government had been broadly sympathetic to the monetarist–new classical approach in designing their macroeconomic policies, believing that unemployment was a predominantly microeconomic problem. Critics of new classical economic policies would argue that not only are demand management policies not impotent but that the impact of the Thatcher Government's deflationary policy since 1979 confirms this conclusion. Given the rigidity of prices and wages in the short run, contractions of aggregate demand initially reduce output and employment levels and cause unemployment to rise above the natural rate. Estimates from the models discussed above suggest that about a quarter of 1985 levels of unemployment and almost half of the rise in unemployment after 1979 were due to contractionary macroeconomic policies. The reduction in inflation has been achieved at considerable cost to British levels of output and employment. The causes of this rise after 1979 in the output gap, potential minus actual real GNP, can be roughly illustrated by Table 7.2.

Table 7.2   Factors affecting UK aggregate demand

| | Taxes as % of GDP at market prices | Government expenditure as % of potential output | | Real short-term interest rates per cent | IMF index of relative unit normal labour costs |
		Real transfers	Goods and services		
1970	37.1	11.4	22.6	– 0.9	110
1975	36.2	11.4	26.4	–14.0	112
1978	33.6	14.0	22.9	3.5	108
1979	34.4	14.4	22.5	– 0.7	125
1980	35.7	13.7	22.8	– 1.5	152
1981	37.6	14.4	21.8	3.4	159
1982	38.6	15.2	21.5	4.6	153
1983	38.3	15.7	22.0	3.9	144
1984	38.7	16.1	21.9	4.7	143

Source: Layard (1986), Table 8, p. 68

If we take all components of fiscal policy then their net contribution compared to GNP has fallen since 1979, largely because of the rise in taxes of over 4 per cent of GNP. At the same time restrictive monetary policy at home and abroad drove short-term real interest rates up by over 5 per cent. This rise in real interest rates together with the impact of North Sea oil exploitation caused the pound to appreciate and reduced the competitiveness of British industry. A different policy mix could have helped prevent such a rapid rise in the pound, albeit at the cost of the some inflation gains. The deflationary package of fiscal and monetary policy adopted by the Conservative Government in 1979 and in general sustained till 1987 was a major cause of high unemployment. This aspect of the Keynesian non-neutrality position appears to have been vindicated by the experience of the last decade.

7.7.4 Special Employment Measures

The rapid rise in British unemployment during the 1970s stimulated a variety of temporary measures aimed at ameliorating the situation. The political expediency of preventing a rapid rise in measured unemployment was combined with a belief that by selectively targeting assistance, the budget deficit and balance of payments costs per unit reduction in unemployment could be minimised. In addition, the policies were designed to produce a more equitable distribution of the burden of unemployment. The first of these measures was the introduction in 1975 of the Temporary Employment Subsidy and the Job Creation Programme and in total there have been about twenty different, often short-lived, schemes. In order to analyse the impact of the various measures and aid the eventual assessment of new proposals, we initially consider the characteristics of an efficient employment policy.

There have been two major forms of Special Employment Measures, those acting to stimulate the demand for labour and those attempting to reduce the supply of labour in the market. The former group have dominated, initially taking the form of a wage subsidy, though later schemes have tended to target specific groups among the unemployed. Any wage subsidy makes labour cheaper compared to capital thereby stimulating employment. Indeed early arguments for a general wage subsidy were based on the need to offset the various subsidies paid to encourage fixed investment and the taxes on employment such as employers' National Insurance contributions. Few economists nowadays anticipate that labour demand is very sensitive to relative factor prices in the short and medium term; most argue that on efficiency grounds to minimise secondary effects discussed below a marginal employment subsidy is preferable. At the macroeconomic level, Layard and Nickell (1980) have argued that an average subsidy would have a similar effect to a marginal subsidy only in a competitive closed economy. This follows because the expansion of output and employment will depend upon the extent to which domestic prices are reduced, and this depends upon the impact of the subsidy on the average cost of the marginal firm. In an open economy, where many firms are price-takers, sales will expand rapidly when marginal costs fall, and a marginal subsidy will produce a bigger employment effect. The appropriateness of the assumption that export prices respond to lower marginal labour costs is questioned by Whitley and Wilson (1983), who reject the macroeconomic argument for preferring a marginal subsidy.

If we accept the efficiency arguments favouring the marginal employment subsidy then it may take the form of either a job-creating subsidy, which pays firms on the basis of additional employees, or a job-preserving subsidy which induces firms to delay redundancies. Generally job-creating subsidies are preferred by economists. Job-preserving subsidies present severe policing problems; counting new jobs is much easier than counting jobs not lost. British experience has also shown that the difficulty in distinguishing between firms and industries in long-term decline from those who given short-term assistance have a 'sound' future, leads to counter-productive support of 'lame ducks'. This problem is compounded by political pressures which may favour the permanent subsidisation of structurally based threatened redundancies rather than offset temporary recession-related redundancies. However, the preferred marginal job-creating subsidy must be designed so that higher turnover is not rewarded, only net recruitments.

Most macroeconomic models suggest the relative attractiveness of these policies over general reflation since they concentrate aid on domestic employment; however, there are several potential problems with such interventions. Where financial inducements are given to firms or workers to adopt certain behaviour, there are always going to be some secondary effects, which must be examined if the net effects of the policy are to be established. Firstly, there will be 'deadweight' effects, subsidies or compensation paid for behaviour which would have been produced without the payments. Secondly, 'displacement' effects are produced when non-subsidised firms and workers are harmed by the competition from subsidised ones. Where additional subsidies are paid to compensate for the effects of payments to other producers, it is termed a 'defensive' or 'domino'; effect. In addition, certain of the policies induce employers to substitute extra workers for extra hours per existing worker. This change in the desired combination of workers and hours merely substitutes underemployment for unemployment, and has ambiguous effects on efficiency and welfare. The problems in actually measuring these secondary effects are severe given the marginal nature of many of the schemes and the small impact upon overall costs; most estimates of these effects are generated by surveys of subsidised and non-subsidised firms. Such surveys require carefully designed questions and sampling if acceptable estimates are to be obtained. Given this overview of the requirements for an efficient policy we now consider British experience.

We initially consider schemes aimed at stimulating or sustaining the level of employment. The frequent changes in the operation of the schemes over the last decade preclude any detailed description here of the eligibility and size of the subsidies paid; Metcalf (1982) and Davies and Metcalf (1985) provide such details. The first and one of the largest schemes was the Temporary Employment Subsidy (TES), a marginal job preservation subsidy scheme introduced in August 1975. At its peak in May 1977 it covered about 200 000 workers, providing employers with a subsidy, £20 per week, to defer redundancies. Although not directly targeted, TES was highly concentrated in manufacturing with 90 per cent of the jobs covered coming from this sector, and half of these jobs being in the clothing and footwear industries. The scheme was output-augmenting and the strong international displacement effect, especially within the EEC, led to the abandonment of TES in 1979 as it was in contravention of the Treaty of Rome. It was replaced by the Temporary Short-Time Working Compensation Scheme (TSTWCS), a subsidy aimed at inducing employers to substitute work-sharing for redundancies; TSTWCS essentially subsidised worker leisure as it substituted underemployment for unemployment, and it covered nearly a million workers at its peak in March 1981. Once again it was in practice highly selective, with 95 per cent of workers supported being in manufacturing, and with an especially high take-up in the metals and engineering industries. Experience with job creation subsidies has been more varied, though on a much smaller scale. The Small Firm Employment Subsidy (SFES) peaked at 76 000 jobs supported in 1979, and the Adult Employment Subsidy (AES) introduced in 1979 never covered more than 1000 workers at a time. Various marginal job creation subsidies have been targeted at young entrants to the labour market. The Recruitment Subsidy for School-leavers (RSSL) and Youth Employment Subsidy (YES) schemes operated in the late 1970s and the New/Young Worker Scheme (YWS) in the mid 1980s. The latter paid employers a subsidy for each youth employed at a 'realistic', i.e. low wage, and covered about 60 000 young workers at the beginning of 1986. More recently the Enterprise Allowance Scheme (EAS) provides a subsidy for unemployed workers to become self-employed; it was expanded to cover 80 000 workers in 1986/87. Overall the Department of Employment estimated that the Special Measures reduced unemployment by about 450 000 in the middle of the 1980s.

Lindley (1986) provides a summary of the limited available evidence on the net employment effects of the above employment subsidies; Table 7.3 reproduces his summary of that evidence. The various studies did not share a common methodology and some caution should be taken in comparing results, nevertheless there are large differences in the size of the net jobs created and of

Table 7.3   Effects of special employment subsidies

	Net jobs created as % supported	Reduction in unemployment count as % supported	Net cost per net job created* (£)	Net cost per unit drop in count (£)
Job preservation				
TES	40	30†	1300	1730
TSTWCS	60	48	1680	2100
Job expansion				
SFES	35	26†	1880	2510
Targeted				
AES	5	5	n.a.	n.a.
RSSL	10	10	2550	2550
YES	5	5	4015	4015
YWS	15–20	15–20	2400	2400
EAS	50	40	2650	2650

Source: Lindley (1986), Table 8.5, p. 167
* Using 1984–85 prices.
† Assuming three-quarters of jobs created filled by unemployed.

the impact on the stock of unemployed workers. The targeted employment subsidies to employers had net job creation effects ranging from 5 to 20 per cent of jobs supported, while the job preservation subsidies appeared to have a larger net effect, ranging from 40 to 70 per cent. The available studies suggest that the displacement effect is lower with job preservation subsidies, but that deadweight effects are smaller with a job creation subsidy. Not all of these net employment effects represent reductions in measured unemployment. If we follow the practice of assuming that subsidies targeted on the unemployed have a 100 per cent impact on unemployment while job preservation schemes have a 75 per cent impact, then estimates can be made of the net cost per job created or per unit reduction in measured unemployment. Such figures are only short term and there may be large differences between the scheme's short- and long-term net costs. The range of figures reported above suggest that, compared to other policies, subsidies are a cheap method of creating jobs and reducing unemployment, a theme we return to later. Job preservation policies appear more effective, largely because targeted subsidies have large substitution and deadweight effects. However, Metcalf's (1986) inter-industry study of redundancy rates suggested that TSTWCS delayed rather than avoided redundancies; contrary to the stated objectives, the scheme did not in practice target jobs with a long-term future. If we therefore consider long-term net costs, job creation subsidies appear more attractive, since a work-sharing subsidy has no output effects, and the positive impact on output of job preservation subsidies is doubtful in the long run. Non-targeted job creation subsidies necessarily produce smaller substitution effects and the early results from the EAS are encouraging in both output and employment terms. Note that the concern with substitution and displacement effects in the labour markets requires that demand is constrained, otherwise these workers are reabsorbed in the employed workforce.

An alternative to supporting employment levels in the private sector is to introduce 'public works' schemes to provide employment opportunities for unemployed workers. Such schemes were popular in the 1930s, and beginning in 1978 several schemes were developed in the UK culminating in the Community Programme scheme (CP). In October 1987 about 230 000 long-term unemployed adults were covered by this scheme, working on projects that promote general community interests, such as environmental or educational facilities' improvements. Although the scheme is open to all long-term unemployed over eighteen years of age, restrictions on rates of pay provide no incentives for those over twenty-five to take a place; in practice the take-up of places is concentrated among the young. The scheme is supposed to cover projects which have no displacement effects. The Community Programme is targeted at a group, the long-term unemployed, who have a high probability of remaining unemployed, and at low-wage labour-intensive projects. In macroeconomic terms the rationale for CP is confused, local authorities being constrained in their ability to finance high-priority schemes such as education and roads, but being encouraged to submit low-priority projects for CP support. At the microeconomic level studies suggest a high benefit/cost ratio of around 2.4. Turner (1985) reports that nearly a quarter of the schemes' participants went into employment on completion, the proportion being higher for young and female workers.

So far the discussion has concentrated on policies to support and stimulate the demand for employees. An alternative response to unemployment is to reduce labour supply. Labour-force participation rates have been falling for older male workers in recent years and most Western countries have introduced early retirement schemes. The Job Release Scheme begun in 1977 provides a financial incentive for older workers to retire early, where their employer agrees to replace them with an unemployed worker. The scheme peaked at 95 000 jobs and was withdrawn at the beginning of 1988; a short-lived version for part-time workers was introduced in 1983. About three-quarters of released workers were in practice replaced, slightly above the average for similar schemes (Mirkin 1987). Also in 1983 a Job Splitting Scheme was introduced and in 1987 extended as Jobshare; this provides employers with a financial incentive to split a full-time job into two part-time ones or consolidate regular overtime hours into part-time employment. The long-term effects of all these schemes must be to reduce the size of the workforce and so permanently lower output. To the extent that the short-term reallocation of unemployment is towards a more equitable distribution, the schemes may be desirable, but because they do not affect the NAIRU they are irrelevant to the basic problem. Further by fostering early retirement as a policy response to unemployment the longer-term consequences of an ageing population are intensified; an increased proportion of national income will have to be devoted to the support of pension schemes. With falling birth rates and consequential decline in the working-age population it is likely that labour forces will no longer increase after this century, and early retirement schemes are therefore unlikely to be sustainable.

7.7.5 Conclusions on current government policies

Macroeconomic policies have added to unemployment and industrial and regional policies seem to have been ineffective. Policies to improve the efficiency of the labour market and reduce wage pressure have had only a marginal impact and too often they have been directed at reducing wages in the lower-paid sectors of the economy, while wage pressure has been strongest among the higher-paid groups. Moreover many of the policies are likely to widen inequality in the labour market and increase the amount of segmentation. Of all the policies that the Conservative Government has adopted since 1979 to combat unemployment the Special Employment Measures appear to have been the least popular with the government but the most effective. This unpopularity reflects fears about their failure to create 'real' jobs, a concept which proves elusive when attempts are made to define it. The apparent success of the Special Measures is in terms of reducing official unemployment figures and there is no evidence that they represent an efficient response to improving the utilisation and allocation of labour. The question is therefore raised as to whether there are alternative policies than can reduce unemployment at acceptable costs.

7.8 Alternative policies to reduce unemployment

The dominant analytical approach to unemployment distinguishes between natural and non-natural unemployment. To reduce the latter requires either time, a contraction of labour supply or increased aggregate demand. However, the consequence of expansionary policies implemented alone will generally be to raise the inflation rate in the medium term. In the case of the 'discouraged' long-term unemployed, because their numbers appear not to influence the level of wage pressure, any expansion of employment among this group will not raise prices, an argument belatedly adopted by government with the Jobstart Allowance. More generally alternative approaches to reducing unemployment start from the need to design reflationary packages which predominantly influence output rather than prices. This requires supply to be increased as well as demand; in other words any comprehensive approach to reducing unemployment requires that policies to reduce the NAIRU are also needed. Earlier it was argued that the major causes of the rise in NAIRU were on the supply side of the labour market; policies are therefore needed to confront these causes.

7.8.1 Is further reflation a viable alternative?

The main reason why governments no longer react to growing unemployment by the traditional Keynesian policies of expansion, is the fear that such an expansion of aggregate demand will predominantly fuel inflation. Such a fear appears to be supported by the bulk of the studies discussed above and is reinforced by fears of the impact of fiscal expansion on the balance of payments. Accordingly we concluded that the key elements of any successful policy to reduce unemployment at a stable inflation rate, is firstly to reduce wage pressure and then to increase real demand by an appropriate amount. Nickell (1985), using the British Government's Treasury model, illustrates the relative dimensions of these influences. A reduction in nominal wage pressure of 2 per cent, while maintaining the same real policy stance, generates only in the order of 60 000–70 000 jobs in the long run. If the same reduction in wage pressure is combined with a modest fiscal stimulus of a 3.25 per cent rise in government spending on goods and services, then the employment effects are 3.5 times greater without any upsurge in inflation. According to the Treasury model the benefits of combining both reduced wage pressure and reflation are therefore large.

There is agreement among economists of all persuasions that general reflation alone is an inefficient means of permanently stimulating employment. As illustration, Davies and Metcalf (1985) calculate that for a given increase in the public sector borrowing requirement (PSBR) of £1bn. then VAT and employers' National Insurance contributions cuts would reduce unemployment by about 17 000, income tax cuts would reduce unemployment by about 21 000, public infrastructure investment by about 38 000, current public spending by 65 000, while expanding the Special Employment Measures by the same amount reduces unemployment by about 480 000. Income tax cuts become even less attractive options when the consequences for the balance of payments are included. While both the short- and long-term impacts on unemployment will clearly depend upon the specific model used, these comparative influences are found in other studies. If it takes about £2000 per annum in net budgetary costs to create a job on the CP and £40 000 in tax cuts to create a job, it is also likely that the output effects of the Special Measures are greater. Simulations on most major UK macroeconometric models and for various costings generally confirm the attractiveness of expanding the Special Employment Measures, especially when targeted at the long-term unemployed (Budd, Levine and Smith 1987; Turner, Wallis and Whitley 1987).

The reasons for such large differences in the impact on unemployment of reflationary packages is that cuts in income taxes and VAT produce withdrawals of demand in the form of increased savings and import purchases. The increased consumption expenditure which does result is biased towards consumer durable goods which have an especially high import content in the UK. It is the size of these leakages which give rise to the ineffectiveness of tax cuts in stimulating employment. Stimulating demand through expansionary public sector capital formation is slightly more effective given the lower import content, but infrastructure investment is capital-intensive. Extra public spending on capital goods in the NHS or even on current spending on defence have especially low impacts on employment. Increasing current public spending generally has a larger impact because such spending is labour-intensive, especially on health and education, and has no first-round withdrawals of spending.

To maximise the employment effects of reflation the expansion needs targeting and combining with an effective incomes policy and possibly devaluation. Effective incomes policies could reduce wage pressure sufficiently to allow the expansion of real demand to levels consistent with the desired level of unemployment. Such Keynesian attempts to subvert market forces and NAIRU have become unfashionable, reflecting disenchantment with the experience of such policies in the 1960s and 1970s. Recent proposals for tax-based incomes policies and for the replacement of the present system of wage determination by one based on profit-sharing are considered in Chapter 8. The political realities of most present Western societies suggest that these proposals are unlikely to be real issues in the short term. Temporary improvements in international price competitiveness by engineered depreciation of sterling appear more politically acceptable.

Accordingly many economists have adopted a more pragmatic approach towards the problem of reducing unemployment. Given that a general reflation is impossible with existing institutional and political forces, how can we maximise the unemployment-reducing effects of current net expenditure levels? Further is there any new way in which government microeconomic policy initiatives can influence the trade-offs between wage pressure and unemployment, and between employment and hours per employee? Targeted employment measures concentrate increased expenditure on reducing measured unemployment; to maximise this effect and avoid bidding-up wages of those in employment, the expenditure needs to be primarily spent on the long-term unemployed and sectors or regions with a high incidence of unemployment. The interest in new forms of job-creating and job-preserving subsidies is examined following a consideration of the lessons learned from other countries' experience.

7.8.2 International experience of employment subsidies

The earlier review of the Special Measures needs to be related to experience of such policies in other countries if we are to reach appropriate conclusions about future policy initiatives. All EEC countries currently use job creation schemes to fight unemployment; some of the individual programmes are described in Bekemans (1985) and Irwin (1987). In most European countries the emphasis has been on producing employment opportunities for the long-term unemployed, often in non-profit-making activities to reduce displacement effects. Ireland has had a job creation subsidy since 1977, Greece since 1982, and the Netherlands and Belgium have such a subsidy for depressed regions in their countries. In the USA the New Jobs Tax Credit (NJTC) was introduced in 1977 and provided a tax credit to firms who hired additional workers. The scheme was biased towards low-paid employees, being payable only up to wage limit, and in 1979 was retargeted at groups with a high risk of unemployment. Assessments suggest that the NJTC had a large employment effect, but that the revised targeted scheme was less successful in stimulating employment prospects for the disadvantaged groups (Haveman and Saks 1985). As yet there appear to have been relatively few evaluations of these schemes outside of the USA where the scale of intervention is fairly small.

There is a widespread belief that marginal employment subsidies are a cheap and effective means of reducing cyclical unemployment. Such schemes appear to work best when subsidies are paid directly, rather than in the form of tax preferences. In the long term it is more difficult to stimulate output and employment by such subsidies but job creation subsidies are likely to be the most effective. Targeting the measures on the long-term unemployed is also likely to produce a more equitable distribution of unemployment. In Denmark the long-term unemployed receive a job guarantee, private sector employers receive a wage subsidy of 50 per cent and public sector places are financed out of local taxes. Irwin (1987) reports that 80 per cent those taking the job in the private sector find permanent employment.

7.8.3 Possible extensions of the Special Measures

Earlier it was concluded that in order to reduce unemployment permanently wage pressure has to be reduced at a given level of employment. Jackman, Layard and Pissarides (1986) argue that restructuring existing taxes on jobs by appropriately designed taxes and subsidies can alter the trade-off between wage and employment levels. Increasing the demand of labour in low-wage markets at the expense of reductions in the demand for higher-paid workers can raise overall levels of employment. Nissim (1984) provided some support for such proposals by showing that in the long run there was a considerable degree of skill substitutability in the mechanical engineering industry. A self-financing tax/subsidy system is suggested where firms pay a wage-bill tax and receive a fixed per-worker subsidy. This generates a net subsidy for low-paid workers producing in aggregate beneficial demand and supply-side responses. To complement, employers' National Insurance contributions could be made more progressive, continuing the 1985 Budget reform. Such a scheme has a close relationship to tax-based incomes policies, in which a tax on the average wage growth of a firm would also increase the relative demand for low-paid employees. What remains unclear in these proposals is the output effects of the bias towards low-paid labour. The encouragement of labour-intensive industries in tradable goods and services sectors of the economy is unlikely to be consistent with long-term growth objectives.

It has been repeatedly argued that increases in the numbers of long-term unemployed do not help to restrain inflation. The size of the NAIRU can therefore be lowered by reducing the numbers of long-term unemployed. In effect the long-term unemployed withdraw from the labour market, either from discouragement or because they are screened out by employers. As they are not part of the effective labour supply to employers they exert no downwards influence on wage pressure. At the same time the long-term unemployed bear a disproportionate share of the costs of being unemployed. If both efficiency and equity require action aimed at this group, what form should it take? Existing schemes include Restart interviews which offer the long-term unemployed a training place or job and threaten the loss of benefits. By the autumn of 1987 there were also about 2000 Jobclubs providing resources and coaching to assist the long-term unemployed's search. The Job Training Scheme (JTS) which was designed to take many of those called to Restart interviews has been previously considered. Layard, Metcalf and O'Brien (1986) argue for a massive expansion of employment opportunities, culminating in a guaranteed one-year placement for all long-term unemployed along the lines of current Danish and Swedish schemes. They argue that because of the difficulty of finding appropriate projects and because unemployed workers receive the most relevant training and work better in a normal work environment, that an alternative to CP is now required. To achieve this expansion of employment opportunities they call for the creation of three-quarters of a million new jobs in construction, other parts of the private sector and the social services. This reflects their belief that such work represents the highest social priorities. If the workers are paid the rate for the job, to encourage a high take-up, the net cost to the PSBR is £2–3bn. when the scheme is fully operating. One reason why the costs of such a large-scale scheme are so low is that in the medium term the substitution and displacement effects disappear. This is because where the long-term unemployed displace other workers, the displaced workers do contribute to the effective labour supply and do produce the normal market adjustments of lower wage pressure which increases employment. The current movement towards a unification of the

CP and JTS for the long-term unemployed represents a movement towards this proposal.

A commonly argued alternative approach is to encourage greater work-sharing in the economy; Jones (1987) provides a survey of recent policy debates in this area. Our review of recent labour market trends in Chapter 3 indicated a growth of peripheral workers which represents a form of work-sharing, albeit sometimes an involuntary one. Since the Second World War the average working week has been reduced by about 1 per cent per annum; this together with the growth of part-time working and fall in activity rates among workers close to state pension age, suggested to many that encouragement of these trends could create a significant impact upon unemployment levels. Whitley and Wilson (1986) estimate that the employment elasticity after three years of a 1 per cent reduction in the length of the working week is around 0.37. This suggests that a reduction in the working week by about 5 per cent could create about 1 million extra jobs, reducing measured unemployment by around 650 000 after seven years. Indirect encouragement to work-sharing could be generated by policies which raise the overtime premium which employers have to pay. Studies in the USA suggest that the employment effects of such measures may be large. These arguments for work-sharing assume that income-sharing linked to the work-sharing prevents wage pressure from rising, since otherwise the NAIRU must rise. The major problem with work-sharing and early retirement policies is that insiders are reluctant to share in the costs of unemployment, hence unit costs rise. Empirical support for this proposition comes from Grubb's (1986) study of OECD labour markets which finds that a decrease in the size of the labour force generates the same wage pressure as an equal increase in employment. The basic problem with such proposals is that they fail to explain the macroeconomic model underlying their rationale, particularly ignoring the consequences for inflationary pressure. They merely substitute underemployment for some unemployment, making the economy poorer at the same time.

The above proposals have not directly confronted the need to improve the supply side of the labour market. Chapter 8 discusses whether tax-based incomes policies or increased profit-sharing could help to offset any socially harmful effects of the present wage-fixing system, and the chapter also considers whether the co-ordination of benefits and taxes can eliminate labour supply distortions. In Chapter 4 it was concluded that the British education and training system compares unfavourably with other developed economies. Improvements in this area along the lines discussed in the earlier chapter can make a long-run contribution to unemployment reduction. Similarly the arguments developed in Chapter 5 suggested that compulsory vacancy notification could improve the efficiency and equity of the job-matching process. Making fuller use of the potential productivity of workers of both sexes and all races by the introduction of anti-discrimination policies discussed in Chapter 6 is also relevant to the objective of reducing the level and costs of unemployment. Additional minor contributions could come from reform of the housing market to encourage locational mobility.

7.9 Conclusions

Unemployment represents an enormously costly economic and social problem for policy-makers and one that requires a large-scale multi-dimensional response. Attention needs to be directed away from the desire to reduce measured unemployment towards the efficient expansion of output and employment. This requires the causes of unemployment to be identified and then reflected in adopted policies. A lack of aggregate demand was discovered to be a major cause of the rise in unemployment in 1979/80. Even the Liverpool model now suggests that the current level of measured unemployment is well above, by around 1.5 million, the equilibrium level of unemployment. Reflationary policies are therefore needed; to be efficient they must be targeted to maximise the employment effects and minimise the inflation effects per pound sterling increase in the PSBR. Expansion should therefore be concentrated on producing job opportunities for the long-term unemployed. Changes in the tax and National Insurance systems and reform of the system of wage determination can also help to encourage the reduction of unemployment. The above review suggests that unemployment needs once again to be viewed as a macroeconomic problem; governments have no more powerful weapon in the short- and medium-term fight against unemployment than fiscal and monetary policies. The microeconomics of reducing the NAIRU is important in the long run and requires a comprehensive policy response to which no single programme is likely to be dominant.

Further reading

The brief 1985 White Paper is now compulsory as a starting-point for further reading. If the limitations and omissions cannot be identified then reread this chapter or consult the other works. Perhaps Davies (1985) provides the most effective and theoretically rigorous critique of recent government policy, while Matthews and Minford (1987) provide the fiercest support of recent British Government policy. Layard's (1986) little book provides a deceptively simple, yet thought-provoking introduction to unemployment theory and policy. Layard read together with Minford *et al.* (1983) will indicate the range of opinion and how hard economists are trying to open up debates to a wider public. While these two books are essentially 'bedtime' reading, Knight (1987) and Sinclair (1987) present more detailed and comprehensive reviews. Ashton's (1986) sociological perspective of unemployment is a thought-provoking palliative after reading the economic literature. As a quick but invaluable introduction to the macroeconomics of unemployment, the short papers by McCallum (1987) and Blinder (1987) should be consulted and enjoyed. The papers in Beckerman (1986) provide many stimulating insights into the developing microeconomics of price and wage rigidity, while the survey by Kniesner and Goldsmith (1987) carefully examine the current state of empirical models of the aggregate labour market. Haveman and Saks's (1985) review of employment and training policies is a good place to start reading on policy.

Chapter 8

WAGE-FIXING, SOCIAL INSURANCE AND TAXATION

If we define labour market policy in its broadest sense as any government intervention into the labour market concerned with promoting efficiency, then the previous discussion has ignored two major areas of importance. Firstly, detailed consideration of the institutional nature of wage-fixing in the economy. Although in Chapter 7 we examined how wage pressure contributed to the short- and long-run movements in inflation and unemployment, we did not consider the structural determinants of that wage pressure. It has been argued that both collectively bargained and unilateral wage-fixing systems will be biased towards inflation as they fail to internalise the externality of the inflationary consequences of the wage fixed. This has led to many proposals for reform of the wage-fixing system, and this issue is considered in the first part of this chapter. The second issue is also concerned with market failure, specifically failure in the provision of insurance for labour market participants. This issue leads directly to a consideration of the potential conflict between efficiency and equity in the labour market. It is widely, but not universally, accepted that government has a role to play in the support of workers facing uncertainty in the labour market. In Chapter 7 we examined the possibility that the social insurance, taxation and transfer systems could produce moral hazard effects upon the supply of labour. To introduce recent debates about reform of taxation and social insurance we need to examine the origins and impact of present policies aimed at influencing the extent, incidence and consequences of poverty, retirement, ill health and unemployment. This is the concern of the second part of this chapter.

One of the components of the Thatcher Government's anti-inflationary policy was to weaken the power of trade unions in collective bargaining; since 1979 four rounds of reform have radically changed the legal environment within which industrial relations are conducted. This policy for controlling wage pressure contrasts with the previously popular use of incomes policies. The academic debate on incomes policies has been rejuvenated in the last fifteen years by the detailed arguments for tax-based incomes policies, which to some economists promise a low-cost and permanent anti-inflationary weapon. More recently following the work of Weitzman and Meade arguments for profit-sharing reappeared, and these have been favourably viewed by the British Government as indicated by the introduction of tax relief for profit-related pay. To consider these policies it is first necessary to re-examine the nature of pay determination in the UK.

8.1 Pay determination

In Chapter 3 it was argued that wage rates in the UK once determined are largely independent of market conditions and profitability. It is money wages which are fixed in both the union and non-union sectors, with employers unilaterally determining employment. We argued in Chapter 2 and again in Chapter 7 that even in non-union firms wage-fixing will be constrained by the need to maintain insiders' morale and loyalty. Although product and labour market conditions influence wage offers, firms will wish to avoid any sudden cuts in money wages or anticipated real wages. The same general conditions will influence wage rates in unionised sectors, market conditions now working through their impact upon relative bargaining strength. In addition in unionised sectors the desire to exercise that bargaining power, what is usually termed union or employer militancy, will determine outcomes. Union bargaining behaviour may also reflect insiders' concern with maintaining consistent increases in real wages, demanding compensating money wage increases for any tax changes. In both sectors any sudden and unanticipated changes in the level of prices, say by a change in the terms of trade, will cause the actual real wage to deviate from the anticipated real wage. The adjustment of real wages to this shock determines the longer-term movement of inflation and employment.

In Chapter 3 we noted that single-employer bargains are the most important form of collective bargaining in the British labour market, multi-employer bargaining being more common in industries with a large number of small firms and/or labour-intensive methods of production. In that earlier chapter we also commented on the growth of payment systems based upon job evaluation and work-study techniques. Thus a decentralised national system of bargaining has caused more centralised bargaining within the firm, usually a unified shop steward body agreeing a structured system of internal pay differentials. International comparisons suggest that the UK has both relatively strong trade unions and decentralised bargaining. This lack of centralisation, or what Bruno and Sachs (1985) call 'corporatism', in wage bargaining may contribute to the rigidity of real wages in the UK discovered in Chapter 3. Strong trade unions can bargain successfully for higher money wages to compensate for any price rise, the employment and inflation consequences not being fully internalised. If this analysis is correct then any 'improvement' in the adjustment mechanism requires either that union power is reduced or that corporatism is increased. A similar conclusion is reached by Cornwall (1983) who contrasts the centralised and co-operative industrial relations system of continental Europe and the corporatism of Japan with the fragmented and adversarial industrial relations systems of the UK and USA. Although the present government has taken measures to reduce union bargaining power, both government and trade unions support decentralised wage bargaining, or 'free collective bargaining', having rejected incomes policies. We now consider these alternative policy approaches.

8.2 Reducing union power

Economic theorists have finally begun to analyse seriously the origins and behaviour of trade unions; Oswald (1985) and Malcomson (1987) provide recent introductory surveys of this literature. Much of the above discussion has implicitly adopted a monopoly model of trade unions in which firms retain the right to manage. Unions and employers bargain about wages, with employers adjusting employment: if unions secure higher wage rates for their members the cost is reduced employment opportunities due to lower output and/or more capital-intensive production. Unions may also contribute to rigidities in the labour market such as reducing occupational mobility; this may increase inflationary pressure and thus raise aggregate unemployment. This line of argument implies a competitive model of the labour market with settlements lying on the demand curve, individual workers are not penalized for their lack of bargaining power, and their 'exit' threat is sufficient to prevent exploitation. Given these assumptions then the evidence summarised in Chapter 3, that on average British unions do raise the wage of many of their members significantly above the non-union level, implies that unions raise the NAIRU. In Chapter 7 it was suggested that increases in this differential were a significant cause of rising British wage pressure and hence unemployment in the 1970s. However, the outcome of the above 'right to manage' model has been shown to be inefficient and if unions are concerned with employment levels the 'efficient bargain' model suggests that bargaining decides which combination of wages and employment prevails. If the relative bargaining power of unions and firms differs between employment and wages then Manning (1987) argues that inefficient outcomes may again result, and the legal framework may produce such distortions.

The suggestion that collective bargaining may produce inefficient outcomes does not by itself constitute an argument against trade unions since the assumptions may not hold or unions may offer compensating benefits. Freeman and Medoff (1984) argued that economists have ignored the possibility that unions' collective voice may increase efficiency in the internal labour market. Their model reflects the dominance in much of the labour market of long tenure, reflecting costly turnover to employers and workers. The collective voice which unions provide is an alternative to the exit or quitting threat of the individual worker. Unionised firms will therefore be more responsive to the preferences of the average and less mobile insider, and will design more effective wage and personnel policies. In the primary sector of the labour market the productivity benefits from improved 'voice' may exceed the costs of higher pay, and both workers and firms can benefit from the presence of unions. Such benefits are independent of any 'shock' benefits, where the introduction of unions raises wages and forces management to reduce x-inefficiency. Unfortunately no empirical evidence on British trade unions' impact upon productivity exists and American studies have produced mixed results (Hirsch and Addison 1986; Cameron 1987). Malcomson (1983) provides another explanation of how unions could contribute to economic efficiency: here risk-averse firms may find risk-sharing easier under collective bargaining. Finally, given that unions reallocate income both away from profits and within the wages and salaries share, calculation of their total impact on welfare also requires some judgement upon the desired distribution of income. At present any overall assessment of the impact of unions on the British economy remains an issue of belief rather than one of evidence.

8.2.1 The 'attack on'/'reform of' trade unions

Reductions in union power can be produced by lowering the level of aggregate demand. Recession is likely to reduce union power directly since the strike threat becomes less effective when capacity utilisation and profitability are low and alternative workers abundant. The recession will also indirectly weaken aggregate union power as unionised sectors are more cyclically sensitive. However, such reductions are temporary and costly; the Thatcher Government has tried to modify the legal framework of industrial relations to produce a permanent reduction in the relative bargaining power of unions. The traditional basis of union law is immunity from civil prosecution for torts committed in furtherance of a trade dispute; unlike in most European countries there is no legal right to strike. Legal immunity for a strike with a member's own employer remains broadly intact but a Green Paper, *Trade Unions and their Members* published in February 1987, formed the basis for the fourth major piece of labour legislation enacted by the Conservatives since 1979. The 1980 Employment Act withdrew legal immunities for secondary picketing, required overwhelming support in ballots for new closed shops and provided public funds for secret union ballots. The 1982 Employment Act required periodic balloting to maintain existing closed shops, narrowed the definition of a trade dispute, allowed the selective dismissal of strikers and made the parent union responsible for any unconstitutional actions of lay officers. The Trade Union Act of 1984 required secret ballots before strikes and introduced periodic ballots both to approve political funds and re-elect officers with votes on the union's governing body. The 1987 Employment Bill seeks to counter actions taken by the National Union of Miners during their strike; in particular it aims at protecting individual members who refuse to strike. In addition it aims at ending the post-entry closed shop by making unions liable for any action they take to enforce one and forbidding any dismissal for non-membership of a union. A policing agency, the Commissioner for the Rights of Trade Union Members, is to be established to investigate members' complaints against their unions.

Assessment of the impact of these measures is problematic; the emphasis upon a particular version of union democracy in the legislation will only have a favourable impact upon wage pressure if the membership is less militant than the leadership. Alternatively, if we assume that unions respond to the wishes of the median voter then the legislation is based upon the assumption that the median voter in postal ballots must be less militant than the median voter under the previous system of branch meetings. There is little evidence on this issue. The other objective has been to reduce union bargaining power by making it more difficult for unions to recruit and both organise and sustain a strike. Once again there is as yet no consensus as to the impact of the new legal framework on union power, though clearly the recession has changed relative bargaining strength with deindustrialisation and the growth of the 'peripheral' workforce threatening permanently to reduce union power. The size of the union/non-union wage differential does not appear to have fallen, though Matthews and Minford (1987) conjecture that because unions retain the strike threat for pay disputes the main impact has been to increase productivity by speeding up redundancies. Hence the measures contributed to the rise in unemployment rather than to a reduction in wage pressure as initially envisaged by these authors.

Mayhew (1985) argues that recent changes in British industrial relations, particularly the weakening of trade unions, owe more to the recession than to legislation. Two surveys by Edwards (1985) and Batstone (1984) found that the formal presence of unions at the workplace had changed little, and few companies had tried to reduce or eliminate the role of trade unions. The loss of 2 million union members between 1980 and 1984 seems due to the disproportionate closure of large plants (Millward and Stevens 1986), though the new legislation and changes in the enforcement of previous legislation enabled the defeat of major strikes in the coal-mining and newspaper industries, hastening the contraction of employment. While trade union organisation appears to have survived fairly intact and average real earnings have been rising since 1982, other proxies of union power indicate a different picture. The growth of flexibility, decline in strike frequency, reductions in job demarcations and narrowing of issues subject to collective bargaining, all indicate a decline in union power (Kelly 1987). The 1984 Workplace Industrial Relations Survey suggested that the attack upon the closed shop has reversed the growth trend, though the measures presuppose an inefficiency which managers seem reluctant to identify. Union power has been reduced since the election of a Conservative Government in 1979 but the relative importance of legislation and consequences of this weakening remain unclear. If the major cause of recent changes in relative bargaining strength is recession then the search for a permanent solution to inflationary wage-fixing continues. Policy alternatives start from a presumption that co-ordination is necessary when collective bargaining dominates wage-fixing.

8.3 Conventional incomes policies

8.3.1 Rationale

There is a great diversity in both the form of proposals for incomes policies and their rationale. In general such policies are favoured by those who have moral or efficiency objections to unrestrained market forces dominating the labour market and opposed by those who believe either in the virtues of a competitive environment or that such policies are biased in favour of profits. For one group the benefits of such policies are that they subvert market forces in the determination of labour market prices. An improvement in equity is the rationale for those who believe in the holy grail of 'just' wages and who view market forces as producing an 'unfair' set of labour market prices. For a second group incomes policies improve social welfare by constraining wage pressure associated with a given level of aggregate demand. Incomes policies therefore allow the economy to be run at a higher level of capacity and employment for any given rate of inflation, avoiding the pain of restrictive demand management policies. They can also improve the inflation and unemployment costs of adjusting to supply-side shocks. This argument is often employed by those economists who believe that market forces work slowly and that shocks cause appreciable and lengthy deviations from potential output. Finally, a third group support incomes policies because of what they consider to be a fundamental contradiction between individual wage-fixing and stable inflation, the 'public good' argument. Individual bargainers have no concern for the impact of their bargain on the overall inflation rate since they have no way of ensuring that any restraint they exercise will be duplicated in other bargains. This 'prisoners' dilemma' characteristic of pay bargaining, more fully outlined in Morris and Sinclair (1985), creates a divergence between private and social welfare. This divergence, inevitable in decentralised wage-fixing, is what incomes policies seek to address.

8.3.2 Form

All governments become involved in pay bargaining, largely because of two reasons. Firstly, governments are major employers, with public sector employees making up about 30 per cent of British employees at the beginning of the 1980s. Secondly, government has to accept overall responsibility for managing the economy including fixing and achieving inflation goals. There have been a large number of different types of incomes policies implemented in Western economies since 1960. These have largely been of the 'fire brigade' type, introduced to cope with specific economic problems. For example, balance of payments problems have generated incomes policies in the UK, Canada, Denmark, Finland and the Netherlands. The mildest form of incomes policy is exhortation by government to moderate wage increases to conform usually with some declared 'norm'; this type of policy is called 'jawboning' in the USA. A more formal policy is where an incomes policy is enforced, but only partially. Thus the Thatcher Government while eschewing incomes policies has introduced cash limits and rate-capping which effectively determine pay settlements in the public sector. Only if savings can be made on employment levels can increases exceed the allowed amount in the cash limit. While the police and fire service have special agreements which link wage increases to movements in earnings in the economy as a whole, elsewhere in the public sector the Thatcher Government has moved away from comparability and arbitration and so increased its powers to control public sector pay. The most formal type of incomes policy is one that enforces compliance with a norm or freeze; Robinson (in Morris 1985) provides a chronology of incomes policies in the UK since 1960.

8.3.3 Effects

The arguments against formal incomes policies are twofold. First, they interfere in the market mechanism and prevent adjustment to changes in the pattern of demand and terms of trade. Second, enforcement costs of traditional policies rise rapidly with the duration of the policy and inefficient non-wage adjustment replaces the adjustment of relative wages. Bogus productivity deals, regrading of jobs, improved holiday and sick pay schemes replace wage adjustment. Controlling wages does not necessarily control unit labour costs which presumably is the appropriate target for reducing inflation. The first objection presupposes that labour markets are price competitive and the second that non-wage adjustments are inferior. We now briefly review the present knowledge concerning the impact of incomes policies in the UK.

A major problem which researchers face in evaluating incomes policies is that the diversity of objectives and form of these policies prevents general conclusions being drawn. Most British researchers have concentrated on the impact upon wage inflation, using aggregate wage equations. Although most studies take basic wage rates as the dependent variable, unit labour costs would appear to be the most relevant to an investigation of inflationary consequences. It is usual to estimate the wage equation with either a dummy variable trying to pick up the effect of the introduction and abandonment of the policy or more generally testing for change in the form of the wage equation when a policy is in operation. Different models of the wage equation have produced different results, though Henry (1981) concluded that in all types of models incomes policies had reduced wage inflation during operation, but that real wages caught up rapidly on abandonment. The existence of this 'catch-up' or 'dam burst' effect appears well established (Sumner and Ward 1983), as does the modest nature of the temporary reduction in inflation. In a disaggregated study, Pencavel (1982) suggested that a wage freeze appears to affect the frequency of wage settlements, and that statutory incomes policies have a bigger impact on the size of wage adjustment than do voluntary ones. Incomes policies may reduce the probability of wage adjustment, as well as the size of that adjustment, hence their abandonment generates the catch-up effect. Davies (1979) found some evidence which indicated that pay-based strikes decline during the operation of the policy but increase afterwards, again reflecting this 'dam burst' effect.

One of the major arguments against incomes policies is that they distort wage differentials and relativities and so prevent the efficient allocation of labour in the economy. Although we have been sceptical about the importance of price adjustments in the labour market, the squeezing of skill differentials and emergence of skill shortages in the UK in the 1970s were taken as illustrating the harmful effects of incomes policies. Less skilled manual workers are more commonly paid by results and skilled by time, hence the less skilled can more frequently offset incomes policies by increasing effort and output. However, the narrowing of skill differentials in the UK preceded the flat-rate incomes policies of the mid-1970s. Ashenfelter and Layard (1983) found that most short-term changes in relativities were reversed, suggesting that inflation confuses the labour market decision-maker and that incomes policies may not cause significant distortions in the market.

8.3.4 Conclusions

Conventional incomes policies can have favourable short-term impact upon wage inflation but little net longer-term effect. In a sense the above empirical studies are irrelevant to contemporary debates, since few argue for a return to one-off, 'fire brigade' policies. Modern discussion has concentrated on whether a low-cost permanent incomes policy is feasible. In a developed Western democracy permanence appears to require the free bargaining of wages, ruling out traditional incomes policies. This means that the policy must work through incentives rather than prohibition, by adding a further constraint to individual negotiators' behaviour.

There has been a wide range of alternative reforms suggested for wage-fixing in the UK, most seeking to provide a method to internalise the inflationary consequences of individual bargains. Among the more ingenious was Wood's (1978) scheme where bargains are concerned directly about relativities, only later does the government set the monetary value of the base wage. Of equal ingenuity was Meade's (1984) advocacy of compulsory, pendular arbitration, where either the employer's or union's last offer is awarded. Neither of these policies seems likely to generate widespread tripartisan support and most recently two other suggestions have been widely discussed: a tax-based incomes policy and profit-sharing.

8.4 Tax-based incomes policies

The origins of tax-based incomes policies (TIPS) were in work by the American economists Weintraub and Wallich in the early 1970s and Bosanquet (1983) provides a survey of alternative TIPS proposals. The central argument is that a counter-inflation tax can raise the costs of parties negotiating large increases in wages, as the tax burden shifts towards firms with high pay increases. Layard (1982, 1986) has argued that British political reality, as well as protecting incentives for workers to seek promotion internally and externally, requires the tax to be levied upon employers. The tax base should be average hourly earnings since this has the closest relationship to labour costs, and taxing earnings per worker would penalise overtime working and give a further incentive to the employment of part-time workers. Each year the government should declare a norm for the growth in nominal average hourly earnings, employers who pay in excess of this norm can do so, but excess payments are subject to a tax penalty. To encourage reductions in wage increases to be reflected in lower price increases, Layard suggests that employers' National Insurance contributions be reduced in line with the proceeds of the inflation tax. Workers can still bargain for larger increases, but as their employers face a higher tax bill from granting increases above the norm the employment consequences of pursuing the claim are greater, and the individual firms' demand for labour has become more elastic. The tax therefore raises employers' resistance to negotiating wage increases. A full tax–subsidy scheme which rewarded firms who paid increases below the norm is not advocated due to the perceived political disadvantages of associating the scheme with incentives for real wage cuts. The great virtue of such a proposal is that it avoids centralisation of wage-fixing; free collective bargaining is diluted but not displaced. Given that public sector pay broadly follows private sector pay, discriminatory partial income policies can be avoided. As the Layard scheme can be integrated into the present pay-as-you-earn (PAYE) and National Insurance schemes, administration costs are small, though small firms could be exempt.

Any tax imposes economic costs apart from administration. The tax will penalise adjustments in the labour market, and expanding firms will face higher taxes if they raise wages to attract additional workers. Since the tax base is not unit labour costs productivity deals will be discouraged, and firms will find it more expensive to reward increases in productivity, though exemption of profit-share payments from TIPS would reduce the schemes' distortions. Similarly firms who seek to upgrade their workforce are penalised; the scheme favours the substitution of low-paid, unskilled for higher-skilled employees. While this has the advantages of reallocating demand towards groups suffering high unemployment, it would take British industry even more down market in world trading terms. These labour-intensive industries tend to be slow-growing and fiercely competitive with the growth of the newly industrialised countries (NICs). A further problem is that firms with product market power can more easily pass on the tax to consumers in the form of higher prices or take tax rebates as windfall profits rather than lower their prices. The incentive effect of the tax is therefore undermined and workers in firms unable to pass on the tax may become more militant. In the tradable goods sector of the economy the tax cannot be passed on, but any widening of profitability differences between sectors open and closed to international competition seems undesirable. If one leaves aside the arguments of political support for such policies then the economic arguments depend, yet again, upon one's beliefs about the extent of price competition in the labour market. For many of those who believe that the total unemployment costs of deviations from potential output are large, the misallocation costs of interference in wage-fixing are minor costs to incur in reducing unemployment. For new, classical economists in contrast, shocks cannot be accommodated more easily by inteference in wage-fixing; indeed interference must increase the natural rate of unemployment.

Doubts remain whether individual participants have sufficient incentives to conform with socially desirable behaviour. If unions are sensitive to the unemployment caused by higher wage growth, TIPS succeed; our previous analysis questioned this premiss when insiders face renegotiating contracts with LIFO. In addition while TIPS are ultimately targeted against inflation in practice they usually control only labour market income. Other sources of income, particularly profits, remain uncontrolled, which produces problems of fairness. Even when dividends are also controlled, as in the Layard 1982 scheme, the overall distribution of income between wages and profits is not addressed. Fragmented and adversarial industrial relations have produced embedded patterns of behaviour in which sectional interests dominate, and more than the introduction of TIPS and synchronised wage bargaining may be required to modify behaviour. If the origin of inflationary wage pressure is a disagreement about the aggregate distribution of income then TIPS are irrelevant to the solution of the problem. Cornwall (1983) argues that countries with adversarial industrial relations cannot implement successful incomes policies unless industrial policies are introduced which foster co-operation and co-determination. Strong internal labour markets can aid this development as can the development of profit-related pay.

8.5 Share economy

For the minority of Japanese workers who are permanent employees about a quarter of their total earnings are in the form of biannual bonus payments loosely based upon current profitability. This share system contrasts with the wage system of the UK where profit-related pay is much less important. This relative lack of flexibility in British wages was examined in Chapter 2; in Chapter 7 it was argued that this caused greater unemployment adjustment costs for any given shock. The British Government's 1986 Green

Paper, *Profit Related Pay* (Cmnd 9835) claimed that increased profit-sharing would not only stabilise cyclical fluctuations and raise overall employment levels but also promote productivity growth through improvements in co-operation and motivation. The formal arguments have been popularised, though with a different emphasis, by Weitzman (1984, 1985, 1987).

8.5.1 Theory of profit-sharing

Consider arguments at the micro level first: if workers receive a reduced fixed wage plus a share of profits, the marginal cost of labour is reduced. Only the fixed wage component enters into the firm's employment decision. Provided that this base wage is sufficiently low, the wedge between average and marginal labour costs encourages the expansion of employment. In Weitzman's (1984: 91) terms the 'share firm always wants to hire more labour than it is actually able to hire'; in the share economy unemployment disappears. A similar argument in support of profit-sharing concerns enhanced wage flexibility. By directly linking pay and performance, changes in product or raw material market conditions can be quickly accommodated by labour market adjustments; the greater flexibility of wages means reduced adjustments of employment. In addition to lowering the marginal cost of labour and promoting employment stability, profit-sharing promotes co-operation, raising the marginal product of labour and hence the demand for labour. The supposed mechanisms here are similar to those discussed in the efficiency wage arguments of Chapter 7. The share system reduces absenteeism and lowers turnover, improves industrial relations and raises employee effort. The wage system finds it difficult to resolve the problems caused by the asymmetry of information in the workplace; the worker can choose his effort level but the employer cannot. The wage system implies that increased efforts by workers merely raise profits, while reduced efforts cannot be easily attributed to individual workers and therefore escapes penalties. In contrast the share system establishes a link between worker effort and remuneration, the greater the share of incremental profits and degree of group production the stronger will be this link. However, where the workforce is large and fragmented 'free-rider' problems are likely to emerge and individual incentive schemes will be more effective in stimulating productivity growth. At the macro level Weitzman argues that as the share system promotes full employment, governments can concentrate demand management on achieving the inflation target. Restrictive monetary policy need no longer cause unemployment, the number of independent policy instruments has been increased and employment and inflation targets need no longer conflict.

Traditional objections to profit-sharing schemes are that they are biased against hiring new workers and investment expenditure since both dilute insiders' shares. Further distortions in firms' decision-taking result from the short time horizons of workers. Estrin, Grout and Wadhwani's (1987) assessment of Weitzman's argument reviews recent critical comments which have concentrated upon weaknesses in the dynamics of profit-sharing arguments. They question how base wages can remain low in an economy with excess demand for labour and risk-averse workers, and whether higher turnover costs may distort the relationship between wage and labour costs. If firms view the total remuneration per worker, rather than base wage, as the marginal cost of additional workers then profit-sharing will have little impact upon employment or inflation. A general weakness of profit-sharing proposals is that once again they pay little attention to the motivation of workers. Workers (insiders) exchange increased employment stability for greater income instability, increased flexibility meaning increased instability from the other side of the bargaining table; this completely reverses the assumed objectives of workers in implicit contract theory. If the firm has established practices for determining redundancies and workers are risk-averse then it is difficult to see how the average employee can be persuaded of the benefits of profit-sharing. All employees will have an incentive to restrict hirings and so increase their share of profits. Indeed Sinclair (1987) shows in his model that with most combinations of firm and household attitude to risk-taking the share economy does not produce greater utility for the representative worker than the wage system. Weitzman (1985: 946) acknowledged the conflict between socially and individually rational behaviour in a footnote, arguing that: 'strong material incentives, such as favourable tax treatment of the profit-sharing component of a worker's pay will probably be needed to convince senior workers to acquiesce in a profit-sharing scheme'. In his 1987 insider–outsider model the need for preferential tax treatment is more directly recognised, as in this model insiders always prefer wages to a share of profits.

To avoid some of the problems with Weitzman-style profit-sharing Meade (1986) proposes an alternative remuneration system, the discriminating labour–capital partnership (DCLP). This is a form of capital–labour partnership where additional workers are hired under different conditions from existing workers and additional capital shares are issued to finance new investment. Hence investment is no longer discouraged since labour's share is automatically adjusted downwards as investment occurs. The introduction of a multi-tier pay structure allows firms to hire additional workers at lower rates of pay while safeguarding current workers' remuneration. This indicates that the DCLP firm will be less resistant to employment expansion then a share firm or labour co-operative where workers have no incentive to expand employment above the level which maximises profit per worker. By removing some conflicts of interest between capital and labour the DCLP will allow greater worker participation in decision-taking. Doubts have been expressed (Wadhwani 1987c) on whether a multi-tier pay structure is a viable solution to the 'insider–outsider' conflict which profit-sharing exacerbates. However, it may be that the increased 'flexibility' of British labour markets represents in practice a movement towards multi-tier pay structure as in Japan, where 'temporary' workers tend to receive inferior rates of pay and conditions compared to 'permanent' workers. All this is in striking contrast to our analysis in Chapter 6; we now find economists encouraging labour market discrimination, with women and other labour market minorities being likely to gain employment only on inferior conditions to those of existing workers. Discriminatory pay structures, we suggested earlier, are likely to produce new conflicts of interest which may be as harmful to productivity and employment growth as the old ones we are seeking to eliminate.

In common with TIPS, existing proposals for profit-sharing take a rather naïve view of industrial relations, co-operation is discussed but not co-determination, and the issue of industrial democracy rarely surfaces in contemporary economic literature. Traditional antagonisms are seen as removable by reforms in wage-fixing alone, even where the average worker receives no direct benefit from that reform. In Weitzman's proposal the broader economic benefits actually depend upon excluding workers from any influence upon employment decisions. There is thus a conflict between the macro and micro arguments for profit-sharing. The macro argument requires insiders to lower their resistance to hires, the micro argument seeks increased productivity by encouraging greater insider involvement in firm performance. Rarely is co-operation in decision-making considered though share-based profit-sharing schemes imply some input into decision-making, but as owners rather than workers. Since the 1974 Bullock Committee of Inquiry on Industrial Democracy, employee participation in decision-making along West

German or Swedish lines has become a peripheral issue in British discussions, notwithstanding its actual growth in British firms.

8.5.2 Profit-sharing in the UK

Disregarding these criticisms, British governments have looked favourably upon the expansion of profit-sharing. The 1972 Finance Act introduced tax advantages to certain types of executive share options, share incentive schemes and share-based profit-sharing. In the following year further concessions to firms and employees operating share option schemes were introduced and again in 1978, 1980 and 1984. Richardson and Nejad (1986) describe these measures and suggest a rapid expansion of qualifying schemes in the early 1980s to take advantage of these deferred tax breaks. The Finance (No. 2) Act 1987 introduced tax relief for profit-related pay following the enthusiastic Green Paper of the previous year. For a government notably reluctant to intervene in markets with tax/subsidies, surprisingly little analysis appeared to lie behind this particular policy; many of the supposed benefits of profit-sharing are internal to the firm and the failure of market forces to ensure efficient payment systems was not identified. In principle such failures could be caused by externalities, management inertia or the resistance by senior employees as discussed above.

By 1984 about 40 per cent of firms in the UK operated some form of sharing scheme, with share ownership schemes most common, but with profit-sharing more frequently found in manufacturing. The 1980 Workplace Industrial Relations Survey suggested that about 10 per cent of workers in British industry were eligible to participate in share ownership schemes, with about half doing so. The 1982 Employment Act required directors of companies with more than 250 employees to include in their annual report a statement of action taken to promote employee involvement. The Department of Employment reports general compliance and a trend towards greater, though diverse, provision of information and consultation (Smith 1986).

8.5.3 Empirical studies

A fundamental problem with empirical studies on this issue concerns the direction of causation between firm performance and profit-sharing. Most empirical studies do not standardise for managerial ability, and if only 'good' managers introduce profit-sharing the causation may be the reverse of the above arguments. Studies in the USA have generally found little evidence of a relationship between share ownership schemes and profitability (see the survey in Blanchflower and Oswald 1987a), though Fitzroy and Kraft (1985) find a significant relationship using German data. Freeman and Weitzman's (1986) study of the Japanese bonus system confirms that bonuses move more cyclically than the base wage, and that higher bonuses are positively correlated with higher employment in most specifications of the employment function. However, the causal relationship appears to be that wages are lower than they would be without profit-sharing, indicating that productivity gains may not be large. Indeed, Wadhwani (1987a) argues that during the thirty years after 1950 Japan did not in reality experience smaller cyclical instability or lower inflation than other industrialised economies. More recently Japanese bonus payments have been reluctant to fall in the face of recent declines in profitability.

Blanchflower and Oswald (1987a) and Estrin, Grout and Wadhwani (1987) provide recent surveys of empirical studies and we limit consideration to the major contributions. Surveys of British workers' and managers' attitudes to profit-sharing suggest only small improvements in morale and productivity (Income Data Services 1986). Until recently there was no direct UK empirical evidence on the effects of profit-sharing on firm and worker behaviour, but in the last few years several studies have been undertaken. Richardson and Nejad (1986) concentrated upon the impact of share ownership schemes upon share prices, the latter postulated to pick up the overall effect upon profits. The link between the short-term movement of share prices and long-term impact of share ownership is a tenuous one and the sample was small and concentrated among larger retail firms. The authors used simple correlation analysis to claim a significant positive association between share prices and share ownership schemes. The direction of causation was not identified and the authors recognised that the most innovative and successful managers may have introduced share ownership schemes, hence reversing their hypothesis. Estrin and Wilson (1986) considered the metalworking sector and concluded surprisingly that share ownership and profit-sharing schemes together significantly increased employment; Wadhwani (1987b) studying larger firms produced the same result. In both cases the positive influence on employment appeared to be through the boost given to productivity. Blanchflower and Oswald (1987a) examined the impact of employee share ownership schemes on the employment and investment performance of firms in manufacturing. They fail to find any significant difference in the behaviour of investment or on the level of employment and speed of adjustment between establishments which operate share ownership schemes and those who do not. Their study of all establishments with any system of profit-sharing schemes (Blanchflower and Oswald 1987b) also failed to discover any influence upon financial performance. Bradley and Estrin (1987) present a detailed comparison of the performance of one of the UK's largest employee-owned companies, John Lewis Partnership. Their estimates suggest that the firm has greater wage flexibility and higher employment than conventionally owned competitors.

8.5.4 Conclusion

The evidence concerning the impact of profit-sharing upon firm performance is not encouraging for the Weitzman model. If the Weitzman approach is rejected then any benefits are internal and there appears no economic rationale for a permanent government subsidy for profit-sharing. However, most schemes in the UK are small scale, on average only about 3 per cent of pay, and shares are often held in trust for up to five years. It may therefore be premature to write off profit-sharing as a vehicle for improving economic performance. Though whether it is superior to individual incentive schemes or alternative policies to encourage productivity growth remains to be investigated. The divorce between profit-sharing and co-determination in discussions of British schemes is in marked contrast to Scandinavian debates. The operation of the Swedish Employee Investment Fund (Hashi and Hussain 1986) which directly aims at increasing employee participation in the running of companies, albeit through trade union representatives, is likely to generate much interest in other Western economies.

8.6 Social insurance and taxation

The concern of this book has been government intervention into the labour market, and we have been concentrating upon issues involving improving labour market efficiency rather than labour market equity. As such we have neglected any systematic discussion of low pay and poverty, not because of their unimportance but because these topics are largely unrelated to our central concern. However, the operation of the social insurance and taxation system will impinge upon labour market behaviour. In Chapter 3 we noted that social security expenditure now accounts for about 30 per cent of central government expenditure and we saw how National Insurance contributions distort the relations between both gross and net earnings and between wage costs and labour costs. In Chapter 7 we mentioned the impact which the insurance and tax system could have upon the supply of labour and hence measured unemployment. In this section we are largely concerned with the reasons for state intervention in the insurance market and with the consequences of the present social security and tax system for individual labour market behaviour; we do not attempt to assess their impact upon inequality and poverty. However, we do note the argument of Piachaud that: 'Much attention is rightly given to benefit levels and the distribution of incomes. But relatively little attention is given to policies affecting the generation of incomes, or, more generally, the opportunities available to different individuals and groups' (1987: 41). Policy debates have tended to ignore the interactions between the distribution of work and distribution of income: efficiency and equity effects have too often been treated separately.

8.6.1 The rationale for social insurance

The dominant form of social security provision in the UK is the National Insurance Scheme which operates a quasi-insurance scheme in which compulsory contributions in the form of payroll taxes largely finance benefits to the sick, unemployed and retired. The form and extent of social insurance provision have been the subject of much controversy and it is important initially to consider the objectives of a social insurance system. The economic arguments usually rest upon economic efficiency arguments though they inter-mix with arguments reflecting particular value judgements. Specifically, most arguments concern the extent of market failures in the insurance and capital markets and the desirability of achieving a redistribution of income. In our previous analysis we have already considered some of the complications which uncertainty produces in labour markets. Risk of undesirable outcomes together with widespread risk aversion suggests a demand for insurance against income losses due to illness or unemployment. Self-insurance will generally be inadequate where the costs of the unpleasant event are large, fires and thefts for example, and where individuals are highly risk-averse. Hence specialist insurers develop to arrange groups to pool risks, as with life insurance for example. In the labour market employers may become 'sellers' of insurance, as suggested by the implicit contract theory discussed in Chapter 7. However, where heterogeneity is pervasive, causing information to be costly and incomplete or where externalities are important, market failure may occur and prevent the private market from producing efficient levels of insurance.

Creedy and Disney (1985) survey the forms of market failure which can occur in the insurance and capital markets. Firstly, private insurance cannot cope with situations where risks are non-diversifiable, since if all suffer the risks cannot be pooled. Thus wars or persistent mass unemployment risks would have to be excluded from private insurance markets. The government could not produce real insurance contracts in these cases either, but value judgements may induce it to provide support to those who suffer from these events beyond their individual control. A second source of market failure occurs when low-risk groups seek to reduce their costs of insurance and gravitate towards insurance companies who operate effective risk-rating, that is premiums reflecting the probability of claim. This may have the result that perceived or known high-risk groups face prohibitive insurance costs and are in practice excluded from the market. Where risk-rating is difficult then insurers may operate via almost arbitrary rules, again excluding certain groups from the market. Problems from adverse selection have been considered in previous chapters and in this case a compulsory state insurance scheme could prevent low-risk groups from opting out. Higher-skilled workers with a low probability of unemployment may be forced to subsidise the unemployment insurance costs of the less skilled workers who are more liable to suffer longer spells of unemployment. If individuals are unaware of these differential risks then even intervention which results in redistribution may be Pareto efficient. A further source of market failure and one that dominates much discussion on this issue concerns moral hazard. This concerns the possibility that once insured the recipients change their behaviour in a way which increases the likelihood of the insurance benefits being paid. For example, sickness insurance alters the relative price of work and sickness and may reduce the toleration of discomfort at work or encourage absenteeism or reckless behaviour. While private companies employ no-claims bonuses and deductibles to reduce incidence, it has been argued that the state has a greater ability to monitor and enforce behaviour. Ever since debates about Poor Law reform, where many classical economists argued that relief for poverty should be provided only 'indoor'(poorhouses) and at levels below customary subsistence, moral hazard effects have aroused bitter controversies. In the UK unlike the USA, this controversy has concentrated exclusively upon disincentives to work, rather than moral hazards to employers and disincentives to workplace accidents and redundancies.

Capital markets may fail as well as insurance markets and the arguments for a state retirement scheme are largely based upon this possibility. Workers saving for retirement face designing a portfolio of assets which combines security and financial return, and for the small inexperienced investor information costs may be prohibitive. Perhaps more importantly because private companies do not offer indexed investments, inflation poses a chronic problem for workers wishing to save for retirement. A social insurance scheme which includes an element of forced saving and inflation-proofing can avoid these failures.

An allied argument to that of market failures is that the government may have cost advantages in the provision of insurance in the labour market. Selling costs of insurance appear comparatively high and information costs may also be severe in a competitive market. The economies of scale possible in information gathering and decision-taking and the disappearance of selling costs under a compulsory scheme may make state provision efficient, though administration costs will depend upon the type of schemes operated. In the UK flat-rate universal schemes such as child benefit have administration costs of less than 3 per cent of benefits, while means-tested benefits such as rent rebates can have proportions five times as great (Hansard, 23 February 1982).

If the state scheme does not apply risk-related premiums then income redistribution must occur. If high risk of unemployment or sickness is positively correlated with low incomes then inequality may be reduced as a consequence. For those with value judgements which equate reduced inequality with greater equity this represents a further advantage of social insurance. However, it may well be that social insurance, as well as incomes policies discussed previously, are relatively inefficient and indirect mechanisms for achieving redistribution, an argument supported by the weak link between labour market income and total income discovered in Chapter 3. The tax and transfer system may appear a much more powerful and direct policy for influencing income distribution. This argument implies a much clearer distinction between the social insurance and tax systems than is the case in the real world. Governments can increase taxable capacity by encouraging the insurance 'myth' that contributions to social insurance finance an individual's future benefits. In the UK the National Insurance Fund was in sizeable surplus for virtually all of the 1970s and the surcharge on employers' National Insurance contributions between 1976 and 1984 was explicitly introduced as a revenue-raising device. If it is accepted that the National Insurance Scheme should not operate like an insurance system where high risks are excluded, then the reason for this separation of taxation and social security becomes even more obscure.

A final reason for the provision of social insurance may be the paternalistic belief that individuals cannot be trusted to pursue their own interests. This belief poses particular problems for economists given their attachment to rational behaviour in aggregate. However, if individuals cannot obtain sufficient information on the distribution of risk they face then misallocation may result. Thus the unforeseen election of a government committed to different methods and objectives of demand management may alter the probability of becoming unemployed and invalidate previous insurance decisions. Of course, uncertainty regarding the probability of events can lead to either under- or over-insurance. Myopia or extreme risk adversity could provide further support to essentially paternalistic rationales for state provision. We now proceed to consider the relevance of these propositions to the actual system of social insurance in the UK.

8.6.2 The British system

Recent detailed descriptions of the British system are contained in Dilnot, Kay and Morris (1984), Hemming (1984) and Beenstock (1987b). Widespread concern with the operation of the social security system culminated in the Social Security Act (1986). Initially we consider these perceived weaknesses of the scheme in the mid-1980s. The British social security system was originally based upon the belief that the state should operate a quasi-insurance system, where compulsory contributions financed benefits payable upon certain contingencies. Surprisingly, redistribution played little role in the evolution of the system and studies indicate that the largest scheme, state pension, produces only a small amount of redistribution. To meet the needs of the poor a system of transfers financed out of general taxation was developed separately. Contributory benefits accounted for less than 60 per cent of total social insurance benefits, and less than 40 per cent of expenditure on unemployment, though sickness and invalidity benefits were financed by contributions. This gradual demise of insurance principles led to National Insurance contributions becoming *de facto* taxes, and regressive ones at that (Creedy and Disney 1985). Strikingly, nominal expenditure on unemployment benefits has at times fallen as the stock of unemployment rises; in 1987 less than one-third of the UK unemployed were receiving unemployment benefits, instead nearly three-quarters received means-tested supplementary benefits. This resulted from the system for payment of unemployment benefits being based upon what Chapter 7 showed were false assumptions, namely unemployment spells are brief, infrequent and randomly distributed through the workforce. Like the unemployed, the sick also experience a decline in exit probability with duration, though the sickness and invalidity scheme was reformed in the early 1980s to take account of this tendency. With an extreme bimodality of spell distributions among the sick and extensive private occupational schemes, reform concentrated resources on the long-term claimants.

A fundamental problem with the whole system was its complexity; the original social insurance scheme was supplemented with non-contributory and means-tested benefits, such as family income supplement, which were introduced without any attempt to harmonise with existing benefits. In addition the tax and benefit system operated independently and the result is anomalies or 'traps'. Here marginal rates of taxation of over 100 per cent confront either those in work on low incomes ('poverty trap') or those unemployed seeking work ('unemployment trap'); labour market disincentive effects were therefore potentially important. Dilnot and Kell (1987) present the example of mothers married to unemployed men: they faced a large range of incomes from part and full-time work where the marginal tax rate was 100 per cent. The complexity of the system also resulted in other inefficiencies such as: high administrative costs; low take-up of benefits, and poor targeting of benefits to individuals in need. The choice between non-targeted schemes such as child benefit which are expensive in terms of impact achieved, and targeted benefits such as supplementary benefit which are expensive in terms of administration, was avoided by having both!

8.6.3 The impact of welfare and taxation upon labour supply

Few topics in economics have provoked more controversy and misunderstandings than the assessment of the effect of tax and benefits upon the supply of labour. In part this results from reliance upon hypothetical families to illustrate the size of replacement rates;

such data series suggest that replacement rates have not risen in the UK since the mid-1960s. Kay and Morris (1983) attempted to describe the actual replacement ratios, income out of work over income in work, faced by the employed in the early 1980s. In the long term, when National Insurance benefits and tax rebates are exhausted, only supplementary benefits are generally payable and their study suggests that few in employment had a high long-term replacement rate. In the short run, defined as the first thirteen weeks of unemployment, only about 5 per cent of employees would have had a replacement rate of 90 per cent or more in the early 1980s. For the unemployed, Moylan *et al.* (1984) found that for a group of male entrants into unemployment in 1978, taking the average replacement rate in weeks 5–13, about a third had replacement rates of 80 per cent or more. This proportion fell to a quarter when tax rebates were excluded. In comparison with other OECD countries the UK does not appear to have an especially high replacement ratio for unemployed workers (Chan-Lee, Coe and Prywes 1987).

However, the level of the replacement rate tells us nothing about how labour supply reacts or whether any supply response influences the incidence or level of unemployment. To estimate the size of benefit-induced unemployment it is necessary to test models of labour market behaviour. Aggregate studies require some hypothetical series to be produced for the replacement rate, and the variety of assumptions made to produce this series, together with theoretical differences in model specification, have produced a wide range of empirical results. Minford *et al.* (1983) estimate the implicit partial long-run elasticity of unemployment to the replacement rate to be as high as 4.5, which suggests that a 10 per cent reduction in benefits would reduce unemployment by over 1.25 million. In the Liverpool model a cut of 10 per cent in unemployment benefits alone reduces unemployment by 342 000 in four years, over twice the impact of any other macro model (Wallis *et al.* 1984). Nickell and Andrews (1983) at the other extreme find a small and statistically insignificant elasticity of unemployment to the replacement ratio. Unfortunately few studies are available on the contribution made to the rise in unemployment since 1979, though Pissarides (1986) suggests that about a tenth of the rise can be attributed to this cause, confirming the results of Layard and Nickell reproduced in Chapter 7.

In individual cross-sectional studies there appears to be more agreement about the size of the elasticity. Studies primarily examine the impact of the replacement rate on the duration of unemployment rather than inflow to unemployment. Given our earlier conclusion about the stability of inflow this appears appropriate. Narendranathan, Nickell and Stern (1985) examined a sample of benefit recipients entering unemployment in 1978. Their model assumes that the duration of unemployment will depend upon the probabilities of being offered and accepting a job, and that it is this latter probability which will be influenced by the replacement rate. The statistically significant effects of benefits on duration were confined to the first six months and to workers under forty-five years of age. Elasticities were higher for younger workers and ranged from 0.26 to 0.67. Using the same data but adopting a search model, Narendranathan and Nickell (1985) obtained lower estimates for younger workers. While other studies reject the detailed age and duration differences found by these studies, all obtain low elasticities (Micklewright 1986; Beenstock 1987b). Thus at the micro level there appears a consensus that variations in individuals' replacement rates were not associated with any large differences in unemployment duration.

The possibility remains that although the levels of benefit made seemingly little contribution to the rise in unemployment, the administering of benefits may have encouraged a reduction in search intensity. In principle individuals are not allowed to get unemployment benefits unless they are available and willing to accept suitable work. Disqualification from unemployment benefits also initially reduces supplementary benefits and continual refusal to work runs the risk of prosecution for failing to maintain oneself and family. Figures suggest that the late 1970s saw a reduction in the number of unemployment benefit cases referred for investigations and in cases prosecuted. However, the proportion of cases investigated which ended with benefits being denied has fallen, and there is no firm evidence that the system has become more tolerant of the 'work-shy'. Institutional changes, such as the abolition of the need to register at Jobcentres, may have been significant but evidence is lacking. However, the impact of the Restart Programme, whereby the long-term unemployed are interviewed and offered a job or training place the refusal of which jeopardises benefits, will provide further evidence. Between April and August 1987 only 1 in 200 Restart interviews resulted in the claimant being placed in employment.

We have so far concentrated upon the labour supply effects of high marginal 'tax' rates for low-income workers, but the 1979 Conservative Government also inherited a system with high marginal tax rates upon high-income groups. The differential on unearned income has been abolished and the higher marginal rates and average income rates reduced. Overall however, including

National Insurance and other taxes, the marginal tax rate on average earners was above the 1979 level until the mid-1980s. Assessment of the impact of taxes on the supply of labour of those in employment is equally controversial to the previous discussion. In theory a change in the tax rate is like a change in the wage rate discussed in Chapter 2. Thus a rise in the tax rate produces a substitution effect which encourages the substitution of less costly leisure for work and an income effect which increases work if leisure is a normal good. Both of these propositions appear empirically supported (Brown 1983). Overall the surveys by Pencavel (1986) and Killingsworth and Heckman (1986) indicate that for men it appears that the wage elasticity of labour supply is small and negative (around −0.16), whereas for women it is positive and larger (0.1–3.0). However, because the tax and benefit systems are generally progressive and themselves contribute to a non-linear budget constraint it is very difficult to produce any assessment of the overall impact of taxation changes on the supply of labour. To ascertain the impact of tax changes it is necessary to know the labour elasticities, the precise form of the tax change and the distribution of individuals on their budget constraints. Thus even to isolate the effects of cutting back the basic rate of taxation to 25 per cent is extremely problematic, with the effects on participation and supply of hours and effort likely to depend upon the sex, income level and family position of the worker. Current research does not indicate any large overall impact upon labour supplied from cuts in the tax rate which leave aggregate demand unaffected, though there may be other benefits, increased tax revenue or savings, from tax reductions. Supply-side economics must look elsewhere for academic respectability.

8.6.4 Reform of social security

In most OECD countries the 1980s have seen a reversal of previous trends towards microeconomic policies which provide increased social insurance and worker protection (Chan-Lee, Coe and Prywes 1987). Underlying this change was a widespread belief that labour market efficiency had been severely harmed by the moral hazard effects of prevailing policy on worker behaviour. In the UK the main response has been the Social Security Act (1986) and the Social Security Bill (1987) which are targeted at increasing the incentives for low wage-earners to seek employment. Supplementary benefits which represented the 'poverty line' benefit to the unemployed, disabled, retired and single parents was replaced by 'income support'.

The latter has eliminated many of the 'special needs' payments of the previous system and is designed to ensure that no one can be financially better-off unemployed. To this end family credit replaces the family income supplement to provide more generous support to low-paid working families and housing benefit became targeted on the lowest income families. Average losers from the changes include pensioners, young unemployed and unemployed without children, while the principal gainers include families with children and most sick and disabled. The 1987 Social Security Bill further tightens conditions for unemployment and sickness benefits, in particular halting benefit claims from sixteen- and seventeen-year-olds.

While the worst of the 'unemployment trap' is eliminated by these changes, the actual impact upon labour market behaviour remains uncertain. Only about half of families entitled actually received family income supplement and increased incentives to work for low wage-earners depend upon the take-up of family credits. In so far as incentives are strengthened then the changes should lower wages at the bottom of the labour market, further reducing the relative wages of unskilled workers. The change is thus akin to a subsidy to employers of unskilled workers and the response of demand to this change in relative price becomes critical. Marshall and McCormick's (1985) review indicates the relatively small response of employment to the abolition of Wages Councils; it suggests that the impact of the above changes is unlikely to be large. In addition the apparently small moral hazard effects on labour supply identified in the empirical work above together with the continuation of 'traps' due to the failure to co-ordinate tax and benefit systems, also suggest a relatively small impact upon the labour market.

8.6.5 Conclusions

Recent changes in the British system of social security continue previous trends towards selectivity and away from the Beveridge social insurance origins. Assessment of such reform depends upon the relative importance of the incentive and income support functions of a welfare system, which itself depends upon the relative importance of voluntary and involuntary unemployment. The problems of targeting and administration costs which selectivity produces have yet to be reduced by the combining of the tax, insurance and benefit systems, and changes have therefore replaced old anomalies by new ones. There are neglected alternatives to present policy; negative income taxes and minimum wage laws to avoid some of the disincentives of means-tested benefits and could be complementary to the extension of workfare. Worries persist that the labour market implications of reforms in this area have not been fully considered. The encouragement to employees to opt out of the earnings-related component of the state pension scheme is a useful illustration of the reasons for such a worry (Beenstock 1987a). Since National Insurance contributions are based broadly on a pay-as-you-go basis, rather than being actuarially based, employers have no incentive to vary the composition of their full-time permanent workforce by age or sex to limit their contributions. With an employer's occupational pension scheme there is an incentive to employ workers who are actuarially inexpensive. Adverse selection is therefore extended since it follows that other workers will be offered lower wages or suffer disproportionately from unemployment. Similarly the encouragement which the British Government has given to increasing numerical flexibility seems at odds with changes which increase the National Insurance contributions required to claim sickness and unemployment benefits.

Further reading

Hirsch and Addison's (1986) book provides a comprehensive introduction to the economic analysis of trade unions. The economics of profit-sharing is a growth area at present and the survey by Estrin, Grout and Wadhwani (1987) is a good place to investigate this literature. Beenstock (1987b) reviews many of the arguments and empirical studies on the disincentive effects on labour supply and Creedy and Disney (1985) analyse the economics of social insurance policy.

Chapter 9

CONCLUSIONS

The investigation of labour market policy has been integrated with an examination of relevant labour economics. Notwithstanding that wage equations may be a major factor in American litigation of disputes concerning labour market discrimination (Ashenfelter and Oaxaca 1987), the link between theory and policy has not been as strong as might have been imagined at the outset. There are several reasons for the absence of a close relationship between the two. Firstly, the origins of many labour market policies are not a concern with economic efficiency, however defined. Anti-discriminatory legislation and educational reforms are examples where other object-ives have usually motivated legislation. Secondly, the theoretical divide between competitive and structuralist explanations of labour market behaviour rarely produce a consensus regarding appropriate policy responses to perceived problems. Crucially, policy advice is constrained by the failure to resolve the dispute over whether it is more accurate to view 'good' workers as creating 'good' jobs or whether causation is the reverse. Thirdly, and related to the previous point, formal evaluation of policy is rare, thus evidence on many issues is lacking; examples are the absence of any evidence concerning the impact of different types of education and search on labour market productivity and efficiency. However, our combination of theory and policy has brought out some of the general principles which should underlie labour market policy. These principles are now outlined.

1. Labour markets are diverse

Chapters 2 and 3 concluded that policy needs to be based upon the realisation that the labour market contains both price- and quantity-adjusting markets. While the auction model is a useful description of many, mainly low-skilled, labour markets, it does not describe actual behaviour in many higher-skilled markets where wages are not the primary adjustment mechanism, especially during contractions. This distinction is not exclusively determined by the level of skill, however; examples of auction and structured internal labour markets appear to be found throughout the labour markets and their relative importance will vary over the cycle. This diversity appears to be largely a consequence of the size and composition of the non-wage costs of employing labour together with the sensitivity of labour productivity to personnel policies. Individual firms find different solutions to the minimisation of unit labour costs, though in general where training and turnover costs are low greater wage flexibility will be found.

2. Objectives need to be related to economic welfare

The objectives of policy need to be clearly stated and such objectives should reflect efficiency, output or equity objectives, rather than the attainment of a target which is unrelated or poorly related to economic welfare. For example, reducing the level of measured unemployment is unlikely to be a suitable target for labour market policy since it is only very loosely related to those objectives. Similarly the current practice of adopting unit costs as measurements of the effectiveness of the management of labour market policy is unlikely to promote efficiency. For all its limitations as a guide to policy-making, at least cost–benefit analysis recognised that costs needed to be related to benefits.

3. Efficiency and equity need not conflict

The concern in this book has been with labour market efficiency rather than equity, though we have been reluctant to accept conventional definitions of the former. However, these two objectives may not conflict; the previous consideration of discrimination and search suggested that intervention could promote both objectives. Since the distribution of income reflects the distribution of work as well as the distribution of labour market incomes, equity and efficiency are always to some extent interdependent. Making better use of female and black labour may promote efficiency and equity. Similarly, long-term unemployment and the restricted labour market opportunities faced by many northern or inner-city residents constrain economic welfare. Policies which expand opportunities promise efficiency and equity benefits.

4. Conventional policies affect primarily secondary labour markets

Given that price adjustment is not universal in the labour market, small, marginal taxes and subsidies on employment or training may have only a limited impact on employer behaviour. Targeting taxes and subsidies can strengthen their impact but since it is the secondary sector which is price-responsive, the impact will be concentrated in this sector of the labour market. Government will find it difficult to create additional employment opportunities in the primary sector through such measures, since insiders can resist competition from outsiders. Hence policy needs to recognise that unemployed and/or discriminated workers find it difficult to price or search themselves into 'good' jobs. The creation of additional 'good' jobs may require industrial and trade policies which target these high-wage–high-productivity sectors.

5. Direct controls need not have large efficiency costs

If unregulated labour markets tend to produce insider–outsider problems, especially in prolonging adjustments to contractionary shocks, then corporatist policies are one solution. Alternatively, the weakness of the price-adjustment mechanism in the labour market means that the efficiency costs of direct controls may be much lower than predicted by competitive models. Incomes policies, positive discrimination and compulsory vacancy registration may not create significant distortions in the market.

6. Policies need credibility and consistency

Modern economic analysis emphasises the importance of forward-looking decision-makers; it is therefore likely that consistency and credibility are important in policy-making. The lessons nearly learnt from regional policies in the 1970s need to be applied to labour market policies: continual changing of regulations and incentives tends to lead to policy being discounted in long-term decision-making.

7. Policies need to be consistent with long-term objectives

The possible conflict between short- and long-term objectives needs to be recognised by policy-makers. A depressed labour market suggests that priority be given to policies which target unskilled workers since they are over-represented among the unemployed. Such policies are unlikely to foster long-run competitiveness as they favour low-technology, labour-intensive production, that is, products whose world markets have grown relatively slowly in recent years and in which the NICs have competed most successfully. In the long term these policies are likely to be as counter-productive as the previously discredited measures aimed at reducing the supply of labour.

References

Abraham K, Farber M 1987 Job duration, seniority and earnings. *American Economic Review* 77(3): 278–97

Adams M, Maybury R, Smith W 1988 Trends in the distribution of earnings. *Employment Gazette* Feb: 75–82

Addison J 1975 On the interpretation of labour market earnings dispersion. In King J. (ed.) *Readings in labour economics.* Oxford University Press, 311–19

Adnett N 1986 On-the-job search in the recession. *Applied Economics* 18: 333–45

Adnett N 1987 State employment agencies and labour market efficiency. *Cambridge Journal of Economics* 11: 183–96

Akerlof G 1976 The economics of caste and of the rat race and other woeful tales. *Quarterly Journal of Economics* 90: 591–617

Akerlof G 1981 Jobs as dam sites. *Review of Economic Studies* 48: 37–49

Akerlof G 1982 Labor contracts as a partial gift exchange. *Quarterly Journal of Economics* 97: 543–70

Akerlof G 1984 *An economic theorist's book of tales.* Cambridge University Press

Akerlof G, Yellen J (eds) 1986 *Efficiency wage models of labour markets.* Cambridge University Press

Aldrich M, Buchele R 1986 *The economics of comparable worth.* Ballinger, Cambridge, Mass.

Allen S, Waton A, Purcell K, Wood S 1986 *The experience of unemployment.* Macmillan

Altonji J, Shakotko R 1987 Do wages rise with job seniority? *Review of Economic Studies* LIV: 437–61

Andrews M, Bell D, Fisher P, Wallis K, Whitley J 1985 Models of the UK economy and the real-wage. *National Institute Economic Review* 112: 41–52

Armstrong H, Taylor J 1987 *Regional policy: the way forward.* Employment Institute

Arrow K 1972 Some mathematical models of race in the labour market.

In Pascal A (ed.) *Racial discrimination in economic life.* Lexington Books, D C Heath, Lexington, Mass., 83–102

Ashenfelter O, Layard R 1983 Incomes policy and wage differentials. *Economica* 50: 127–43

Ashenfelter O, Layard R 1986 *Handbook of Labor Economics.* North-Holland, Amsterdam.

Ashenfelter O, Oaxaca R 1987 The economics of discrimination: economists enter the courtroom. *American Economic Review* 77(2): 321–5

Ashton D 1986 *Unemployment Under Capitalism.* Wheatsheaf Books

Atkinson J, Meager N 1986 Is flexibility just a flash in the pan? *Personnel Management* Sept: 26–9

Bain G (ed.) 1983 *Industrial relations in Britain.* Basil Blackwell

Barnow B 1987 The impact of CETA programs on earnings: a review of the evidence. *Journal of Human Resources* XXII: 157–93

Barron J, Bishop J, Dunkelberg W 1985 Employer search – the interviewing and hiring of new employees. *Review of Economics and Statistics* 67: 43–52

Barron J, Gilley O 1981 Job search and vacancy contacts. *American Economic Review* 71: 683–91

Barron J, Mellor W 1982 Labour contract formation, search requirements and use of a public employment service. *Economic Inquiry* XX: 381–7

Bassi L 1983 The effect of CETA on the post program earnings of participants. *Journal of Human Resources* XVIII: 539–56

Batstone E 1984 *Working order.* Basil Blackwell

Becker G 1957 *The economics of discrimination.* University of Chicago Press, Chicago

Becker G 1975 *Human capital: a theoretical and empirical analysis* 2nd edn. National Bureau for Economic Research, New York

Becker G 1985 Human capital, effort and the sexual division of labour. *Journal of Labor Economics* 3: S33–S58

Beckerman W (ed.) 1986 *Wage Rigidity and Unemployment.* Johns Hopkins University Press, Baltimore

Beckerman W, Jenkinson T 1986 How rigid are wages anyway? In Beckerman W (ed.) *Wage rigidity and unemployment.* Duckworth, 21–42

Beenstock M 1987a Pensions and labour market structure. *Oxford Economic Papers* 39: 568–76

Beenstock M 1987b *Work, welfare and taxation.* Allen and Unwin

Bekemans L 1985 Job creation schemes in Europe: a review. *International Journal of Social Economics* 12: 27–36

Beller A 1978 The economics of enforcement of anti-discriminatory law, Title VII of the Civil Rights Act of 1964. *Journal of Law and Economics* 21: 359–80

Biebly W, Baron J 1986 Sex segregation within occupations. *American Economic Review* 76(2): 43–7

Björklund A 1984 A look at the male–female unemployment differentials in the Federal Republic of Germany, Sweden, United Kingdom and the United States of America. In Schmid G (ed.) *Sex discrimination and equal opportunity.* Gower

Blackaby D 1986 An analysis of male racial earnings differentials in the UK using the GHS. *Applied Economics* 18: 1233–42

Blanchflower D 1984 Unions relative wage effects: a cross-sectional analysis using establishment data. *British Journal of Industrial Relations* 22: 311–32

Blanchflower D 1986 What effect do unions have on relative wages in GB? *British Journal of Industrial Relations* 24: 195–204

Blanchflower D, Oswald A 1987a Profit-sharing – can it work? *Oxford Economic Papers* 39: 1–19

Blanchflower D, Oswald A 1987b *Profit related pay: prose discovered.* Centre for Labour Economics, London School of Economics, Discussion Paper 287

Blanchflower D, Oswald A, Garrett M 1987 Insider power in wage determination. Mimeo

Blaug M 1976 The empirical status of human capital theory: a slightly jaundiced survey. *Journal of Economic Literature* 14: 827–55

Blaug M 1985 Where are we now in the economics of education? *Economics Education Review* 4: 17–28

Blaug M, Dougherty C, Psacharopoulos G 1982 The distribution of education and the distribution of earnings: ROSLA in 1972. *Manchester School* 50: 24–50

Blinder A 1987 Keynes, Lucas and scientific progress. *American Economic Review* 77(2): 130–6

Bluestone B, Stevenson M 1981 Industrial transformation and the evolution of dual labour markets: the case of retail trade in the United States. In Wilkinson F (ed.) *The dynamics of labour market segmentation.* Academic Press

Board of Inland Revenue 1987 *Inland Revenue statistics.* HMSO

Board of Inland Revenue 1988 *International comparisons of direct tax on employment income.* HMSO

Bosanquet N 1983 Tax-based incomes policies. *Oxford Bulletin of Economics and Statistics* 45: 33–49

Bosanquet N, Doeringer P 1973 Is there a dual labour market in Great Britain? *Economic Journal* 83: 421–35

Bosworth D, Wilson R 1980 The labour market for scientists and technologists. In Lindley R (ed.) *Economic change and employment policy.* Macmillan

Bowles S, Gintis H 1976 *Schooling in capitalist America.* Basic Books, New York

Bradley K, Estrin S 1987 *Profit sharing in the retail trade sector: the relative performance of the John Lewis Partnership.* Centre for Labour Economics, London School of Economics, Discussion Paper 279

Britton A 1986 Employment policy in the public sector. In Hart P (ed.) *Unemployment and labour market policy.* Gower

Brown C 1982 The federal attack on labor market discrimination: the mouse that roared? In Ehrenberg R (ed.) *Research in labor economics* vol. 5. JAI Press, 33–68

Brown C V 1983 *Taxation and the incentive to work* 2nd edn. Oxford University Press

Bruno M, Sachs J 1985 *The economics of worldwide stagflation.* Basil Blackwell

Budd A, Levine P, Smith P 1987 Longer-term unemployment and the labour market: some further results. *Economic Outlook* **11**: 28–31

Bulow J, Summers L 1986 A theory of dual labor markets with application to industrial policy, discrimination and Keynesian unemployment. *Journal of Labor Economics* **4**: 376–414

Cain G 1985 Welfare economics of policies toward women. *Journal of Labor Economics* **3**: 375–96

Cain G 1986 The economic analysis of labour market discrimination: a survey. In Ashenfelter O and Layard R (eds) *Handbook of labour economics*. North-Holland, Amsterdam, 693–785

Cameron S 1987 Trade unions and productivity: theory and evidence. *Industrial Relations Journal* **18**: 170–6

Carline D 1985 Trade unions and wages. In Carline D, Pissarides C, Siebert W and Sloane P *Labour economics*. Longman, 186–232

Carline D, Pissarides C, Siebert W, Sloane P 1985 *Labour economics*. Longman

Carruth A, Oswald A 1986 *Testing for Multiple Natural Rates of Unemployment in the British Economy*. Centre for Labour Economics, London School of Economics, Discussion Paper 265

Carruth A, Oswald A 1987 Wage inflexibility in Britain. *Oxford Bulletin of Economics and Statistics* **49**: 59–78

Casey B 1986 The dual apprenticeship system and the recruitment and retention of young persons in West Germany. *British Journal of Industrial Relations* **24**: 63–82

Catt H 1984 Recruiting manual workers in high unemployment: an employer's experience. *Industrial Relations Journal* **15**: 90–3

Caves R 1980 Productivity differences among industries. In Caves R and Krause L (eds) *Britain's economic performance*. Brookings Institute, Washington D.C. 175–98

Central Statistical Office 1986 *Guide to Official Statistics*. HMSO

Central Statistical Office 1987 *Social trends*. HMSO

Chan-Lee J, Coe D, Prywes M 1987 Macroeconomic changes and the macroeconomic wage disinflation in the 1980s. *OECD Economic Studies* **7**: 121–58

Chapman P, Tooze M 1987 *The Youth Training Scheme in the United Kingdom*. Avebury Press

Charter for Jobs 1987 Declining unemployment: a statistical illusion? *Economic Report* **2**(7)

Chiplin B, Curran M, Parsley C 1980 Relative female earnings in Great Britain and the impact of legislation. In Sloane P (ed.) *Women and low pay*. Macmillan, 57–126

Coe D 1985 Nominal wages, the NAIRU and wage flexibility. *OECD Economic Studies* **5**: 87–126

Collier P, Knight J 1985 Seniority payments, quit rates and internal labour markets in Britain and Japan. *Oxford Bulletin of Economics and Statistics* **47**: 19–32

Congressional Budget Office 1982 *CETA training programs – do they work for adults?* Washington D.C.

Corcoran M, Courant P 1987 Sex-role socialization and occupational segregation: an exploratory investigation. *Journal of Post-Keynesian Economics* **9:** 330–46

Cornwall, J 1983 *The conditions for economic recovery*. Martin Robertson

Craig C, Garnsey E, Rubery J 1984 *Payment structures and smaller firms: women's employment in segmented labour markets*. Department of Employment Research Paper 48

Creedy J, Disney R 1985 *Social insurance in transition: an economic analysis*. Clarendon Press.

Creedy J, Hart P 1979 Age and the distribution of earnings. *Economic Journal* **89:** 280–93

Creedy J, Thomas B (eds) 1982 *The economics of labour*. Butterworths

Creedy J, Whitfield K 1986 Earnings and job mobility: professional chemists in Britain. *Journal of Economic Studies* **13:** 23–37

Cross R 1983 Long-term unemployment, hysteresis and the natural rate of unemployment. *Business Economist* **14:** 4–15

Crossley J 1970 Theory and methods of national manpower policy. *Scottish Journal of Political Economy* **17:** 127–146

Daly A 1982 The contribution of education to economic growth in Britain: a note on the evidence. *National Institute Economic Review* **101:** 48–56

Daly A 1986 Education and productivity: comparison of Great Britain and the United States. *British Journal of Industrial Relations* **24:** 251–66

Daly A, Hitchens D, Wagner K 1985 Productivity, machinery and skills in a sample of British and West German manufacturing plants: results of a survey. *National Institute Economic Review* **111:** 48–61

D'Amico T 1987 The conceit of labour market discrimination. *American Economic Review* **77**(2): 310–15

Daniel W, Millward N 1983 *Workplace industrial relations in Britain*. Heinemann

Danziger S, Gottschalk P 1987 Earning inequality, the spatial concentration of poverty and the underclass. *American Economic Review* **77**(2): 211–15

Datcher-Loury L 1986 Racial differences in the stability of high earnings among young men. *Journal of Labour Economics* **4:** 301–16

Davies G 1985 *Government can affect unemployment*. Employment Institute

Davies G, Metcalf D 1985 *Generating jobs: the cost-effectiveness of tax cuts, public expenditure and SEM in cutting unemployment*. Simon and Coates

Davies R 1979 Economic activity, incomes policy and strikes: a quantitative analysis. *British Journal of Industrial Relations* **18:** 205–23

Deakin B, Pratten C 1987 Economic effects of YTS. *Employment Gazette* Oct: 491–7

Department of Employment 1986 Unemployment flows and durations. *Employment Gazette* Sept: 358–64

Department of Employment 1988 Training in Britain: key statistics. *Employment Gazette* March: 130–42

Dex S 1986 Earnings differentials of school-leavers. *Manchester School* **54:** 162–79

Dex S 1987 *Women's occupational mobility: a lifetime perspective*. Macmillan

Dex S, Shaw L 1986 *British and American women at work: do equal opportunities policies matter?* St Martin's Press, New York

Dex S, Sloane P 1988 Detecting and removing discrimination under equal opportunities policies. *Journal of Economic Surveys* **2**: 1–27

Dickens W, Katz L 1987 Inter-Industry wage differences and industry characteristics. In Lang K and Leonard T (eds) *Unemployment and the structure of the labor market*. Basil Blackwell

Dickens W, Lang K 1987 Where have all the good jobs gone? De-industrialization and labour market discrimination. In Lang K and Leonard J (eds) *Unemployment and the structure of the labour market*. Basil Blackwell, 90–102

Dilnot A, Kay J, Morris C 1984 *The reform of social security*. Clarendon Press

Dilnot A, Kell M 1987 Male unemployment and women's work. *Fiscal Studies* **8**: 1–16

Dilnot A, Morris C 1983 Private costs and benefits of unemployment; measuring replacement rates. *Oxford Economic Papers* **35**, Supplement: 321–40

Doeringer P 1986 Internal labour markets and non-competing groups. *American Economic Review* **76**(2): 48–52

Dolton P, Makepeace G 1986 Sample selection and male–female earnings differentials in the graduate labour market. *Oxford Economic Papers* **38**: 317–41

Dolton P, Makepeace G 1987 Marital status, child rearing and earnings differentials in the graduate labour market. *Economic Journal* **97**: 897–923

Donaldson M *et al.* 1987 *Skills for the future*. Sheffield University Education Division

Dornbusch R, Layard R (eds) 1986 *The performance of the British economy*. Oxford University Press

Edwards P 1985 Managing labour relations through the recession. *Employee Relations* **7**(2): 3–7

Elliot R, Murphy P 1986a The determinants of the coverage of PBR systems in Britain. *Journal of Economic Studies* **13**(3): 38–50

Elliot R, Murphy P 1986b The theory of net advantages. *Scottish Journal of Political Economy* **33**: 46–57

Elliot R, Murphy P 1987 The relative pay of public and private sector employees 1970–84. *Cambridge Journal of Economics* **11**: 107–32

Estrin S, Grout P, Wadhwani S 1987 Profit-sharing and employee share ownership: an assessment. *Economic Policy* **4**: 13–61

Estrin S, Wilson N 1986 *The micro-economic effects of profit-sharing*. Centre for Labour Economics, London School of Economics, Discussion Paper 247

Ferber M, Green C, Spaeth J 1986 Work power and earnings of women and men. *American Economic Review* **76**(2): 53–6

Figart D 1987 Gender, unions and internal labour markets: evidence from the public sector in two states. *American Economic Review* **77**(2): 252–6

Fischer C 1987 Toward a more complete understanding of occupational sex discrimination. *Journal of Economic Issues* **21**: 113–38

Fitzroy F, Kraft K 1985 Profitability and profit-sharing. *Journal of Industrial Economics* **35**: 113–30

Fleisher B, Kniesner T 1984 *Labor economics: theory, evidence and policy.* Prentice-Hall

Ford J, Keil E, Beardsworth A, Bryman A 1982 How employers see the public employment service. *Employment Gazette* **90**: 466–72

Freeman B 1981 Black economic progress after 1964; who gained and why? In Rosen S (ed.) *Studies in the labour market.* University of Chicago Press, 247–94

Freeman R 1986 Demand for education. In Ashenfelter O and Layard R (eds) *Handbook of labor economics.* North-Holland, Amsterdam, 357–86

Freeman R, Medoff J 1984 *What do unions do?* Basic Books, New York

Freeman R, Weitzman M 1986 *Bonus and employment in Japan.* National Bureau of Economic Research, Working Paper 1878

Fuchs V 1986 His and hers: gender differences in work and income. *Journal of Labour Economics* **4** Supplement: S245–72

Gallagher C, Stewart H 1986 Jobs and business life-cycle in Britain. *Applied Economics* **18**: 875–900

George K, Shorey J 1985 Manual workers, good jobs and structured internal labour markets. *British Journal of Industrial Relations* **23**: 424–47

Ginsberg H 1983 *Full employment policy: the United States and Sweden.* D C Heath

Goldin C, Polachek S 1987 Residual differences by sex: perspectives on the gender gap in earnings. *American Economic Review* **77**(2): 143–51

Gordon A 1983 *How to choose school leavers for jobs.* Gower

Gordon I 1986 Comments on chapter 4. In Hart P (ed.): *Unemployment and labour market policies.* Gower, 75–79

Gottschalk P, Maloney T 1985 Involuntary terminations, unemployment and job matching: a test of job search theory. *Journal of Labour Economics* **3**: 109–23

Gray D, King S 1986 *The Youth Training Scheme: the first five years.* MSC

Green A *et al.* 1986 What contribution can labour migration make to reducing unemployment? In Hart P (ed.) *Unemployment and labour market policies.* Gower, 52–74

Green F, Hadjimatheou G, Smail R 1985 Fringe benefits distribution in Britain. *British Journal of Industrial Relations* **23**: 261–80

Greenhalgh C 1980 Male–female wage differentials in GB; is marriage an equal opportunity? *Economic Journal* **90**: 751–75

Greenhalgh C, Stewart M 1985 The occupational status and mobility of British men and women. *Oxford Economic Papers* **37**: 40–71

Greenhalgh C, Stewart M 1987 The effects and determinants of training. *Oxford Bulletin of Economics and Statistics* **49**: 171–90

Greenwald B 1986 Adverse selection in the labor market. *Review of Economic Studies* **LIII**: 325–47

Gregory R 1986 Wages policy and unemployment in Australia. *Economica* **53** Supplement S53–S74. Reprinted in Bean C, Layard R and Nickell S (eds) *The rise in unemployment.* Basil Blackwell

Gregory M, Lobban P, Thomson A 1987 Pay settlements in manufacturing industry 1979–84: a micro data study of the impact of product and labour market pressures. *Oxford Bulletin of Economics and Statistics* **49**: 129–50

Gregory R, Duncan R 1981 Segmented labour market theories and the Australian experience of equal pay for women. *Journal of Post-Keynesian Economics* **3**: 403–28

Grubb D 1986 Topics in the OECD Phillips curve. *Economic Journal* 96: 55–79

Grubb D, Jackman R, Layard R 1983 Wage rigidity and unemployment in OECD countries. *European Economic Review* **21**: 11–39

Hadjimatheou G 1986 Why has Britain not had full employment since the early 70s? *Journal of Post-Keynesian Economics* **8**: 359–70

Hahn F, Solow R 1986 Is wage flexibility a good thing? In Beckerman W (ed.) *Wage rigidity and unemployment*. Johns Hopkins University Press, Baltimore, 1–20

Hakim C 1981 Job segregation: trends in the 1970s. *Employment Gazette* Dec: 521–9

Hakim C 1987a Homeworking in Britain. *Employment Gazette* Feb: 92–104

Hakim C 1987b Trends in the flexible workforce. *Employment Gazette* November: 549–560

Hall S, Henry S 1987 Wage models. *National Institute Economic Review* **119**: 70–5

Hamermesh D 1986 The demand for labour in the long run. In Ashenfelter O and Layard R (eds) *Handbook of labor economics*. North-Holland, Amsterdam, 429–71

Hamermesh D 1987 The costs of worker displacement. *Quarterly Journal of Economics* **102**: 51–75

Hart P 1987 Small firms and jobs. *National Institute Economic Review* **121**: 60–3

Hart P, Trinder C 1986 Employment protection, national insurance, income tax and youth unemployment. In Hart P (ed.) *Unemployment and labour market policies*. Gower, 28–48

Hart R 1984 *The economics of non-wage labour costs*. Allen and Unwin

Hartley K 1982 Why state intervention in industrial training? *Journal of Industrial Affairs* **2**: 84–9

Hashi I, Hussain A 1986 The Employment Investment Fund in Sweden. *National Westminster Bank Review* May: 17–27

Haveman R, Saks D 1985 Transatlantic lessons for employment and training policy. *Industrial Relations* **24**: 20–36

Haveman R, Wolfe B 1984 Schooling and economic well-being: the role of non-market effects. *Journal of Human Resources* **19**: 377–407

Hedges B 1983 *Survey of employers' recruitment practices*. Social and Community Planning Research

Hemming R 1984 *Poverty and incentives: the economics of social security*. Oxford University Press

Henry S 1981 Incomes policy and aggregate pay. In Fallick J and Elliot R (eds) *Incomes policies, inflation and relative pay*. George Allen and Unwin, 23–44

Henry S, Payne J, Trinder C 1985 Real wages and unemployment: the role of unemployment and social security benefits and unionisation. *Oxford Economic Papers* **37**: 330–45

Hey J, McKenna C 1979 To move or not. *Economica* **46**: 175–85

Heywood J 1987 Wage discrimination and market structure. *Journal of Post-Keynesian Economics* **9**: 617–28

Hirsch B, Addison J 1986 *The economic analysis of unions: new approaches and evidence.* Allen and Unwin

HM Treasury 1985 *The relationship between wages and employment.* HM Treasury

Hoffman S, Link C 1984 Selectivity bias in male wage equations: black and white comparisons. *Review of Economics and Statistics* **66**: 320–3

Holzer H 1987 Informal job search and black youth unemployment. *American Economic Review* **77**(3): 446–53

House of Commons, Public Accounts Committee 1984 *Regional industrial incentives: report and minutes of evidence.* HC378 HMSO

Howitt P, McAfee P 1987 Costly search and recruiting. *International Economic Review* **28**: 89–107

Hughes G, McCormick B 1981 Do council housing policies reduce migration between regions? *Economic Journal* **91**: 919–37

Hughes G, McCormick B 1985 Migration intentions in the UK: which households want to move and which succeed? *Economic Journal* **95** Supplement: 76–95

Hughes G, McCormick B 1987 Housing, unemployment and labour market flexibility in the UK. *European Economic Review* **31**: 615–45

Hughes P, Hutchinson G 1986 The changing nature of male unemployment in GB 1972–81. *Oxford Bulletin of Economic and Social Research* **48**: 309–30

Hunter L 1978 *Labour shortages and manpower policy.* MSC

Incomes Data Services 1986 *Profit Sharing and Share Options.* Incomes Services Study No. 357, London

Institute for Employment Research 1987 *Review of the economy and employment.* University of Warwick

Irwin P 1987 European policies to help the long-term unemployed people. *Employment Gazette* Nov: 541–7

Jackman R 1985 *Search behaviour of the unemployed men in Britain and the United States.* Centre for Labour Economics, London School of Economics, Working Paper 550.

Jackman R, Layard R, Pissarides C 1986 Policies for reducing the natural rate of unemployment. In Butkiewicz J, Koford K, Miller J (eds) *Keynes' economic legacy.* Praeger, New York

Jackman R, Roper S 1987 Structural unemployment. *Oxford Bulletin of Economics and Statistics* **49**: 9–35

Jencks C et al. 1979 *Who gets ahead?* Basic Books, New York

Jenkins R 1984 Acceptability, suitability and the search for the habituated worker: how ethnic minorities and women lose out. *International Journal of Social Economics* **11**: 64–76

Jenkinson T 1987 The natural rate of unemployment: does it exist? *Oxford Review of Economic Policy* **3**: 20–6

Johnson T, Dickinson K, West R 1985 An evaluation of the impact of ES referrals on applicants' earnings. *Journal of Human Resources* **20**: 117–37

Joll C, McKenna C, McNabb R, Shorey J 1983 *Developments in labour market analysis*. George Allen and Unwin

Jones D, Martin R 1986 Voluntary and involuntary turnover in the labour force. *Scottish Journal of Political Economy* **33**: 124–44

Jones I 1985 Skill formation and pay relativities. In Worswick G (ed.) *Education and economic performance*. Gower, 25–39

Jones I 1986 Apprentice training costs in British manufacturing establishments: some new evidence. *British Journal of Industrial Relations* **24**: 333–62

Jones S 1987 The economics of worksharing in western Europe: some policy considerations. *British Review of Economic Issues* **9**: 91–117

Jonung C 1984 Patterns of occupational segregation by sex in the labour market. In Schmid G (ed.) *Sex discrimination and equal opportunity*. Gower

Joshi H, Layard R, Owen S 1985 Why are more women working in Britain? *Journal of Labour Economics* **3** Supplement: 147–76

Jovanovic B 1987 Work, rest and search: unemployment, turnover and the cycle. *Journal of Labour Economics* **5**: 131–48

Katrak H 1982 Labour skills, research and development and capital requirements in the international trade and investment of the UK 1968–78. *National Institute Economic Review* **101**: 38–47

Kaufman R 1984 On wage stickiness in Britain's competitive sector. *British Journal of Industrial Relations* **22**: 101–12

Kay J, Morris C 1983 The IFS position on unemployment benefits. *Fiscal Studies* **4**: 66–73

Keeley M, Robins P 1985 Government programs, job search requirements and the duration of unemployment. *Journal of Labour Economics* **3**: 327–62

Keil T, Ford J, Bryman A, Beardsworth A 1984 Does occupational status matter? *International Journal of Social Economics* **11**: 32–48

Kelly J 1987 Trade unions in the recession 1980–84. *British Journal of Industrial Relations* **25**: 275–82

Killingsworth M, Heckman J 1986 Female labor supply; a survey. In Ashenfelter O and Layard R (eds) *Handbook of labor economics*. North-Holland, Amsterdam, 103–204

King S 1988 Temporary workers in Britain. *Employment Gazette* April: 238–47

Klau F, Mittelstädt A 1986 Labour market flexibility. *OECD Economic Studies* **6**: 7–46

Kniesner T, Goldsmith A 1987 A survey of alternative models of the aggregate US labour market. *Journal of Economic Literature* **25**: 1241–80

Knight K 1987 *Unemployment: and economic analysis*. Croom Helm

Kuhn P 1987 Sex discrimination in labor markets. *American Economic Review* **77**: 567–83

Layard R 1982 Is incomes policy the answer to unemployment? *Economica* **49**: 219–39

Layard R 1986 *How to beat unemployment*. Oxford University Press

Layard R, Metcalf D, O'Brien R 1986 A new deal for the long term unemployed. In Hart P (ed.) *Unemployment and labour market policies*. Gower, 181–90

Layard R, Nickell S 1980 The case for subsidizing extra jobs *Economic Journal* 90: 51–73

Layard R, Nickell S 1985a The causes of British unemployment. *National Institute Economic Review* 111: 62–85

Layard R, Nickell S 1985b Unemployment, real wages and aggregate demand in Europe, Japan and US. *Carnegie–Rochester Conference Series on Public Policy* 23: 143–202

Layard R, Nickell S 1986 Unemployment in Britain. *Economica* Supplement 210: S121–70. Reprinted in Bean C, Layard R, Nickell S (eds) *The rise in unemployment*. Basil Blackwell, 121–70

Layard R, Nickell S 1987 The performance of the British labour market. In Dornbusch R and Layard R (eds) *The performance of the British economy*. Oxford University Press, 131–79

Leijonhufvud A 1968 *On Keynesian economic and the economics of Keynes.* Cambridge University Press

Leonard T 1986 What was affirmative action? *American Economic Review* 76(2): 359–63

Leslie D 1987 Real wages and real labour cost growth 1948–81: a disaggregated study. *Applied Economics* 19: 635–50

Lindbeck A, Snower D 1985 Explanations of unemployment. *Oxford Review of Economic Policy* 1(2): 34–59

Lindbeck A, Snower D 1986 Wage rigidity, union activity and unemployment. In Beckerman W (ed.) *Wage rigidity and unemployment*. Duckworth, 97–126

Lindbeck A, Snower D 1987 Efficiency wages versus insiders–outsiders. *European Economic Review* 31: 407–16

Lindley R 1975 The demand for apprentice recruits by the engineering industry 1951–71. *Scottish Journal of Political Economy* 22: 1–24

Lindley R 1986 Labour demand: microeconomic aspects of state intervention. In Hart P (ed.) *Unemployment and labour market policies*. Gower, 154–75

Lockwood B 1986 Transferable skills, job matchings and the inefficiency of the natural rate of unemployment. *Economic Journal* 96: 961–74

Lucas R 1981 *Studies in business cycle theory*. Basil Blackwell

Lucas R 1986 *Models of business cycles*. Paper prepared for Yrjo Jahnsson Lectures, Helsinki, Finland

Lucas R, Sargent T 1981 *Rational expectations and econometric practice.* Allen and Unwin

Lundberg S, Startz R 1983 Private discrimination and social intervention in competitive labour markets. *American Economic Review* 73: 340–7

McCallum B 1987 The development of Keynesian economics. *American Economic Review* 77(2): 125–9

McCallum J 1986 Unemployment in OECD countries. *Economic Journal* 96: 942–60

McCormick B 1986a Evidence about the comparative earnings of Asian and West Indian workers in GB. *Scottish Journal of Political Economy* 33: 97–110

McCormick B 1986b Employment opportunities, earnings and the journey to work of minority workers in GB. *Economic Journal* **96**: 375–97

McCormick B 1988 Quit rates over time in a job-rationed labour market: the British manufacturing sector, 1971–1983. *Economica* **55**: 81–94

McDonald I, Solow R 1985 Wages and employment in a segmented labour market. *Quarterly Journal of Economics* **100**(4): 115–41

Mace J 1979 Internal labour markets for engineers in British industry. *British Journal of Industrial Relations* **17**: 50–63

McKee M, Visser J, Saunders P 1986 Marginal tax rates on the use of capital and labour. *OECD Economic Studies* **7**: 45–102

McKenna C 1985 *Uncertainty and the labour market: recent developments in job search theory*. Wheatsheaf Books

McNabb R 1987 Testing for labour market segmentation in Britain. *Manchester School* **55**: 257–73

McNabb R, Psacharopoulos G 1981a Further evidence on the relevance of the dual labour market hypothesis for the UK. *Journal of Human Resources* **16**: 442–8

McNabb R, Psacharopoulos G 1981b Racial earnings differences in the UK. *Oxford Economic Papers* **33**: 413–25

Madden J 1987 Gender differences in the cost of displacement: an empirical test of discrimination in the labour market. *American Economic Review* **77**(2): 246–51

Maddison A 1987 Growth and slowdown in advanced capitalist economies. *Journal of Economic Literature* **25**: 649–98

Main B 1982 The length of a job in GB. *Economica* **49**: 325–33

Malcomson J 1983 Trade unions and economic efficiency. *Economic Journal* Conference Papers **93**: 50–64

Malcomson J 1987 Trade union labour contracts: an introduction. *European Economic Review* **31**: 139–48

Mallier A, Rosser M 1987 *Women and the economy: a comparative study of Britain and the USA*. Macmillan

Manning A 1987 Collective bargaining arrangements, closed shops and relative pay. *Economic Journal* **97**: 140–56

Manpower Services Commission 1977 *Annual report 1976–77*. MSC

Manpower Services Commission 1978 *Jobcentres: an evaluation*. MSC

Manpower Services Commission 1987a *Annual report 1986/87*. MSC

Manpower Services Commission 1987b *Labour market quarterly report*. February, MSC

Manwaring T 1984 The extended internal labour market. *Cambridge Journal of Economics* **8**: 161–87

Manwaring T, Wood S 1984 Recruitment and the recession. *International Journal of Social Economics* **11**: 49–63

Marin A, Psacharopoulos G 1982 The reward for risk in the labour market: evidence from the UK and reconciliation with other studies. *Journal of Political Economy* **90**: 827–53

Marsden D 1983 Wage structure. In Bain G (ed.) *Industrial relations in Britain*. Basil Blackwell, 263–90

Marsden D 1986 *End of economic man?: Custom and competition in the labour market*. Wheatsheaf Books

Marsden D, Ryan P 1986 Where do young workers work? Youth employment by industry in various European economies. *British Journal of Industrial Relations* 24: 83–102

Marsh A 1982 *Employee relations policy and decision making*. Gower

Marshall G, McCormick B 1985 Minimum wages and unemployment: the reform of the Wages Councils. *Industrial Relations Journal* 16: 38–46

Matthews K, Minford P 1987 Mrs Thatcher's economic policies. *Economic Policy* 5: 57–102

Mayhew K 1985 Reforming the labour market. *Oxford Review of Economic Policy* 1: 60–79

Mayhew K, Rosewell B 1978 Immigrants and occupational crowding in Great Britain. *Oxford Bulletin of Economics and Statistics* 40: 223–48

Mayhew K, Rosewell B 1979 Labour market segmentation in Britain. *Oxford Bulletin of Economics and Statistics* 41: 81–116

Meade J 1984 *Wage fixing revisited*. Institute of Economic Affairs, Occasional Paper 72

Meade J 1986 *Different forms of share economy*. Public Policy Centre

Meager N 1986 Skill shortages again and the UK economy. *Industrial Relations Journal* 17: 236–48

Medoff M, Dick P 1978 A test for relative demand functions in American manufacturing. *Applied Economics* 10: 61–73

Merrilees W 1983 Alternative models of apprentice recruitment: with special reference to the British Engineering Industry. *Applied Economics* 15: 1–21

Merrilees W 1984 Do wage subsidies stimulate training? An evaluation of the Craft Rebate Scheme. *Australian Economic Papers* 23: 235–48

Metcalf D 1982 Special employment measures: an analysis of wage subsidies, youth schemes and worksharing. *Midland Bank Review* Autumn/Winter: 9–21

Metcalf D 1986 Employment subsidies and redundancies. In Blundell R and Walker I (eds) *Unemployment, search and labour supply*. Cambridge University Press, 103–20

Metcalf D, Nickell S 1982 Occupational mobility in Great Britain. In Ehrenberg R (ed.) *Research in labour economics* vol 5. JAI Greenwich, Connecticut

Micklewright J 1986 Unemployment and incentives to work: policy and evidence in the 1980's. In Hart P (ed.) *Unemployment and labour market policies*. Gower, 104–27

Milgrom P, Oster S 1987 Job discrimination, market forces and the invisibility hypothesis. *Quarterly Journal of Economics* 52: 453–74

Miller M 1985 Measuring the fiscal stance. *Oxford Review of Economic Policy* 1: 44–57

Miller P 1987 The wage effect of the occupational segregation of women. *Economic Journal* 97: 885–96

Millward N, Stevens M 1986 *British workplace industrial relations 1980–4*. Gower

Mincer J 1962 On the job training: costs, returns and some implications. *Journal of Political Economy* Supplement **70**: S50–79

Mincer J 1985 Inter-country comparisons of labour force trends and of related developments: an overview. *Journal of Labour Economics* Supplement **3**: S1–32

Minford P *et al.* 1983 *Unemployment: cause and cure*. Basil Blackwell

Mirkin B 1987 Early retirement: an international overview. *Monthly Labour Review* **110**(3): 26–33

Mitchell D 1986 Explanations of wage inflexibility: institutions and incentives. In Beckerman W (ed.) *Wage rigidity and unemployment*. Duckworth, 47–76

Morris D (ed.) 1985 *The economic system in the UK* 3rd edn. Oxford University Press

Morris D, Sinclair P 1985 The unemployment problem in the 1980's. *Oxford Review of Economic Policy* **1**: 1–19

Mortensen D 1986 Job search and labor market analysis. In Ashenfelter O and Layard R (eds) *Handbook of labor economics*. North-Holland, Amsterdam, 849–919

Moylan S, Millar J, Davies R *et al.* 1984 *For richer, for poorer?* DHSS Research Report 11. HMSO

Narendranathan W, Nickell S 1985 Modelling the process of job search. *Journal of Econometrics* **29**: 29–49

Narendranathan W, Nickell S, Metcalf D 1982 *An investigation into the incidence and dynamic structure of sickness and unemployment*. Centre for Labour Economics, London School of Economics, Discussion Paper 142

Narendranathan W, Nickell S, Stern J 1985 Unemployment benefits revisited. *Economic Journal* **95**: 307–29

National Economic Development Council 1987 *The training of managers*. NEDC

National Economic Development Office 1984 *Competence and competition: training and education in the Federal Republic of Germany, the United States and Japan*. NEDO

de Neubourg C 1985 Part-time work: an international quantitative comparison. *International Labour Review* **124**: 559–76

Nickell S 1982 The determinants of equilibrium unemployment in Britain. *Economic Journal* **92**: 555–75

Nickell S 1985 The government's policy for jobs: an analysis. *Oxford Review of Economic Policy* **1**: 98–115

Nickell S, Andrews M 1983 Trade unions, real wages and employment in Britain 1957–79. *Oxford Economic Papers* **35** Supplement: 183–206

Nissim J 1984 The price responsiveness of the demand for labour by skill in the British mechanical engineering industry 1963–78. *Economic Journal* **94**: 812–25

Nolan P 1983 The firm and labour market behaviour. In Bain G (ed.) *Industrial relations in Great Britain*. Basil Blackwell, 263–90

Nolan P, Brown W 1983 Competition and workplace wage determination. *Oxford Bulletin of Economics and Statistics* **45**: 269–87

Nord S 1987 Schooling and changes in the inequality in male and female earnings in the United States over the 1970's. *Applied Economics* **19**: 1083–105

Norwood J 1985 Perspectives on comparable worth: an introduction to the numbers. *Monthly Labor Review* **108**(12): 3–5

Oaxaca R 1973 Male–female wage differentials in urban labour markets. *International Labour Review* **14**: 693-709

Office for Population Censuses and Surveys 1983 *Recently moving households: a follow-up to the 1978 National Dwelling and Housing Survey.* HMSO

Okun A 1970 *The political economy of prosperity.* Brookings Institute, Washington D.C.

Okun A 1981 *Prices and quantities: a macroeconomic analysis.* Basil Blackwell

Oliver J, Turton J 1982 Is there a shortage of skilled labour? *British Journal of Industrial Relations* **20**: 195–200

O'Neill J 1985 The trend in the male–female wage gap in the United States. *Journal of Labor Economics* **3** Supplement: S91–116

Organisation for Economic Co-operation and Development 1984 *The public employment service in a changing labour market.* OECD, Paris

Organisation for Economic Co-operation and Development 1986 *Flexibility in the labour market.* OECD, Paris

Osterman P 1982 Employment structures within firms. *British Journal of Industrial Relations* **20**: 349–59

Osterman P 1987 Choice of employment systems in internal labor markets. *Industrial Relations* **26**: 46–67

Oswald A 1985 The economic theory of trade unions: an introductory survey. *Scandinavian Journal of Economics* **87**: 160–93

Oswald A 1986a Is wage rigidity caused by lay-offs by seniority? In Beckerman W (ed.) *Wage rigidity and unemployment.* Duckworth, 77–96

Oswald A 1986b Wage determination and recession: a report on recent work. *British Journal of Industrial Relations* **24**: 181–94

Oswald A 1987 *Efficient contracts are on the labour demand curve: theory and facts.* Centre for Labour Economics, London School of Economics, Discussion Paper 284

Oswald A, Turnbull P 1985 Pay and employment determination in Britain: what are labour contracts really like? *Oxford Review of Economic Policy* **1**: 80–97

Owen S, Joshi H 1987 Does elastic retract? The effects of recession on women's labour force participation. *British Journal of Industrial Relations* **25**: 125–43

Paldam M 1987 How much does a 1% growth change the unemployment rate? A study of 17 OECD countries. *European Economic Review* **31**: 306–14

Pencavel J 1982 The effects of incomes policies on the frequency and size of wage changes. *Economica* **49**: 147–59

Pencaval J 1986 Labor supply of men: a survey. In Ashenfelter O and Layard R (eds) *Handbook of labor economics.* North-Holland, Amsterdam, 3–102

Peston M 1985 Comments on Chapters 3-5. In Worswick G (ed.) *Education and economic performance*. Gower, 76–79

Phelps E 1972 The statistical theory of racism and sexism. *American Economic Review* **62**: 659–61

Phelps E *et al.* 1970 *Microeconomic foundations of employment and inflation*. Macmillan

Piachaud D 1987 The distribution of income and work. *Oxford Review of Economic Policy* **3**: 41–61

Pike M 1985 The employment response to equal pay legislation. *Oxford Economic Papers* **37**: 304–18

Pissarides C 1979 Job matchings with state employment agencies and random search. *Economic Journal* **89**: 818–33

Pissarides C 1981 Staying on at school in England and Wales. *Economica* **48**: 345–63

Pissarides C 1982 From school to university: the demand for post-compulsory education in Britain. *Economic Journal* **92**: 654–67

Pissarides C 1984 Search intensity, job advertising and efficiency. *Journal of Labor Economics* **2**: 128–43

Pissarides C 1985 Job search and the functioning of labour markets. In Carline D *et al. Labour economics*. Longman, 159–85

Pissarides C 1986 Unemployment and vacancies in Britain. *Economic Policy* **3**: 499–541

Pissarides C, McMaster I 1984a *Sector specific and economy wide influences on industrial wages*. Centre for Labour Economics, London School of Economics, Working Paper 571

Pissarides C, McMaster I 1984b *Regional migration, wages and unemployment: empirical evidence and implications for policy*. Centre for Labour Economics, London School of Economics, Discussion Paper 204

Postlethwaite T 1985 The bottom half in lower secondary schooling. In Worswick G (ed.) *Education and economic performance*. Gower, 93–100

Prais S 1981 Vocational qualifications of the labour force in Britain and Germany. *National Institute Economic Review* **98**: 47–59

Prais S 1985 What can we learn from the German system of education and vocational training? In Worswick G (ed.) *Education and economic performance*. Gower, 40–51

Prais S 1987 Educating for productivity: comparisons of Japanese and English schooling and vocational preparation. *National Institute Economic Review* **119**: 40–56

Prais S, Steedman H 1986 Vocational training in France and Britain: the building trades. *National Institute Economic Review* **116**: 45–55

Prais S, Wagner K 1983 Schooling standards in England and Germany: some survey comparisons bearing on economic performance. *National Institute Economics Review* **102**: 53–76

Prest A, Coppock R (eds) 1986 *The UK economy: a manual of applied economics* 11th edn. Weidenfeld and Nicholson

Psacharopoulos G 1978 Labour market duality and income distribution: the case of the UK. In Krelle W and Shorrochs A (eds) *Personal income distribution*. North-Holland, Amsterdam

Psacharopoulos G 1985 Returns to education: a further international update and implications. *Journal of Human Resources* **20**: 583–604

Psacharopoulos G (ed.) 1987 *Economics of Education: research and studies.* Pergamon Press

Psacharopoulos G, Arriagada A 1986 The educational composition of the labour force: an international comparison. *International Labour Review* **125**: 561–74

Rajan A, Pearson R 1986 *UK occupational and employment trends to 1990.* Butterworths

Ray G 1987 Labour costs in manufacturing. *National Institute Economic Review* **120**: 71–4

Reynolds L, Masters S, Moser C 1987 *Economics of labor.* Prentice-Hall

Rice P 1987 The demand for post-compulsory education in the UK and the effects of educational maintenance allowances. *Economica* **54**: 465–75

Richardson R, Nejad A 1986 Employee share ownership in the UK – an evaluation. *British Journal of Industrial Relations* **24**: 233–50

Roberts K, Dench S, Richardson D 1986 *The changing structure of youth labour markets.* Department of Employment, Research Paper 59

Robinson D 1986 *Monetarism and the labour market.* Oxford University Press

Robinson D 1987 How inflexible are negotiated wages in Britain? *Oxford Bulletin of Economics and Statistics* **49**: 37–58

Rosen S 1985 Implicit contracts. *Journal of Economic Literature* **23**: 1144–75

Rosewell B, Robinson D 1980 Reliability of vacancy statistics. *Oxford Bulletin of Economics and Statistics* **42**: 1–17

Rossi V, Walker J, Todd D, Lennan K 1986 Exchange rates, productivity and international competitiveness, *Oxford Review of Economic Policy* **2**: 56–73

Ryan P 1981 Segmentation, duality and the internal labour market. In Wilkinson F (ed.) *The dynamics of labour market segmentation.* Academic Press, 3–20

Sako M, Dore R 1986 How the Youth Training Scheme helps employers. *Employment Gazette* June: 19–204

Salop S 1973 Systematic job search and unemployment. *Review of Economic studies* **40**: 191–201

Schmid G 1984 The political economy of labour market discrimination. In Schmid G (ed.) *Sex discrimination and equal opportunity.* Gower, 264–308

Schoer K 1987 Part-time employment: Britain and West Germany. *Cambridge Journal of Economics* **11**: 83–94

Schwab S 1986 Is statistical discrimination efficient? *American Economic Review* **76**: 228–34

Shah A 1985 Does education act as a screening device for certain British jobs? *Oxford Economic Papers* **37**: 118–24

Shorey J 1980 An analysis of quits using industry turnover data. *Economic Journal* **90**: 821–37

Shorey J 1984 Employment discrimination and the employer taste model. *Scottish Journal of Political Economy* **31**: 157–75

Short C 1986 Equal pay – what happened? *Journal of Industrial Relations* **28**: 315–35

Siebert W 1985 Developments in the economics of human capital. In Carline D *et al. Labour economics.* Longman, 5–77

Siebert W, Sloane P 1981 The measurement of sex and marital status discrimination at the workplace. *Economica* **48:** 125–41

Sinclair P 1987 *Unemployment: economic theory and evidence.* Basil Blackwell

Sloane P 1985 Discrimination in the labour market. In Carline D *et al. Labour economics.* Longman, 78–158

Smith E 1988 Vacancies and recruitment in Great Britain. *Employment Gazette* April: 211–13.

Smith G 1986 Profit sharing and employee share ownership in Britain. *Employment Gazette* Sept: 380–5

Smith J, Welch F 1987 Race and poverty: a forty-year record. *American Economic Review* **77**(2): 152–8

Smith R 1987 *Unemployment and health.* Oxford University Press

Snell M, Glucklich P, Povall M 1981 *Equal pay and opportunity.* Department of Employment, Research Paper 20

Sobel I 1982 Human capital and institutional theories of the labour market: rivals or complements? *Journal of Economic Issues* **16:** 255–72

Solow R 1986 Unemployment: getting the question right. *Economica* **53** Supplement: S23–34. Reprinted in Bean C, Layard R, Nickell S (eds) *The rise in unemployment.* Basil Blackwell, 23–34

Southworth M 1987 Counting the jobless 1979–1986. *Economics* **23:** 178–81

Standing G 1986 Meshing labour flexibility with security: an answer to British unemployment. *International Labour Review* **125:** 87–106

Steedman H 1987 Vocational training in France and Britain: office work. *National Institute Economic Review* **120:** 58–70

Stewart M 1983a Racial discrimination and occupational attainment in the UK. *Economic Journal* **93:** 521–41

Stewart M 1983b Relative earnings and individual union membership in the UK. *Economica* **50:** 111–25

Stewart M 1987 Collective bargaining arrangements, closed shops and relative pay. *Economic Journal* **97:** 140–56

Stewart M, Greenhalgh C 1984 Work history patterns and occupational attainment of women. *Economic Journal* **94:** 493–519

Stigler G 1962 Information in the labour market. *Journal of Political Economy* **70:** 94–105

Stiglitz J 1986 Theories of wage rigidity. In Butkiewicz J, Koford K, Miller J (eds) *Keynes' economic legacy: contemporary economic theories.* Praeger, New York, 152–221

Stiglitz J 1987 The causes and consequences of the dependence of quality on price. *Journal of Economic Literature* **25:** 1–49

Sumner M, Ward R 1983 The reappearing Phillips' curve. *Oxford Economic Papers* **35:** 36–20

Tachibanaki T 1987 Labour market flexibility in Japan in comparison with Europe and the US. *European Economic Review* **31:** 647–84

Taubman P 1976 The determination of earnings. Genetics, family and the environments: a study of male twins. *American Economic Review* **66**: 858–70

Taubman P, Wachter M 1986 Segmented labor markets. In Ashenfelter O, Layard R (eds) *Handbook of labor economics*. North-Holland, Amsterdam, 1183–1217

Taylor J 1979 Staggered wage setting in a macro model. *American Economic Review* **69**(2): 108–13

Thomas B, Deaton D 1977 *Labour shortages and economic analysis: a case study of occupational labour markets*. Basil Blackwell

Thompson Q, Walford V 1986 A challenge to complacency. *Employment Gazette* Jan: 28–30

Turner D, Wallis K, Whitley J 1987 Evaluating special employment measures with macroeconomic models. *Oxford Review of Economic Policy* **3**: xxv–xxxvi

Turner P 1985 After the Community Programme – results of the first follow-up survey. *Employment Gazette* Jan: 9–14

Tzannatos Z, Zabalza A 1984 The anatomy of the rise in British female relative earnings in the 1970's. Evidence from the N.E.S. *British Journal of Industrial Relations* **22**: 177–94

Tzannatos Z, Zabalza A 1985 The effect of sex anti-discriminatory legislation on the variability of female employment in Britain. *Applied Economics* **17**: 1117–34

Wadhwani S 1987a The macroeconomic implications of profit sharing: some empirical evidence. *Economic Journal* **97** Supplement: 171—83

Wadhwani S 1987b The effects of profit sharing on wages and employment: some micro-econometric evidence. London School of Economics, mimeo

Wadhwani S 1987c Profit-sharing and Meade's discriminating labour–capital partnership: a review article. *Oxford Economic Papers* **39**: 421–42

Wallis K et al. 1984 *Models of the UK economy*. Oxford University Press

Way K 1984 Labour market operation, recruitment strategies and workforce structures. *International Journal of Social Economics* **11**: 6–31

Weitzman M 1984 *The share economy*. Harvard University Press, Cambridge, Mass.

Weitzman M 1985 The simple macroeconomics of profit-sharing. *American Economic Review* **75**: 937–53

Weitzman M 1987 Steady state unemployment under profit-sharing. *Economic Journal* **97**: 86–105

Welch F 1973 Black–white wage differences in the returns to schooling. *American Economic Review* **63**: 893–907

Whitley J, Wilson R 1983 The macro-economic merits of a marginal employment subsidy. *Economic Journal* **93**: 862–80

Whitley J, Wilson R 1986 The impact on employment of a reduction in length of the working week. *Cambridge Journal of Economics* **10**: 43–60

Williams B 1984 Long term trends of working time and the goal of full employment. In OECD *Employment growth in the context of structural changes*. OECD, Paris

Williams G 1985 Comments on Chapters 8–10. In Worswick G (ed.) *Education and economic performance*. Gower, 131–35

Williamson O et al. 1975 Understanding the employment relation: the analysis of idiosyncratic exchange. *Bell Journal of Economics* **6**: 250–80

Willis R 1986 Wage determination: a survey and reinterpretation of human capital earnings functions. In Ashenfelter O, Layard R (eds) *Handbook of labor economics*. North-Holland, Amsterdam, 525–601

Wilson R 1981 Rates of return. Institute for Employment Research, University of Warwick, mimeo

Wilson R 1987 The determinants of the earnings of professional engineers in GB in 1981. *Applied Economics* **19**: 983–94

Wood A 1978 *A Theory of pay*. Cambridge University Press

Wood S 1985 Recruitment systems and the recession. *British Journal of Industrial Relations* **23**: 103–20

Worswick G (ed.) 1985 *Education and economic performance*. Gower

Zabalza A, Arrufat J 1985 The extent of wage discrimination in Great Britain. In Zabalza A, Tzannatos Z *Women and equal pay: the effects of legislation on female employment and wages in Britain*. Cambridge University Press, 70–96

Zabalza A, Kong P 1984 *Pay determination in the public and private sectors*. Centre for Labour Economics, London School of Economics, Working Paper 574.

Zabalza A, Tzannatos Z 1985a Effects of Britain's anti-discriminatory legislation on relative pay and employment. *Economic Journal* **95**: 679–99

Zabalza A, Tzannatos Z 1985b *Women and equal pay: the effects of legislation on female employment and wages in Britain*. Cambridge University Press

Zalokar N 1986 Generational differences in female occupational attainment – have the 1970's changed women's opportunities? *American Economic Review* **76**(2): 378–81

Ziderman A 1975 Costs and benefits of manpower training programmes in Great Britain. *British Journal of Industrial Relations* **13**: 223–43

INDEX

ability and schooling, 67, 74
accelerationist hypothesis, 181
acceptance wage, *see* reservation
  wage
activity rates, 32–33
Adult Employment Subsidy, 211–12
adverse selection, 115, 117, 242, 250
affirmative action, 158–62, 165
apprenticeships, 76, 91–3
arbitration, 232

black workers
  earnings, 133–4, 152–3
  unemployment, 117–18, 134, 154
Bolton Committee, 35

Career Development Loans, 95–6
Civil Rights Act (1964), 130, 161, 165
child care provision, 156, 165
closed shop, 45, 205, 227
codetermination, 237, 240
collective bargaining, 45, 51, 224–5,
  228–9
collective voice, *see* exit/voice
  model
Community Programme, 7, 213,
  216, 219–20
comparable worth, 158, 161, 164
Comprehensive Employment and
  Training Act 1973, 94, 96–7
contracts, 45–6, 185–6
corporatism, 3–4, 225
credentialism, 79

demand for labour, 11–13
  elasticity of, 12–13, 48–9
Department of Employment, 6–7
differentials, *see* wage differentials
discouraged worker effects, 151

discrimination, *see* labour market
  discrimination
discriminatory labour-capital
  partnerships, 236–7
Donovan Commission, 3
dual labour markets, 21–5, 28, 53–6

earnings, *see* wages
earnings function, 53–4, 73–7,
  146–50
education
  participation, 62–5
  social returns, 81, 96
  and economic performance, 82–5
  and earnings, 53–4, 73
  and human capital theory, 61–71
  and screening, 71–80
efficiency wage theory, 23–5, 186–7
efficient bargaining model, 18, 226
employer search, 111–17
employment, 32–9
  by occupation, 33–4, 84
  by sex, 32–3, 164
  by sector, 33–4
  flexibility, 35–7, 47–50
  part-time, 36
  projections, 34–5
  temporary, 37, 50
Employment Act (1980), 227
Employment Act (1982), 227
Employment and Training Act
  (1973), 3, 91
Employment and Training Act
  (1981), 93
Employment Bill 1987, 227
employment exchanges, *see*
  Jobcentres
employment protection legislation,
  193–4, 202–3, 205

employment service, 103–4, 110–12, 117, 119–21
Employment Training, see Job Training Scheme
Employment Transfer Scheme (ETS), 126
Enterprise Allowance Scheme, 7, 211–13
enterprise zones, 128
Equal Pay Act (1970), 3, 162
Equal Rights Amendment, 3
exchequer costs
  of Special Measures, 7, 211–13, 216
  of unemployment, 172
  of YTS, 7
exit/voice model, 226–7
extended internal labour market (EILM), 116–18, 120

Fair Wages Resolution, 193
family allocation of labour, 13–14, 136
feasible v target real wage, 190, 198–9
female workers, see women workers
fixed costs of employment, 20, 52, 70, 76, 187
flexible workers, 35–6
France
  education and training, 63–5, 100

General Household Survey, 59, 73, 104, 148
geographical mobility, 121–6
growth accounting, 60–1, 82

housing and migration, 125–7
hours worked, 39, 49, 220
human capital theory, 17, 61–71
  and anti-poverty policy, 71–3
  and earnings structure, 54, 68, 134–8
  and training, 69–71, 91
hysteresis: unemployment, 197–8

implicit contract theory, 185–6
income tax
  policy changes, 206–7, 216
  and labour supply, 156, 201–2, 245–8
incomes policy, 163, 216–7, 229–234
Industrial Training Act (1964), 3, 88
Industrial Training Boards, 4, 88, 93
inner cities, 129
insider-outsider models, 21, 25, 144–6, 187–8, 234, 237, 253

internal labour markets, 21–5, 115
  importance, 52–8
  occupational, 22, 56
  and discrimination, 144–6
  and job search, 116–18
  and returns to human capital, 53–4, 77–80
  and unemployment, 187–9
internal rate of return, 67–8

Japan
  educational system, 63–4, 85
  labour market flexibility, 47–50
  seniority, 57
  and profit-sharing, 234, 237
Jobcentres, 7, 103, 114, 119–21, 247
Job Clubs, 7
Job Creation Programme, 5–6, 209
job ladders, 21–2, 55–56
Job Release Scheme, 213–14
job search
  form, 102–6, 123–4
  theory, 19, 101, 106–10
    and employer search, 111–17
    and on-the-job search, 108–9, 198
    and state employment agencies, 111–12
    and unemployment benefits, 108, 120, 192
Job Search Scheme, 126
Jobstart, 215
Job Training Scheme (JTS), 7, 219–20

Keynesian analysis, 4, 169, 178–9, 182–3

labour force participation, see activity rates
labour costs
  international comparisons, 40, 203
labour demand, see demand for labour
labour market discrimination, 28
  competitive theories
    human capital theory, 134–40
    statistical, 141–3
    tastes, 140–1, 154–5
  defined, 134–9
  empirical studies
    by race, 152–4
    by sex, 148–52
  occupational, 138, 150–1
  pre-entry, 138–40
  policy implications, 154–60
  positive, 158–62

structuralist approaches, 117–19,
    144–6
wage, 138, 163–4
and social customs, 23
and unemployment, 117–118
labour productivity, 39, 101
international comparisons, 40, 82
LIFO, 46, 188, 234

Manpower Development and
    Training Act, 73, 94, 96–7
Manpower Services Commission,
    see Training Commission
marginal product of labour, 11–12
median voter models, 188, 228
middle class work ethic, 16
migration, 122–3
neoclassical theory, 121–6
minimum wage legislation, 28
mismatch, 101
and the NAIRU, 180, 190, 195, 198
mobility of labour, 37–8, 52–3
geographical, 121–9
occupational, 53, 156
and housing, 125–7
and job search, 109
and unemployment, 180, 190, 195
monetarism, 106
monopoly, 140, 155
bi-lateral, 18
monopsony, 18
and discrimination, 144, 155
moral hazard, 242

NAIRU, natural rate of
    unemployment, 179–81,
    189–94, 196–200, 203
National Insurance Contributions,
    39, 202–3, 206–7, 241–50
National Mobility Scheme, 126
National Vacancy Circulation
    System, 124
neoclassical model, 10–16, 31
assessment, 25–27, 57–8
extensions, 16–21, 177–8
neoclassical search theory, see job
    search
nepotism, 69
net advantages, 17, 51, 124
new classical theory, 181–3
New Earnings Survey, 59
New Jobs Tax Credit (1977), 217–18
New Training Initiative, 93

occupational crowding, 132, 138,
    150–1, 153, 165
Okun's Law, 49–50

OPEC and labour market
    adjustments, 49
overtime working, 39

participation rates, see activity rates
pay discrimination, see labour
    market discrimination: wage
payment systems, 223–5, 232
payment by results (PBR), 40
personnel policies
and internal labour markets,
    23–5, 116–17
and labour turnover, 70
Phillips Curve, 2, 106, 178
poaching of labour, 70, 91
poverty, 44, 241
and human capital theory, 28
poverty trap, 192, 207, 245
primary labour markets, 21
and discrimination, 144–145
and training, 79–80
and unemployment, 187–9
professional labour markets, 22–3,
    55
profit-sharing, 41, 234–40
public sector
employment, 46
pay comparisons, 46, 206, 230

Race Relations Act (1968), 3, 166–7
racial discrimination, see labour
    market discrimination
radical theories, 23–5, 79, 144–6
Recruitment Subsidy for School-
    leavers, 211–12
regional policy, 3, 127–9
replacement ratio, 191, 210
international comparisons, 245–6
and unemployment, 192, 201–2,
    245–8
reservation wage, 106–9, 113
Restart programme, 7, 247
risk aversion, 19, 71, 186, 241–4

school-leavers, 62, 84, 140
pattern of employment, 64
schooling, see education
screening hypothesis, 77–80
search, see job search
secondary labour markets, 21, 116,
    145, 188
segmented labour markets, 21–5,
    52–7, 145
self-employment, 37
seniority, see tenure
seniority payments
service sector, 33–4, 36–7

sex discrimination, *see* labour market discrimination
Sex Discrimination Act (1975), 162
share economy, *see* profit-sharing
shift-working, 36
skill shortages, 60–1, 89–90, 100
Skillcentres, 80, 94–5
small firms, 35, 151, 211
social security, *see* social insurance
Social Security Act (1986), 207, 244, 248–9
social insurance, 240–50
special employment measures, 128, 170, 204, 209–14, 216, 218–21
statistical discrimination, 79, 141–3
stereotypes, 141–3
structuralist theories, 21–25, 52–8
    empirical evidence, 52–7
    and discrimination, 144–6, 155
    and education and training, 53–4, 77–80
    and job search, 115–117
    and unemployment, 187–8
subsidies, *see* wage subsidies
supply of labour, 13–15, 245–50
Sweden
    bargaining system, 4
    profit-sharing, 240
    training, 97

target real wage, 190, 198–9
tastes, for discrimination, 140–1
tax-based incomes policy (TIPS), 220, 232–4
Technical and Vocational Education Initiative (TVEI), 7, 86
Temporary Employment Subsidy, 209, 211–12
temporary lay-offs, 50, 189
Temporary Short Time Working Compensation Scheme, 211–13
tenure, 37–8, 56–7
Trade Union Act (1984), 227
trade unions, 18, 44–6, 188
    bargaining power, 201, 205–6, 225–9
    reform, 227–9
    and inflationary bias, 224–5
    and insider-outsiders, 188
    and unemployment, 191, 199–201
training
    costs of training, 65, 69–70, 91–2
    general, 69, 91
    off-the-job, 94–7
    on-the-job, 77, 90–4
    specific, 17, 70

Training Commission
    development, 2–8
    and training policy, 93–4, 97–100
Training Opportunities Scheme, 94–5
Travel to Interview Scheme, 126
turnover of labour, 37–8, 104
    costs of, 20–22, 70–6, 187–8

unemployment
    causes of recent British, 194–203
    characteristics, 176–7
    costs, 171–3
    defined, 170–1
    duration of, 174–5, 247
    frictional, 103, 179
    long-term, 175, 197–8, 219
    measurement
        in Britain, 38, 170–1, 173–5
        international comparisons, 38, 173–6
        stocks and flows, 174–5
    natural rate, 179–81, 189–94, 196–200, 203
    voluntary v involuntary, 183, 191–2
    and aggregate demand, 169, 178–9, 182–3, 207–8, 215–17
    and wage rigidity, 47–50, 177–178, 184–9, 199–200
unemployment benefits
    and job search, 108, 120, 192
    and level of unemployment, 192, 201–2, 245–8
United States
    discrimination, 132–4, 148, 152–3, 251
    education system, 63–5
    labour market adjustment, 47–50
    mobility of workers, 37–8, 122–3

vacancies, 89–90, 101, 120–1
    notification, 103, 175

wage differentials, 41–4, 50–2, 68
    and unions, 46, 71, 228
    by age, 41
    by firm, 19, 43
    by industry, 41–2, 50–1
    by occupation, 43
    by race, 133–4, 152–3
    by sex, 41, 131–2, 163–4
wage discrimination, 138, 163–4
wage rigidity
    international comparisons, 48–50, 183–4
    theories of, 184–9

and unemployment, 47–50,
177–8, 199–200
wage subsidies, 99–100, 121, 157,
209–13, 217–21
wages, 39–44
distribution of, 41, 57
Wages Councils, 4, 47, 193, 202–3,
205–6, 249
West Germany
and vocational training, 64, 83, 96
women workers, 132–3
activity rates, 32

discrimination, 131–152
married, 32, 48, 149, 151, 156
work-sharing, 189, 220

x-inefficiency, 23, 27, 52, 55–6, 92,
145, 226

Youth Employment Subsidy,
211–12
Youth Training Scheme, 7, 64–5,
86–88
Young Worker Scheme, 211–12